D1212892

MACMILLAN
CONNECTIONS
READING PROGRAM

SKETCHES

SENIOR AUTHORS

Virginia A. Arnold   **Carl B. Smith**

AUTHORS

James Flood   **Diane Lapp**

LITERATURE CONSULTANTS

Joan I. Glazer   Margaret H. Lippert

Macmillan Publishing Company
New York

Collier Macmillan Publishers
London

Parts of this work were published in the first edition of CONNECTIONS.
This work is also published in individual volumes under the titles *Discoveries, Memories, Gifts,* and *Changes,* copyright © 1989 Macmillan Publishing Company, a division of Macmillan, Inc.

Macmillan Publishing Company
866 Third Avenue
New York, N.Y. 10022
Collier Macmillan Canada, Inc.

Printed in the United States of America.

ISBN 0-02-174860-8

9 8 7 6 5 4 3 2 1

ACKNOWLEDGMENTS

The publisher gratefully acknowledges permission to reprint the following copyrighted material:

"The Ballad of Davy Crockett" with words by Tom Blackburn and Music by George Bruns. © 1954 Wonderland Music Co., Inc. Reprinted by permission. All Rights Reserved.

"Beezus and Her Little Sister" from pages 134–159 in BEEZUS AND RAMONA by Beverly Cleary. Copyright © 1955 by Beverly Cleary. Adapted by permission of William Morrow & Co. By permission also of Hamish Hamilton Ltd.

"Blue Moose" is from BLUE MOOSE by Manus Pinkwater. Copyright © 1975 by Manus Pinkwater. Adapted and reprinted by permission of Dodd, Mead & Company, Inc.

"Book Report Day" is adapted from TOAD FOOD & MEASLE SOUP by Christine McDonnell. Text copyright © 1982 by Christine McDonnell. Reprinted by permission of the publisher, Dial Books for Young Readers.

"Childtimes" is abridged and adapted from pages 7, 12–17, 55–61, 150–154 and with three photos from CHILDTIMES: A Three-Generation Memoir by Eloise Greenfield and Lessie Jones Little, with Pattie Ridley Jones (Thomas Y. Crowell Co.) Copyright © 1979 by Eloise Greenfield and Lessie Jones Little. Copyright © 1971 by Pattie Ridley Jones. By permission of Harper & Row, Publishers, Inc. and Marie Brown Associates.

"Celebration" by Alonzo Lopez from THE WHISPERING WIND: Poetry by Young American Indians edited by Terry Allen. Copyright © 1972 by Institute of American Indian Arts. Reprinted by permission of Doubleday & Company, Inc.

"The Dancing Man" and selected illustrations from THE DANCING MAN by Ruth Bornstein. Copyright © 1978 by Ruth Bornstein. Reprinted by permission of Ticknor & Fields/Clarion Books, a Houghton Mifflin Company and by permission of Curtis Brown, Ltd.

"Davy Crockett" from AMERICAN TALL TALES by Adrien Stoutenburg. Copyright © 1966 by Adrien Stoutenburg. Reprinted by permission of Viking Penguin Inc. and Curtis Brown, Ltd.

"The Desert Is Theirs" with selected illustrations is adapted from THE DESERT IS THEIRS by Byrd Baylor. Text copyright © 1975 Byrd Baylor. Illustrations by Peter Parnall. Illustrations copyright © 1975 Peter Parnall. Used with the permission of Charles Scribner's Sons.

"Elisabeth and the Marsh Mystery" is adapted from ELISABETH AND THE MARSH MYSTERY by Felice Holman. Copyright © 1966 by Felice Holman. Adapted with permission of Macmillan Publishing Company.

"Feelings About Words" is an excerpt from "Feelings About Words" from WORDS, WORDS, WORDS by Mary O'Neill. Copyright © 1966 by Mary O'Neill. Reprinted by permission of Doubleday & Company, Inc.

"Felita" is adapted from FELITA by Nicholasa Mohr. Text copyright © 1979 by Nicholasa Mohr. Reprinted by permission of the publisher, Dial Books for Young Readers and the author.

"Four Riddles for a Fortune" by Kathleen C. Phillips. Copyright © 1974 by Kathleen C. Phillips. This was originally published in *Cricket* Magazine. Reprinted by permission of the author.

Contents

16

Introducing Level 10

DISCOVERIES

UNIT 1

You never know what discoveries await you! In the stories in this unit, you will meet people who discover new interests, new talents, and new ways to communicate. What are your favorite ways to communicate? How could you help yourself and others discover new interests and talents?

Still round the corner there may wait
A new road or a secret gate ...

J. R. R. Tolkien

THE WEEK MOM UNPLUGGED THE TVs

Terry Wolfe Phelan

Steve spent almost all of his free time watching TV. There were three TVs in his house, so he and his two sisters could always watch whatever they wanted. One day, Steve's mom decided that he and his sisters spent too many hours glued to the screen. She announced that she was pulling out the plugs! Could Steve make it for an entire school week without his shows?

Day 1

The pulling out of the plugs began on Monday. I invited every friend I had to my house after school. I needed them to forget what I was missing on TV.

When my friends left at five o'clock, all the quiet got to me. I screamed. It didn't do any good. Mom ignored me. My oldest sister, Beth, ignored me. My middle sister, Stacey, ignored my screaming, too. You'd think I went around screaming all my life.

Then I just sat there. I heard some crickets clicking outside. I'd never heard crickets in the afternoon before. I went to the window and tried to see them. I looked hard, but I couldn't find them. So I walked around the house sixteen times.

When I came back in, I didn't see Stacey or Beth around. I figured they were doing their homework. I didn't have any homework, so I wrote a letter to my cousin Frank. I asked him if I could come and visit. I signed it, "Save me; your long lost cousin, Steve."

Then I left the house and went to mail my letter. The crickets' clicks were even louder at night. I wished I could see one of them. After I plopped my letter in the mailbox, I started back home. I noticed a star following me.

Later that first night, I lay in bed and listened to the crickets. I pulled my bed close to the window. I wanted to check on that star.

Day 2

Day Two without a TV was almost a rerun of Day One, except I did a few more things. I didn't invite my friends. I oiled my baseball mitt. I searched for the crickets, but I had no luck. I even checked the mail to see if Frank wrote me back.

I got into bed that second night nearly two hours before my usual bedtime. I looked out the window. I couldn't find that star anywhere. I hoped it hadn't followed someone else home. No, that was silly. That star was there somewhere, but I couldn't see it.

I bet if I had a telescope I could see it, I thought. I might even see the crickets. A telescope would be like my own TV. I could tune in anything I wanted. I decided right then I would have something to do on Day Three. I would build a telescope.

Day 3

I raced home from school so I could start building. I didn't even have a snack. I had to get to work.

I used two cardboard tubes—one large one from a paper towel roll and a smaller one from a toilet paper roll. I had two magnifying glasses to use for lenses. I fit the smaller tube into the larger one. Then I glued the lenses in place. I was on my way.

I painted "on" and "off" knobs on the tubes to remind me of a TV. My completed telescope was perfect, except for one thing. It only had a $1\frac{1}{2}$-inch screen. I didn't care too much though. Only my eyeball had to fit in. If the telescope worked right, everything would become ten times their real sizes!

By the time I finished my telescope, it was too dark to see a cricket and too light to see a star. When night finally did come, it was so cloudy I couldn't see a thing. The only thing left for me to do was go to bed. I even had blurred dreams that night.

Day 4

By Day Four, I was really anxious to use my telescope. I had almost forgotten what I was missing on TV. I grabbed my telescope and ran outside.

I noticed a bumblebee on our rose bush. I pulled the tubes back and forth in order to focus on the bee. Even I was surprised with what I saw.

Everything was upside down! A bee looks real funny upside down on a flower. A bird on a branch looks like it's flying upside down with a nest for

shoes. My telescope made every show a daytime comedy.

It took ages for Day Four to finally get dark. But I was ready when the first star appeared. I peered through my telescope and discovered the sky shows looked right side up. Why were the daytime shows upside down? Then I realized the night shows were upside down, too. Stars just look the same right side up or upside down.

While I was focusing, my cousin Frank called. He was ready to save me, but I was too busy to be saved. I told him to write me a letter. I'd answer it if I had time.

That night I dreamt that I discovered a new comet. I got all kinds of awards and medals. The President declared a school holiday to honor me.

Day 5

On Day Five, I was ready to make my comet discovery. I knew I'd have to work fast. I only had five hours until my TV-less life was over. But, I had to wait until it got dark. I used the daytime scenes to practice focusing. Stacey and Beth must have wondered why I hadn't been bothering them lately. They both followed me outside to check on what I was doing. I was focusing on leaves and blades of grass. "Let me see, too," Beth said. "Then me," Stacey said.

I taught them how to use my telescope. Stacey discovered an ant hill that looked like a cone with sprinkles all over it. Beth saw a caterpillar. We hoped we would see it turn into a butterfly.

When I took my turn to watch the caterpillar, a clap of thunder struck. The caterpillar hid under a leaf. "There goes the daytime star," I said.

"As a matter of fact, there go all the outdoor shows. It's going to rain any minute," Beth said.

She was right. The thunder got louder. Lightning began to flash. The sky was dark enough to see a comet, but there was too much rain. We all ran inside.

We were busy watching the downpour through the kitchen window. Not one of us noticed that the refrigerator stopped humming. I went to get a glass of milk. "There's no light in the refrigerator," I said.

Stacey flicked the wall switch. The overhead light didn't go on either. "The storm must have knocked out the power," Stacey said.

Then Mom came. "It's too bad the power had to blow just when you could plug in again," she said.

"What luck," I said. "No TV shows and no outdoor shows either." I felt like screaming again.

"The rain has to stop some time," Stacey said, "so let's be ready."

"What do you mean, 'ready'?" Beth asked.

"Well, Steve has a telescope. Let's make some more equipment to add to his." Stacey began searching for empty milk cartons and pocket mirrors. She was going to build a periscope so we could see around corners. Wow! I thought. With a periscope, I could surely find those hiding crickets.

We were so busy collecting and constructing, I never heard the refrigerator start to hum again. Our equipment was almost ready. It was getting dark enough for the sky shows, too.

Mom *did* hear the refrigerator hum. She flicked on the overhead light. Edison's invention lit up our inventions. Stacey, Beth, and I just stared at each other. No one said a word. The week without a TV was over. We could switch on any program we wanted.

I looked at my watch. It was 6:30—time for the reruns. Then I looked outside and saw the sky was clearing. The reruns were O.K., but I could watch reruns any time. I was after a first run. Maybe I'd even discover a U.F.O. circling that comet this time.

Thinking and Writing About the Selection

1. Why did Steve decide to build a telescope?
2. Did Steve miss watching TV on Days Four and Five? How do you know?
3. How did Steve's project help Stacey and Beth discover new interests?

 4. What kinds of TV programs do you like to watch? Choose one of your favorite shows and tell what you like about it.

Applying the Key Skill
Sequence of Events

Write these headings on your paper:

Day 1   Day 2   Day 3   Day 4   Day 5

Then write each of the following events from "The Week Mom Unplugged the TVs" under the proper heading.

Steve decided to build a telescope.

Steve went to bed two hours before his usual bedtime.

Mom unplugged the TVs.

Frank called Steve, but Steve was too busy focusing on a star to talk.

Stacey looked at an ant hill, and Beth looked at a caterpillar.

Steve wrote a letter to his cousin Frank.

Stacey decided to build a periscope.

Steve built his telescope but couldn't use it.

What's Behind TV?

There's a word story behind TV. You probably know the first part of the story. The letters *TV* come from the two word parts that make up *television*, *tele* and *vision*. Knowing what these two word parts mean will help you understand what television is.

tele	+	**vision**	→	**television**
far off, distant		seeing or sight		distant seeing

Television is a system of sending and receiving pictures over long distances.

Now take *tele* and add *scope*.

tele	+	**scope**	→	**telescope**
far off, distant		instrument for observing		A telescope is an instrument for making distant objects look larger.

Next take *scope* and add it to *peri*.

peri	+	**scope**	→	**periscope**
around		instrument for observing		observing around

A periscope is an instrument for seeing things that are not in a straight line with the viewer.

Here are some words made up of the word parts you have just learned: telephone, telegram, microscope, kaleidoscope, perimeter. How many do you know?

SEQUENCE OF EVENTS

What would you do if you wanted to make a telescope? First you might go to the library to find a book about telescopes. Next you might gather all the materials the book says you will need. Only then could you begin to follow the steps to construct the telescope.

An important part of working on a project is following the steps in order, or **sequence**. Events in a story have an order, or sequence, too. Writers sometimes help their readers to understand the sequence of events by using signal words such as *before*, *after*, *next*, and *then*. Number words such as *first*, *second*, and *third* are also clues to sequence. The author of "The Week Mom Unplugged the TVs" used special sequence clues. What are they?

ACTIVITY A Read the following paragraph about some of the events in "The Week Mom Unplugged the TVs." Look for the words or groups of words that help you keep track of the sequence. Write these words on your paper.

Steve was horrified at the thought of an entire week without TV! What could he do to help himself forget about his TV shows? First, he invited all of his friends over to play. After his friends left, he wrote a letter to his cousin Frank. The next day, he decided to build a telescope. On the third day, he built the telescope, but the sky was cloudy so he couldn't use it. By the fourth day, Steve had almost forgotten TV.

Keeping track of the sequence of events can help you make connections between one event and another. Why did Steve's cousin call him on Day Four? Did you remember that Steve had written to him on Day One?

ACTIVITY B Read the sentences below. Then look back at the story "The Week Mom Unplugged the TVs" to fill in the missing events. Write the completed sentences on your paper.

1. On Day One, Steve noticed a star.
   Steve probably would never have seen the star if he hadn't _____.

2. On Day Five, Stacey suggested that she, Beth, and Steve build a periscope.
   Stacey probably got the idea because _____.

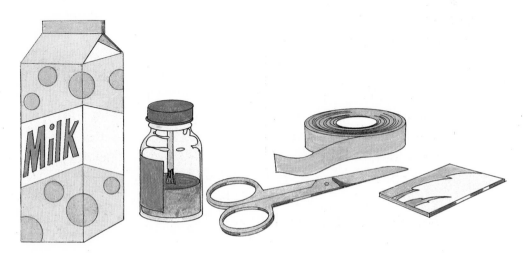

Pippi Finds a Spink

Astrid Lindgren

*You have read about the many new interests
Steve and his sisters discovered during a week
without television. Now you are about to meet
someone who makes discoveries no matter what
week it is. Her name is Pippi Longstocking.
Pippi is not the kind of girl you're likely to meet
every day. She seems to have one adventure after
another. A horse and a monkey are her pets.
Pippi's best friends, Tommy and Annika,
never know what to expect when they visit
her. Join them as they help Pippi make a
discovery that may surprise you.*

One morning Tommy and Annika came skipping into Pippi's kitchen as usual, shouting good morning. But there was no answer. Pippi was sitting in the middle of the kitchen table with Mr. Nilsson, the little monkey, in her arms and a happy smile on her face.

"Good morning," said Tommy and Annika again.

"Just think," said Pippi dreamily, "just think that I have discovered it—I and no one else!"

"What have you discovered?" Tommy and Annika wondered. They weren't in the least bit surprised that Pippi had discovered something because she was always doing that, but they did want to know what it was.

"What did you discover, anyway, Pippi?"

"A new word," said Pippi and looked at Tommy and Annika as if she had just this minute noticed them. "A brand-new word."

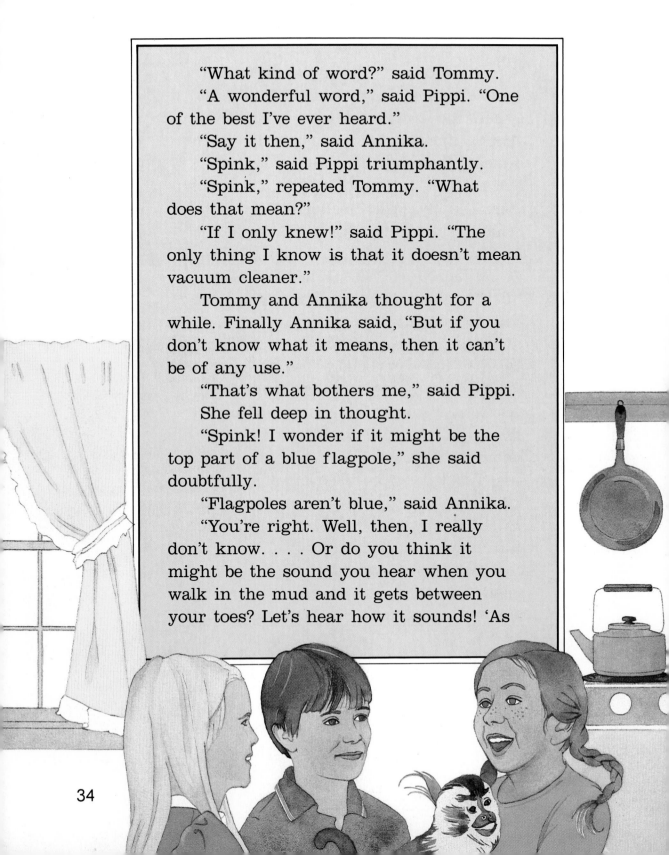

"What kind of word?" said Tommy.

"A wonderful word," said Pippi. "One of the best I've ever heard."

"Say it then," said Annika.

"Spink," said Pippi triumphantly.

"Spink," repeated Tommy. "What does that mean?"

"If I only knew!" said Pippi. "The only thing I know is that it doesn't mean vacuum cleaner."

Tommy and Annika thought for a while. Finally Annika said, "But if you don't know what it means, then it can't be of any use."

"That's what bothers me," said Pippi.

She fell deep in thought.

"Spink! I wonder if it might be the top part of a blue flagpole," she said doubtfully.

"Flagpoles aren't blue," said Annika.

"You're right. Well, then, I really don't know. . . . Or do you think it might be the sound you hear when you walk in the mud and it gets between your toes? Let's hear how it sounds! 'As

34

Annika walked in the mud you could hear the most wonderful spink.'" She shook her head. "No, that's no good. 'You could hear the most wonderful *tjipp*'—that's what it should be instead."

Pippi scratched her head. "This is getting more and more mysterious. But whatever it is, I'm going to find out. Maybe it can be bought in the stores. Come on, let's go and ask!"

Pippi led the horse down from the veranda. "We're in a hurry," she said to Tommy and Annika. "We'll have to ride. Because otherwise there might not be any spink left when we get there."

When the horse came galloping through the streets of the little town with Pippi and Tommy and Annika on his back, the children heard the clatter of his hoofs on the cobblestones and came happily running because they all liked Pippi so much.

"Pippi, where are you going?" they cried.

"I'm going to buy spink," said Pippi and brought the horse to a halt for a moment.

The children looked puzzled.

"Is it something good?" a little boy asked.

"You bet," said Pippi and licked her lips. "It's wonderful. At least it sounds as if it were."

In front of a grocery store she jumped off the horse, lifted Tommy and Annika down, and in they went.

"I would like to buy a bag of spink," said Pippi. "But I want it nice and crunchy."

"Spink," said the lady behind the counter, trying to think. "I don't believe we have that."

"You must have it," said Pippi. "All well-stocked shops carry it."

Then the lady blushed and said, "I really don't even know what spink is. In any case, we don't have it here."

Very disappointed, Pippi walked toward the door. "Then I have to keep on looking," she said. "I can't go back home without spink."

The next store was a hardware store. A salesman bowed politely to the children.

"I would like to buy a spink," said Pippi. "But I want it to be of the best kind, the one that is used for killing lions."

"Let's see," the salesman said. He scratched himself behind the ear. "Let's see." He took out a small rake. "Is this all right?" he said as he handed it to Pippi.

Pippi looked angrily at him. "That's a rake," she said. "It's a spink I wanted. Don't try to fool me."

Then the salesman laughed and said, "Unfortunately we don't have the thing you want."

Pippi looked sad. She said good-by to the salesman, and so did Annika. Tommy bowed. Then they went out to the horse, who was waiting at the fence.

Not far from the hardware store was a high three-story house with a window open on the upper floor. Pippi pointed toward the open window and said, "It wouldn't surprise me if the spink is in there. I'll dash up and see." Quickly she climbed up the water spout. When she reached the level of the window she hoisted herself up by the arms and stuck her head in.

In the room two ladies were sitting chatting. Imagine their astonishment when all of a sudden a red head popped over the window sill and a voice said, "Is there by any chance a spink here?"

The two ladies cried out in terror. "Good heavens, what are you saying, child? Has someone escaped?"

"That is exactly what I would like to know," said Pippi politely.

"Maybe he's under the bed!" screamed one of the ladies. "Does he bite?"

"I think so," said Pippi. "He's supposed to have tremendous fangs."

The two ladies clung to each other. Pippi looked around curiously, but finally she said with a sigh, "No, there isn't as much as a spink's whisker around here. Excuse me for disturbing you. I just thought I would ask, since I happened to be passing by."

She slid down the water spout and said sadly to Tommy and Annika, "There isn't any spink in this town. Let's ride back home."

And that's what they did. When they jumped down from the horse outside the veranda, Tommy came close to stepping on a little beetle which was crawling on the path.

"Be careful not to step on the beetle!" Pippi cried.

All three bent down to look at it. It was such a tiny thing, with green wings that gleamed like metal.

"What a pretty little creature," said Annika. "I wonder what it is."

"It isn't a June bug," said Tommy.

"And no ladybug either," said Annika. "I wish I knew what it was."

All at once a smile lit up Pippi's face. "I know," she said. "It's a spink."

"Are you sure?" Tommy asked doubtfully.

"Don't you think I know a spink when I see one?" said Pippi. "Have you ever seen anything so spink-like in your life?"

She carefully moved the beetle to a safer place, where no one could step on it. "My sweet little spink," she said tenderly. "I knew that I would find one at last. But isn't it funny! We've been hunting all over town for a spink, and there was one right here all the time!"

Thinking and Writing About the Selection

1. What did Pippi discover?
2. Why did Pippi and her friends go to the stores?
3. Did Pippi really find a spink? Could anyone else have told her what a spink was?
4. Make up a new word and tell what it means. Then explain why you think the meaning and the word go well together.

Applying the Key Skill
Multiple-Meaning Words

Use context clues to choose the correct meaning of each underlined word. Write each word and its meaning.

1. Pippi said that all well-stocked shops would carry spink.
   a. to take from one place to another
   b. to have on hand
   c. to approve
   d. to capture

2. Could spink be as light as down, wondered Annika.
   a. fine, soft feathers
   b. sad
   c. to cause to fall
   d. toward the ground

3. Were Pippi's descriptions of the spink sound, wondered Tommy.
   a. healthy
   b. based on fact
   c. a noise
   d. to give a signal

PLUMP

BRICK

ice

SCREAM

ROUND

Lace

BRIGHT

SQUAT

FEELINGS ABOUT WORDS

Mary O'Neill

Some words clink
As ice in drink.
Some move with grace
A dance, a lace.
Some sound thin:
Wail, scream and pin.
Some words are squat:
A mug, a pot.
And some are plump,
Fat, round and dump.
Some words are light:
Drift, lift and bright.
A few are small:
A, is and all.
And some are thick,
Glue, paste and brick.
Some words can fly—
There's wind, there's high;
And some words cry:
"Goodbye . . .
Goodbye. . . ."

NEWS ARTICLE

Prewrite

Pippi Longstocking had a wild imagination. She imagined a spink and then went out to discover what it might be. You can use your imagination just as Pippi did and imagine an unusual discovery of your own.

Look at the chart. These ideas may set your imagination to work. Think about what each discovery might be. The time and place of discovery may help you.

Name of Discovery	Time and Place of Discovery
A marvuna	Lonely beach near the ocean in summer
A blodget	Trip to the planet Jupiter in 2034
A dop	A visit to the mountains in the spring

Many discoveries are reported in newspapers or magazines. Suppose you have been asked to report on your discovery. These questions may help you plan your news article. Make notes about the ideas you will use.

1. What is your discovery? Describe it clearly.
2. When and where did you make the discovery?
3. What events led to the discovery?
   What happened to you first, then, next?
4. What did you do after you made the discovery?

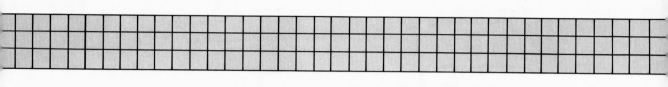

Write

1. Reread your notes. You will need to organize them so you can write your news article. In "Pippi Finds a Spink," the writer told events in time order, that is, what Pippi and her friends did first, next, then, and last. You should use time order, too.

2. List all the events that happened to you before, during, and after your discovery. Number them in the order you will write about them in your news article.

3. Plan to write at least two or more paragraphs. One paragraph should describe your discovery. Another paragraph or two could tell about the events that happened to you.

4. Try to use Vocabulary Treasures in your article.

5. Now write the first draft of your news article.

VOCABULARY TREASURES

astonishment	triumphantly
unfortunately	eventually

Revise

Read your news article. Have a friend read it, too. Think about this checklist as you revise.

1. Could your reader tell the time order of the events?

2. Could your reader describe your discovery?

3. Did you choose words that caught the interest of your reader? Use Vocabulary Treasures and your Glossary for help.

4. Did you proofread your report for correct use of capital letters and end punctuation in sentences?

5. Now rewrite your news article to share.

Eloise Jarvis McGraw

The Galumpagalooses

Do you know what galumpagalooses (gə lum′ pə gə lüs′ əs) are? Jamie, the boy in this story, doesn't know, but he finds out. He also discovers something new about his special interest.

Jamie propped his cheek on one hand and gazed out the schoolroom window. It was raining outdoors. He propped the other cheek on the other hand and looked around the room at his classmates. They were doing their arithmetic or reading their library books. He'd finished everything.

He looked at the clock over the blackboard. It was still twenty minutes till school was out. He propped both cheeks on both hands and sighed. His teacher, Miss Morris, came over to his desk.

"What'll I *do*?" he whispered. "I don't have anything to *do* again."

"Yes, I noticed," she said. "Well, Jamie, I know how much you like to draw. Today I'm going to let you draw some pictures."

"I've already drawn a lot of pictures," said Jamie. He moved his elbows so she could see the five sheets of paper he had covered with drawings.

"You haven't drawn the kind of pictures I'm thinking of," said Miss Morris. She put a fresh sheet of paper on top of his drawings. "I want you to draw five pictures of something nobody's ever seen before."

She walked away, leaving Jamie blinking after her. Something *nobody* had ever seen before?

Jamie reached for his pencil. Then he frowned at the sheet of paper. He'd have to make something up. Something that wasn't like anything else.

He let the pencil touch the paper and sort of do what it wanted to. It drew a blob. Jamie stared at it. It looked like a wad of chewing gum. It looked like a cloud. The longer he studied it, the more things he thought it looked like.

He scribbled it out and drew another sort of thing. This was an animal kind of thing. It had six legs and ears no wider than needles and polka-dots on its back. When he got through, it looked a lot like a bug of some kind. Maybe a ladybug.

He scribbled that out and drew a sort of little Mars-man. Somehow it came out looking like a dog. Then he drew a huge giant Mars-man with a lot of crazy scribbles instead of a head. It turned out to be the best tree he had ever drawn.

He drew seven more pictures in the next ten minutes. Not one of them managed to look like something nobody had ever seen before. In fact, they all looked like things everybody saw every day. By now Jamie had forgotten to watch the clock. When the bell rang, he jumped.

Scowling, Jamie wadded his drawings into a ball. Then he walked up to Miss Morris.

"I didn't get through with the five drawings yet," he told her. "Not *all* through." He didn't want to admit he hadn't got through even one.

"Oh, that's all right, Jamie," said Miss Morris. "Maybe you can't do it anyway."

"I can do it," Jamie said, scowling harder. "I'll bring them tomorrow."

"All right," Miss Morris said cheerfully.

Jamie didn't feel cheerful. He walked the four blocks to the store where his mother worked. She wasn't waiting on anyone, so he went to her counter. "If you were going to draw something nobody's ever seen before, what would you draw?" he asked.

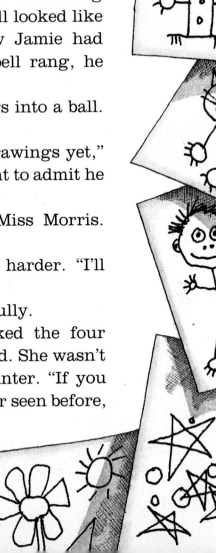

46

She only laughed and hugged him. "Goodness! What do I know about drawing pictures? Why not ask Mr. Rollo?"

"Mr. Rollo? Would he know?" Jamie asked.

"He's an artist, isn't he?" Jamie's mother got her purse and handed him his house key. "Now go straight home and be *careful* crossing Seventh Street. I'll be home about six." She hugged him good-bye.

Jamie and his mother lived in the downstairs half of a house. Mr. Rollo lived in the upstairs half and worked at an advertising agency. Jamie had never thought of him as an artist. He went to an office every day like anybody else. Still, he *had* told Jamie once that all he did at work was draw pictures of things like furniture and TV sets. Jamie had thought he was joking.

When Mr. Rollo came home at five o'clock, Jamie was out in the front hall waiting for him.

"Hi there, Jamie, how's it going?" said Mr. Rollo.

"Mr. Rollo, are you an artist?" Jamie asked him.

"You could say that," answered Mr. Rollo. "I'm not exactly anything else."

"A *real* artist?" said Jamie.

"That's a different question." Mr. Rollo looked down at Jamie. "Ask me something easier."

"Well . . . could you draw a picture of something that nobody's ever seen before?"

Mr. Rollo blinked. Then he said, "Sure. I do that all the time."

"Really?" Jamie exclaimed. "But you said you only drew pictures of furniture and TV sets and—"

"That's at work. At home I draw things nobody's ever seen before." He smiled at Jamie. "Come on up and I'll show you."

Jamie had never been in Mr. Rollo's part of the house. Mostly it was one long room. There were pictures all over the walls. Jamie just stood and stared at them. All of them were pictures of things nobody had ever seen before—every single one.

"What are they, Mr. Rollo?" he asked at last. "I mean, what do you call them?"

"Well, sometimes I call them abstractions. Sometimes I just call them shapes. Now and then I call one a galumpagaloos."

Jamie laughed. This time he knew Mr. Rollo was joking. "How do you draw them? How do you start?" he asked.

Mr. Rollo thought a minute, then said, "I look at something."

"Oh," said Jamie, feeling doubtful. "But it's supposed to be something nobody's ever seen."

"Nobody ever *has* seen it the way I see it, because nobody else is me. Look there, Jamie," said Mr. Rollo. He turned Jamie to face a painting on the wall. "Did you ever see the thing in that picture before?"

Jamie looked carefully, then said, "No."

"Yes, you have," said Mr. Rollo. He turned Jamie to face the window. Outside, you could see a piece of the church, and there was a bowl of oranges on the sill. "That's what you saw. But I saw something nobody'd ever seen before—not even me, until I drew it."

Jamie stared at the painting, and then at the window, and then at the painting again. Slowly he began to understand. It made him feel very excited. "Could I draw one of those galumpagalooses, do you think?" he asked.

"Never know till you try," said Mr. Rollo.

So Jamie tried. He hurried downstairs and found some paper and a pencil. Then he looked at things. He looked until he really *saw* them in his very own way. Then he drew.

Right away he knew he was drawing things *he'd* never seen before. By the time his mother came home, he had four sheets of paper covered with drawings. When he showed them to her, she said *she'd* never seen such things. Jamie still wasn't sure about Miss Morris.

The next morning at school, he drew one last picture. Then he took them all up to Miss Morris's desk. She looked at him and then at the papers in his hand. "Do you mean you've done it?" she asked him.

"I *think* so," Jamie told her. He handed her the last picture he had drawn. "Did you ever see that thing before?"

Miss Morris looked at the picture carefully. Then she said, "No."

Jamie began to smile. He knew she had, but not the way *he* had seen it. "It's a galumpagaloos," he said. He handed her his other drawings. "Here are four other galumpagalooses."

He watched her spread them out on her desk and stare at them. Finally she raised her eyes and said, "You win, Jamie."

"I told you I could do it," said Jamie.

For a minute they just grinned at each other. Then Jamie had a thought. "Miss Morris," he said. "What'll I do today if I finish all my work?"

Thinking and Writing About the Selection

1. What kind of pictures did Miss Morris want Jamie to draw?

2. Were Jamie's first tries at the drawings for Miss Morris successful? Explain your answer.

3. Why do you think Mr. Rollo called some of his pictures *galumpagalooses*?

4. You can draw your own galumpagaloos. Pick an object or place you know. Look at it carefully. Then draw it as you see it.

Applying the Key Skill
Facts and Opinions

Write these headings on your paper:

Facts   Opinions

Then write each sentence below about "The Galumpagalooses" under the proper heading.

1. Miss Morris asked Jamie to draw five pictures of something no one had ever seen before.

2. Jamie was the best artist in his school.

3. Mr. Rollo had pictures all over the walls of his room.

4. Abstractions are the hardest kind of pictures to draw.

5. Jamie probably would have drawn a galumpagaloos without Mr. Rollo's help.

DIFFERENT WAYS OF SEEING

by Judith Nayer

Look closely at the palm of your hand.
Focus your attention on the lines and
creases. Look at the loops the lines make
on your fingertips. Notice the patterns the
lines form.

Now hold your hand as far away from your eyes as you can. The details you saw before are more difficult to see now. The shape of your hand, the outline of your fingers, and the spaces between them are the things you may notice. You are still looking at your hand, but you are seeing it in a different way.

Two people looking at the same thing may see it very differently. Suppose they are looking at the ocean. One person may notice the movement and colors of the water. The second person may see the swimmers riding the waves. For every eye that sees, there is a different way of seeing.

Artists can help us to understand the many different ways of seeing. On the pages that follow, you can discover how some artists have seen people in hats, houses, and arrangements of fruit. As you look at the paintings, you may see things you have not seen or noticed before. You may also discover that you see the paintings in a different way if you look at them more than once. Keep on looking. Let your eyes find different ways of seeing.

Portrait of a Young Man
by Bronzino

Woman with Hat.
by Pablo Picasso

© giraudon-orion press

Self-Portrait with a Straw Hat
by Vincent van Gogh

54

Bright Red Houses
by Oscar Bluemner

Bellevue Garden
by Édouard Manet

Still Life with Apples
by Paul Cézanne

Still Life with Flowers and Fruit
by Ignace Henri Jean Théodore
Fantin-Latour

56

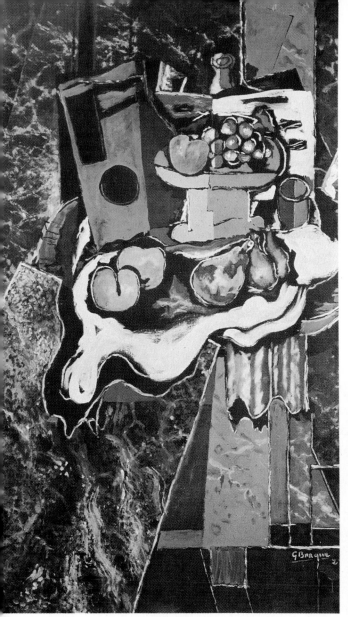

Fruit, Musical Score and Glass
by Georges Braque

Still Life with Crystal Bowl
by Roy Lichtenstein

57

FACTS AND OPINIONS

Read the sentences below. Think about the kind of statement each makes.

- Eloise Jarvis McGraw wrote "The Galumpagalooses."
- "Different Ways of Seeing" is an interesting article.

The first sentence states a fact. **Facts** can be checked and can be proven to be true. How can you check the truth of the first sentence?

The second sentence is an opinion. **Opinions** express personal feelings. Opinions cannot be proven or disproven. Opinions are often general statements. When people state an opinion, they often begin by saying, "*In my opinion*" or "*I think*." Other words that signal opinions are *should*, *ought*, *must*, *best*, and *least*.

ACTIVITY A Number your paper from 1 to 6. Read each sentence. Decide whether it is a fact or an opinion. Write **Fact** or **Opinion** next to each number.

1. Astrid Lindgren wrote more than one story about Pippi Longstocking.
2. "Pippi Finds a Spink" is her best.
3. Paintings by Picasso and Van Gogh are found in many museums.
4. The most beautiful paintings are abstractions.
5. Everyone should learn how to draw.
6. People who look at the same scene may see different things.

Sometimes people make statements that *seem* to be facts. Read the sentences below:

- "The Galumpagalooses" was written by Astrid Lindgren.
- "The Galumpagalooses" was written by Eloise Jarvis McGraw.

Only one of these statements is true. The other is false. You can use the Contents to find out which statement is true and which is false.

ACTIVITY B Number your paper from 1 to 5. Read each sentence below. If the sentence is true, write **True**. If it is false, write **False**. Then rewrite each false statement to make a true statement by changing the necessary word or words.

1. Mr. Rollo is a character in "Pippi Finds a Spink."
2. Miss Morris suggested that Jamie talk to Mr. Rollo for help.
3. "The Galumpagalooses" is a photo-essay.
4. Mr. Nilsson is the name of a monkey in "Pippi Finds a Spink."
5. Jamie told his teacher that the picture he had drawn was a spink.

MARIA'S HOUSE

Jean Merrill

Maria loved her Saturday art classes at the museum. She looked forward to discussing her pictures with Miss Lindstrom, her art teacher. But one Saturday, Maria did not want to go to art class. She had a problem, and this story tells how she solved it with some help from Mama.

The Saturday before, Miss Lindstrom had given the class an assignment to do at home. She had asked the class to make drawings of the houses where they lived. Usually, Maria was very happy when Miss Lindstrom gave assignments. This time was different. As Maria walked down Market Street after class, she decided that she could not draw a picture of the building in which her family and fourteen other families lived.

It was just an old building. It was squeezed into the middle of a block of other buildings. Each one was as tired and worn-out looking as the next. How could she make a beautiful picture of 79 Market Street?

Maria was sure that when Miss Lindstrom said to draw a house, she was thinking of a house where one family lived. She was thinking of a neat, freshly painted building set apart from other houses by grass, gardens, and shade trees. Maria imagined that the other children in the art class all lived in such houses. None of them lived in buildings like those on Market Street.

Maria had put off doing the assignment all week. Then, last night, Friday night, she had opened her drawing pad on the kitchen table.

She had a new set of markers that Mama had bought her. She wanted to do a drawing with the markers. She tried all the colors on the cover of the pad. Then she sat for a long time, staring at a clean sheet of drawing paper. Finally, she started to draw.

She drew a large white house with picture windows. The windows looked out over a wide lawn. Then she sketched in a driveway with birch trees on either side.

Mama looked over at the drawing. "Pretty," she said. "Like a picture in a magazine. But what are you drawing for art class?"

"This is for class," Maria said.

"A *magazine* picture?" Mama asked.

Mama had learned a lot about art. She knew by now that art was not like a picture in a magazine.

"We have to draw a house this week," she said.

"Just a house?" Mama asked. "Any house?"

Maria did not answer for a minute. Then she said, "It's supposed to be the house where we live."

"Oh," Mama said. She looked at Maria's picture again. "Our house?" she asked.

"No," Maria said. "I can't draw our house."

"Can't *draw* it?" Mama asked. "Before you ever went to art class, you could draw a whole block of houses burning down and five fire engines and a hundred people in the picture. Now you can't draw one house?"

"That's not what I mean," Maria said. She tried to explain that a three-room apartment on Market Street wasn't the same as a house. In order to do the assignment, she would have to imagine a house.

"But a three-room apartment is *in* a house," Mama said. "So it's a big house—an apartment house. Your teacher means draw where you live."

"Oh, Mama!" Maria cried. "This house is no good to draw. How can I make a beautiful picture of this house? I was trying to make a beautiful picture."

Mama looked down at the house Maria had drawn and shook her head. "It's nice that art should be beautiful," she said. "But it should also be true. Your teacher asks you to draw what you know." Mama sighed. "I am not an artist," she said. "All I know is that art must be true."

Mama went on talking as she ironed a shirt. "It must be true to how you feel. True to how you see. If you're a rabbit—true to how a rabbit sees. But true. Always true."

Maria looked again at the house she had drawn. It did look like a magazine picture. Mama was right

about that. Maria tore the picture from her drawing pad and slipped it into her portfolio. She started another drawing.

She sketched the outline of the house she lived in. With angry slashes of her marker, she drew the rusted fire escape zigzagging down the front of the building. She drew the crumbling cement steps leading up to the front door.

She was drawing very fast. She put in all the things that made the building look so sad, old, and tired. Mama would see that she could not take a picture like this to Miss Lindstrom.

Maria stopped and looked at her drawing. It was 79 Market Street all right. She hadn't even had to go out and look at the building. She knew exactly how it looked.

Mama came over to look at the picture. She studied it for a long time. "It's true," she said finally. "It's Market Street." Mama sighed. "Will you take it to art class?"

"Mama! I can't!" Maria cried. She ripped the picture off the pad and stuffed it into her portfolio. She put away her markers and pencils, washed, and went to bed.

Mama did not say much at breakfast the next morning. Maria wanted to say, "Please, Mama, try to understand," but she couldn't say it. When Mama went to wake up Papa, Maria knew what she had to do.

She opened up her portfolio and took out the drawing of the white house. She tore it up and threw it away.

Mama must have known. She nodded her head in a proud stern way as Maria went out the door.

Most of the kids in the class were already at their easels when Maria came in. They were pinning up the drawings they had done during the week.

Coming in late, Maria felt as if everyone was watching her. Quickly, she took out her drawing and tacked it to her easel. She was afraid someone might laugh, but no one did.

Maria's hands felt cold when Miss Lindstrom moved over to her easel. Her mouth felt dry. She wanted to run out of the room. But she just stood there by her easel, watching Miss Lindstrom.

Maria caught the brief look of surprise on Miss Lindstrom's face. She wished she could sink through the floor. Miss Lindstrom did not say anything for a minute. Then she put an arm around Maria's shoulder. "Everyone come here," she called. The rest of the class crowded around Maria's easel.

Miss Lindstrom asked the class if any of them had ever been through the old part of town.

"I have," a boy named Jasper said. "My uncle goes there to buy fish."

"Those of you that have," Miss Lindstrom said, "will see how well Maria has caught the feeling of that neighborhood."

"Look." Miss Lindstrom bent over Maria's drawing. "See here," she said, "—and here—and here—" The art teacher's hands touched the paper lightly. "I can almost hear the kids yelling in the street," Miss Lindstrom said. "I can hear people laughing inside the apartments. I can even smell spaghetti cooking."

"Not me," Jasper said. "I smell fish."

Miss Lindstrom laughed. "You're right, Jasper. I can smell that, too. There's so much going on in this house. Does everyone see what is so good about Maria's drawing?" Miss Lindstrom asked.

"All those little details," one girl said.

"No," another girl said. "All those bits are nice. Maria can draw anything. But what's really good is that her picture isn't just a picture of a building. You feel as if you know the people who live in it."

"Yes," Miss Lindstrom said. "That's it. It's a beautiful drawing, Maria. Full of life and feeling. The nicest thing you've done this year." She gave Maria a hug and moved on to another easel.

Maria stood staring at her picture. Miss Lindstrom had hugged her and told her that her picture was beautiful. But it wasn't Miss Lindstrom that Maria was seeing as she stared at her picture.

She was seeing Mama. Mama standing dark and stern over the ironing board. Mama saying, "Art must be true."

Thinking and Writing About the Selection

1. Why didn't Maria want to draw her own house?
2. What did Mama mean when she said, "Art must be true"?
3. Why do you think Maria decided to draw her own house and take her picture to art class?
4. What do you think Maria will tell Mama about what happened in art class?

Applying the Key Skill
Facts and Opinions

Read the sentence pairs below. Write the sentences that state opinions.

1. Maria lived at 79 Market Street.
   Her apartment building was the best one on the block.
2. Maria didn't want to draw her house.
   Maria's drawing of the white house was beautiful.
3. Learning how to draw is more important than learning how to play the piano.
   Some museums offer art classes for young students.
4. When Maria grows up, she will be a great artist.
   Miss Lindstrom liked Maria's drawings.

MURAL ON SECOND AVENUE

Lilian Moore

Someone
stood here
tall on a ladder,
dreaming
to the slap of a
wet brush,

painting
on the blank
unwindowed wall of
this old house.

Now the wall is a
field of wild
grass,
bending to a wind.

A unicorn's grazing there
beside a
zebra,

A giraffe
is nibbling a
treetop

and in a sky of
eye-blinking
blue

a horse is flying.

All
right at home in the
neighborhood.

69

SEQUOYAH:
THE CHEROKEE WHO CAPTURED WORDS
Lillie Patterson

*S*equoyah (si kwoi' ə) was born in a Cherokee village on the Tennessee River about the year 1773. As a child, he suffered from an illness that left one leg weaker and shorter than the other. This caused him to walk with a limp, so he was called "The Lame One."

One day, Sequoyah saw some soldiers reading their mail. They explained to him that the marks on the paper were letters. The letters were used to write words. Sequoyah decided that the Cherokees should have the power to write, too.

Words are like wild animals
I must learn to capture them
I will catch them and tame them
And put them in writing.

Sequoyah sang a Song for Thinking. As he sang, he slowly scratched the picture of a horse on a stone.

"*Ha-ya!*" he sang out. "I will draw our Cherokee language. I will make a picture for every word we speak."

71

Still singing, he limped to the forest. He began to cut thin strips of bark from birch trees. All the while he sang a Song for Starting New Things.

Working beside his house, Sequoyah drew pictures on the smooth inside of the strips. His little daughter, Ah-yoka (ä yō′ kə), came to look on with wide eyes. She picked up a bark picture. "This is a house."

"Yes, Little One," Sequoyah said. "Each picture will show a different word. Look! This is for the word *pot*. This is for *fox*. And this is for *fish*."

When cold weather came, Sequoyah took his drawings indoors. He worked at a wooden table. Sometimes he cut pictures into the bark with a small knife. Sometimes he used the burnt end of a stick or a piece of coal as a crayon. Other times he painted with a brush.

Ah-yoka sat beside her father and kept him company. She seemed to know that he was doing something important.

Winter changed to spring, and one season followed another. Sequoyah's friends seldom saw him anymore. Some made jokes. "The Lame One plays with bark pieces all day."

Some of Sequoyah's friends worried. "The poor man acts like someone in a dream." They often left fish and meat beside his door.

The pile of bark grew higher. There were thousands of words in the Cherokee language. Each word stood for at least one thing or idea. Sequoyah faced several hard problems. A picture of a girl could stand for Ah-yoka. But it could stand for other little girls as well. "How can I show the difference?" Sequoyah asked himself.

Many words could not be made into pictures. "How can I show words such as *good* and *bad*?" Sequoyah wondered aloud. "What can I use for *today* or *tomorrow*?" In time he hit upon a new plan. He began to make up symbols, or signs, for different words. Soon he had so many symbols, he could not remember which one stood for which word. If he forgot, how could other people remember?

"There must be a better way," he said aloud. "I can never make enough signs for every Cherokee word. Never!"

A few days later Sequoyah came across something that gave him new ideas. He found a child's spelling book beside a road. A teacher, sent by a church, had opened a school nearby for Cherokee children. They were taught in English, but this was a foreign language to them.

"Our tribe would move ahead much faster if we had books in our own language," Sequoyah told Ah-yoka. He took the speller home and began to study it. He had no idea what the names of the letters were or what each meant. Day after day he looked at the black marks printed in rows.

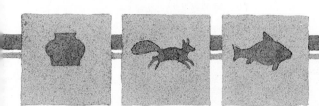

"See," he showed them to Ah-yoka. "The same marks are put down again and again." He counted them. "Yes, there are 26 of the strange shapes. The whole book is made up of only 26 different signs." Of course, Sequoyah was looking at the letters of our alphabet, *a* to *z*.

Late one night he sat studying the speller. A pine log burning in the fireplace gave him light. Suddenly the answer came to him. "Sounds!" he cried out. "Each sign is for a different sound. Put together, the sounds make words."

Next morning he got a fresh bundle of bark. "This time I know I am on the right track," he told Ah-yoka.

"What will you do now?" Ah-yoka asked.

"*Ha-ya!*" Sequoyah swung her high into the air. "I do not need a different sign for every single word. I can break our Cherokee words into parts. All I need is a sign for the sound each part makes."

"Oh, can I help?" Ah-yoka asked.

"Yes, you can," Sequoyah answered. "You are young, but you think quickly. You have keen ears and sharp eyes."

Sequoyah began to draw. "Sequoyah," he sang his name. "Se-quoy-ah. It has three parts. I can make a sign for each. When I put the three signs together, they will show my whole name."

"Can you show my name?" Ah-yoka wanted to know.

"Ah-yo-ka," sang the Lame One. "Ah. The first part of your name is like the last part of mine. They will take the same sign. I can use the same symbols for the same sounds in different words."

"How many signs will you need?" Ah-yoka asked.

Sequoyah tried to find the answer in the months that followed. He tried to remember all the words he had ever said or heard. He broke each word into parts, or syllables—"Hee-tun-hah-yu-hoo." He said each syllable while Ah-yoka listened. Then she sounded words for him to hear.

He was working on a way of writing called a syllabary. It is like an alphabet, yet different. An alphabet has a sign for any one of the tiny sounds that make up a word. Each letter stands alone. A syllabary has a sign for each spoken syllable. For example, an important city in Tennessee has the Cherokee name, Chat-ta-noo-ga. It is

spelled with eleven letters of the alphabet. It is written with only four of Sequoyah's symbols, or letters.

Sequoyah counted 100 of these big sounds, or syllables, in the Cherokee language. After that he decided on a symbol to match each one. He picked out many of the letters of the alphabet, chiefly the big letters, or capitals. They were easy to make. Sequoyah used English letters, but he gave them Cherokee speech sounds. He also made up signs himself.

Sequoyah knew that some members of the Cherokee Nation had moved beyond the Mississippi River. Sequoyah decided to join them.

"We will go far away and build a new home," he told Ahyoka one day in 1818.

"What about the signs?" Ah-yoka asked.

"I will draw them on deerskin," Sequoyah said. "I will keep working on them when I get to the West."

Sequoyah and his family traveled to the Arkansas Territory. Sequoyah set up a trading post. There he met many people.

He listened carefully to the words they spoke. "Say that word again," he would ask strangers. If he heard a new word sound, he made a new sign for it.

Sequoyah worked on his word signs at night. "They must be easy to make and easy to learn," he told his family. After a year of hard work, he found that he needed only 86 signs, not 100. Any Cherokee word could be written by using one or more of them.

Sequoyah picked out the 86 symbols he liked best. He kept many letters of the alphabet, but changed them to his liking. He drew some upside down, others sideways or backward. Sometimes he added little squiggles and fancy lines. He wanted each symbol to express meaning and feeling. At last his 86 signs, or letters, were ready.

"Now they must be taught to others," Sequoyah said. "My first students will be my own family."

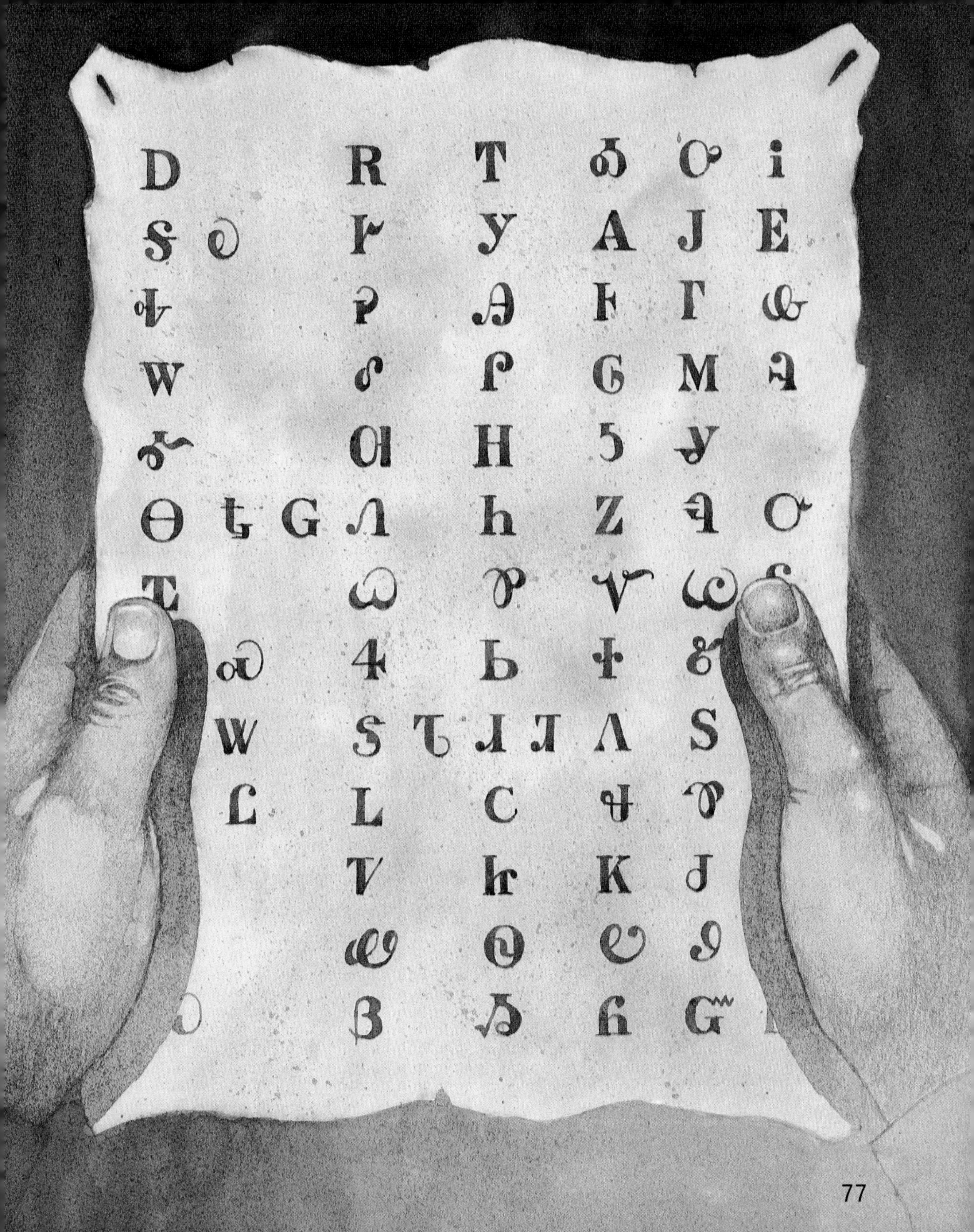

Every evening the family sat around a table near the stone fireplace. One person would call out a word. The others wrote it. Soon they began writing short sentences.

Sequoyah was happy. His writing signs were easy to learn. After years of hard work, he had captured Cherokee words on paper. His dream had come true.

The Lame One did not realize that he had done what no other person had ever done before. He had invented a way to write a spoken language *all by himself*. Other written languages had been developed slowly over the years by many people.

Sequoyah wanted to teach his writing to everyone in the Cherokee Nation. "I will get permission from the leading chiefs," he told his family. "I must go back East."

"Please take me," Ah-yoka cried excitedly.

Sequoyah hugged his ten-year-old daughter. "You have been my helper all along. You should go with me now."

Before he left, Sequoyah taught his symbols to some of the young Cherokees nearby. He helped them to write letters to their families in the East.

These he would take with him. The letters were put on bark or animal skin.

One morning father and daughter mounted two fine horses and waved good-bye. They would follow the overland trails to the Great Smokies. They went singing. They had a dream to sell.

When Sequoyah returned to the East, he received permission from the chiefs to teach his writing to the Cherokee people. Soon the Cherokees were writing letters to their families and friends. For the first time, Cherokees from the East and West could communicate with each other. By 1828, the Cherokees had their own newspaper, books, and schools. They also had the Cherokee laws written down and printed. Sequoyah was honored by his own people and by the United States government. Before Sequoyah died, he went to Mexico to teach even more Cherokees his written language.

Thinking and Writing About the Selection

1. Sequoyah realized that it was a problem to have pictures stand for words. Why did he reach that conclusion?
2. How many symbols would Sequoyah have used to write the word *Cherokee*?
3. Why is a written language useful?

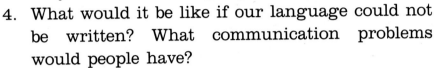 4. What would it be like if our language could not be written? What communication problems would people have?

Applying the Key Skill
Figurative Language

Read each sentence below. Then write the sentence that has the same meaning.

1. Words are like wild animals.
   a. Words cannot be tamed.
   b. Some words sound like animals.
   c. It is not easy to catch wild animals, and it is not easy to learn how to write words.

2. Sounds are the key to written words.
   a. Letters stand for sounds.
   b. Once you know that letters stand for sounds, you can "unlock," or understand, written words.
   c. You can say or write words.

3. Sequoyah's syllabary was his dream come true.
   a. Sequoyah had finally discovered how to write the Cherokee language.
   b. Sequoyah's friends said he acted like someone in a dream.
   c. Sequoyah had a dream about how he could use symbols to write.

YOU NAMED IT!

Have you ever wondered how certain things got their names? You might have thought about this as you read the last selection. Did you think that the tree we call the sequoia might have something to do with **Sequoyah?** If you did, you were right. The giant evergreen of the Pacific coast was named in honor of the man who invented the Cherokee system of writing.

Many words we use today came from people's names. Another man who worked with words gave his name to a system of reading and writing for the blind. His name was **Louis Braille.** Braille, who was blind himself, worked out a code for the alphabet made up of raised dots. The dots could be read by touch.

Samuel Maverick was a Texan who didn't brand his calves. Soon a stray calf or unbranded range animal came to be known as a maverick. After a while, the word *maverick* came to mean an independent person who does not go along with others.

Below are some more words that started out as someone's name. Use a dictionary or encyclopedia to find out about them.

sandwich   **pasteurize**   **cardigan**   **leotard**

FIGURATIVE LANGUAGE

Sometimes writers use words in special ways. One way they do this is by using **figurative language**. Look at the pairs of sentences below. The sentences in each pair mean the same thing. One sentence in each pair uses an example of figurative language. Which sentence in each pair do you think is more interesting?

1. She wished she could sink through the floor.
2. She was so embarrassed she wanted to disappear.

3. Words are like wild animals.
4. Once words are spoken, they are gone.

5. Now the wall is a field of wild grass.
6. The wall is painted to look like a field of grass.

Sentence 1 uses an idiom. An **idiom** is an expression that means something different from the individual words in it. We use idioms every day. For example, when you say, "You're putting me on," you mean, "You're kidding me" or "You're not telling me the truth." "Butterflies in my stomach," and "hit it on the nose" are other examples of idioms.

Sentence 3 is a simile and Sentence 5 is a metaphor. Similes and metaphors are comparisons. They are often used in poetry. A **simile** is a comparison using the words *like* or *as*. A **metaphor** is a comparison without the use of *like* or *as*. In a metaphor, the writer says one thing *is* another thing.

ACTIVITY A Number your paper from 1 to 4. Read each sentence. Write **Idiom**, **Simile**, or **Metaphor** to tell what kind of figurative language is used in each.

1. Sequoyah was like a hunter of words.
2. Maria finished the picture as quick as a wink.
3. Art is truth.
4. Sequoyah knew he was on the right track.

ACTIVITY B Number your paper from 1 to 4. Write the meaning of each numbered sentence on your paper.

1. The cupboard was as bare as a tree in winter.
   a. There were no leaves in the cupboard.
   b. There was nothing in the cupboard.
   c. The cupboard was full.

2. He and I don't often see eye to eye about things.
   a. He and I don't look at one another when we talk.
   b. He and I can't see things in the distance.
   c. He and I don't often agree about things.

3. The lake was a mirror.
   a. Reflections could be seen in the lake.
   b. The lake was frozen.
   c. The lake didn't look real.

4. The room was like an oven.
   a. The room was very small.
   b. The room was dark and airtight.
   c. The room was very hot.

Four Riddles for a Fortune

Kathleen C. Phillips

A riddle is like a word puzzle. You have to understand how words can be turned around to mean different things. Then you can solve the puzzle and find the answer to the riddle. In this folk tale, a young man sets out to seek his fortune. Along the way, he discovers how helpful and fun words can be.

One spring morning Waldo was awakened by his father calling, "Up, Waldo, up! The sun is in the sky."

His mother called, "Your oldest brother is already out herding his cows."

His grandmother called, "Your second brother is already herding his sheep."

"It is time," his father said, "for you to set forth to seek your fortune."

"But I like it here," Waldo said. "Why can't I stay home?"

"Because you are the third son," his father explained. "Third sons always set forth to seek their fortunes."

"We could get some pigs, and I could be a swineherd," Waldo said, "or some bees, and I could be a beeherd."

"Beekeeper, not beeherd," said his father. "No, third sons must set forth to seek their fortunes. You must find shelter for your head from sun and rain."

"A palace," said his mother, "or a fine mansion."

"You must find a companion for your lonely hours," his father went on.

"A princess for a wife," said his grandmother, "or a beautiful young maiden."

"And," his father said, jingling some coins, "you must find something of value for your pocket. I have given you your instructions. Now set forth to seek your fortune."

"I shall give you some good advice," his mother said. "Don't speak to strangers."

"Mother," Waldo said, "the world is strange to me so everyone I meet will be a stranger. I may have to speak to someone."

"So much for good advice," his mother said. "I'll give you a loaf of bread instead."

"And I," his grandmother said, "shall give you four riddles."

So, with his father's instructions, his mother's loaf of bread, and his grandmother's riddles, Waldo started out.

At the gate he looked back at his parents' cottage and red barn, at the fields sprinkled with flowers. He looked at the first hill where his oldest brother herded cows, and at the second hill where his second brother herded sheep. He looked at the third hill where he would like to be herding something. Waldo sighed. Home was where he wanted to be, but he must seek his fortune.

All day Waldo walked, and at evening he came to a crossroads. There, under a willow tree, a large man was eating an apple while holding a huge rock.

"Good evening, lad," the man said. "Going far?"

"Going to seek my fortune," answered Waldo. "What are you doing?"

"Exercising, lad. Your fortune lies in your own strong arms and back. Lift a rock or two."

Waldo was tired and hungry, so instead he sat down and pulled out his loaf of bread.

"Share our suppers, lad?" the man asked.

So Waldo gave the man part of his bread, and the man gave Waldo an apple.

When they had eaten, Waldo said, "You look like a very strong man."

The man nodded. "Strongest man you've ever seen." He took a gold coin out of his pocket and flipped it into the air. "Make a wager, lad?" He looked about, at the boulders along the roadside, at a fallen tree. "Name something I can't hold."

"I have no coins," Waldo said.

"If you win, you have my gold coin," said the man. "If I win, I have the rest of your bread."

"Very well," said Waldo. "Listen to this:

Light as a feather,
Lighter than a flower,
The strongest man can't hold it
For a quarter of an hour."

"Didn't reckon on riddles, lad," the man said. "Tell me what I can't hold for a quarter of an hour."

"*Your breath*, sir," said Waldo, and he pocketed the coin. Then he curled up and slept the night under the willow tree.

The next morning Waldo started on his way again, taking the road to his left. At evening he came to another crossroads. There, sitting by a stream, was a man with a large umbrella. He was eating a piece of cheese, and he was crying.

"Evening, lad," the man said. "Are you far from home?"

"Far from home and family," Waldo said. "I am seeking my fortune. Why are you crying?"

"I am crying," the man said, "because I am an orphan and have no family. Your family is your fortune, lad, and your fortune is your family. Share our suppers?"

So Waldo gave the man part of his bread, and the man gave him some cheese.

After they had eaten, Waldo said, "How about a riddle? If you guess it, you win my bread. If you can't guess it, you give me the answer."

"If I give you the answer, *I'll* have won," said the man.

"No," Waldo said, "if you give me the answer, *I'll* have won. Here is the riddle:

What can go up a chimney down,
But can't go down a chimney up?"

The man thought and thought. Finally he said, "I give up. I don't know, so how can I give you the answer?"

"Then I have won," said Waldo. "The answer is *an umbrella*. So you must give me your umbrella."

Waldo curled up and slept the night under the big umbrella.

The next morning Waldo started on his way again, down the road to his left. At evening he came to another crossroads. There, sitting with his back against an oak tree, was a young man drinking cider and reading a book.

"Do you journey far?" the young man asked.

"I am seeking my fortune," Waldo said.

"I have been many places," the young man told him, "and I have found that one's fortune is in one's head. Brains."

"What are you reading?" Waldo asked.

"A dictionary. It's full of words but no chatter, information but no gossip. Shall we share our suppers, lad?"

So Waldo gave the young man part of his bread, and the man gave Waldo some cider.

After they had eaten, Waldo said, "How about a riddle? If you guess it, you win my bread. If you can't, you must give me the answer."

"If I give you the answer, *I'll* have won," said the man.

"No," said Waldo. "Here is the riddle:

Where is the place that Friday comes before Thursday?"

The young man thought and thought. Finally he said, "I don't know, so how can I give you the answer?"

"I win," said Waldo. "The answer is *in the dictionary*. So you must give me your dictionary."

Waldo curled up under the oak tree and slept.

The next morning Waldo started on his way again, following the road to his left. At evening he came to a crossroads. By the side of the road, an old woman stood over a fire stirring something in a kettle.

"Good evening, lad," the old woman called. "Have you come far?"

"Yes," Waldo said. "I'm seeking my fortune."

"It's tiresome, lonesome work, seeking one's fortune," the old woman said. "Shall we share our suppers?"

So the old woman gave Waldo some soup, and Waldo divided his last slice of bread.

After they had eaten, Waldo said, "How about a riddle? If you guess it, I'll carry your kettle for you tomorrow. If you don't, you tell me my fortune, for I'm tired of seeking it."

"Very well," said the old woman. "Ask your riddle."

So Waldo said:

"It's always going from here to there,
Yet moves not an inch, any time,
anywhere."

The old woman thought and thought. Finally she said, "I don't know. Tell me the answer."

"It's a *road*," Waldo said. "Roads run everywhere, yet they never move an inch. Now it's your turn. Tell me my fortune."

"So be it," the old woman said. "It is also a riddle:

It belongs to you,
So you can't flee it;
Always ahead of you,
But you can't see it."

Waldo thought and thought. He thought about the riddle all night long. In the morning he said, "I give up. What belongs to me so I can't flee it, and is always ahead of me but I can't see it?"

"Your future," the old woman said.

"That's where your fortune lies. Turn left at the crossroads and keep walking."

"The way to the right is greener," said Waldo.

"A matter of opinion," the old woman answered. "Turn to the left for your fortune."

So Waldo started on his way again, and as he walked, the road grew smooth, and the brown fields turned green. In the distance he saw three green hills and a red barn and a cottage. Near the cottage he saw an old woman.

"Grandmother!" Waldo called. "I'm home!"

"Waldo!" cried his grandmother. "You're back! I was looking for you."

Waldo's mother came running out of the house, and Waldo's father hurried from the barnyard. "Have you found your fortune?" they asked.

"Well," said Waldo, "the Strong Man said my fortune would be in my strong arms and back. The Reading Man said it would be in my head. The Orphan Man said my fortune was with my family, and the Old Woman said it was in my future. So, here I am, back at home with my family, ready to make a fortune with my brains and my strong back."

"But where is your palace?" asked his mother.

"And your beautiful wife?" asked his grand-mother.

"And your gold?" asked his father.

"You told me to find shelter for my head from sun and rain, a companion for my lonely hours, and something of value for my pocket," Waldo said.

"This is shelter for my head." And Waldo put up his umbrella.

"This is a companion for my lonely hours." He pulled the dictionary out of his pack.

"And this is something of value for my pocket." He flipped the gold coin high in the air and caught it as it came spinning down. "With this I shall purchase a pig and become a swineherd, or bees and become a beeherd."

"Bee*keeper*," his father said.

Waldo smiled. "I shall live with my family and keep my pigs or bees among the clover and daisies on the third green hill. I shall sit under my umbrella when the sun is hot or the rain is cold. I shall find company by reading my dictionary. And we shall all live happily ever after."

And they probably did.

Thinking and Writing About the Selection

1. What three things did Waldo's family want him to seek?
2. How did Waldo feel about going on a journey?
3. How can a dictionary be a companion?

 4. Think about a journey or trip you have taken. What did you discover while you were away? How did it feel to return home?

Applying the Key Skill
Multiple-Meaning Words

Use context clues to choose the correct meaning of each underlined word. Write each word and its meaning.

1. You can't hold your breath for a <u>quarter</u> of an hour.
   a. twenty-five cents
   b. three months
   c. one-fourth
   d. fifteen minutes before or after every hour

2. The empty kettle would be a <u>light</u> load to carry.
   a. not dark
   b. not serious
   c. not heavy
   d. not cheerful

3. Turn left and <u>keep</u> walking along the road.
   a. to store or put
   b. to be faithful to
   c. to hold back
   d. to continue

4. Waldo found <u>company</u> by reading the dictionary.
   a. a business firm
   b. companionship, fellowship
   c. a part of an army
   d. guests

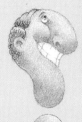

CAN YOU GUESS

Try to guess the answers to these riddles.
Then find out if you were right
by turning your book upside down!

In what room can a lion watch TV?

The den.

How can you keep cool at a baseball game?

Sit next to a fan.

When is ink like a sheep?

When it's in a pen.

What kind of coat is made without buttons and put on wet?

A coat of paint.

What kind of keys don't fit any locks?

Piano keys.

How are the answers to these riddles alike?
Each answer has a multiple-meaning word.

99

DICTIONARY

In "Four Riddles for a Fortune," Waldo asked the Reading Man what he was reading. "A dictionary," said the man. "It's full of words but no chatter, information but no gossip."

A **dictionary** is a book that contains information about words. The dictionary shows you how to spell words and how to pronounce them. It also tells you the meanings of words. The dictionary can help you when you need it—if you know how to use it.

How do you find a word in a dictionary? In the last story, Waldo asked, "Where is the place that Friday comes before Thursday?" The answer was "in the dictionary." The reason *Friday* comes before *Thursday* in the dictionary is that the words in a dictionary are listed in alphabetical order.

Use the sample dictionary page to learn about these other dictionary features.

guide words   **pronunciation**
entry words   **part of speech**

rhythm/ride

rhy·thm (rith′ əm) *n.* **1.** a regular or orderly repetition of sounds or movements: *the rhythm of drumbeats.* **2.** movement marked by such regular or orderly repetition. **3.** Music. **a.** a repeated pattern of beats. **b.** a particular or characteristic form of this: *That song is written in waltz rhythm.*

rib (rib) *n.* **1.** one of the series of curved bones attached in pairs to the backbone and enclosing the chest cavity. **2.** a cut of meat including one or more ribs. **3.** anything like a rib: *the ribs of an umbrella.* **4.** a raised ridge, as in a knitted sweater of sock. **5.** the main vein of a leaf.

rich (rich) *adj.* **1.** having great wealth: *a rich man, a rich country.* **2.** well-supplied with something: *The old house was rich in memories.* **3.** productive; fertile: *rich soil, a rich imagination.* **4.** deep and full: *a rich baritone voice, a rich brown color.* **5.** (of foods) having a heavy, strong flavor or containing large amounts of nutritious, sugary, or creamy ingredients; *a rich sauce.* **6.** not thin or diluted: *a rich mixture of fuel.* —**rich·ly**, *adv.* —**rich·ness**, *n.*

ric·o·chet (rik′ ə shā′) *n.* the skipping or glancing of an object off a flat surface. —*v.* **ric·o·cheted** (rik′ ə shād′), **ric·o·chet·ing** (rik′ ə shā′ ing). to skip or glance off a flat surface: *The ball ricocheted off the wall and accidentally hit a bystander.*

rid (rid) *v.,* **rid** or **rid·ded**, **rid·ding**. to clear or free, as from something unpleasant or undesirable: *What can we do to rid the house of ants?*

rid·dle[1] (rid′ əl) *n.* **1.** a puzzling problem or question. **2.** a person or thing that is hard to understand. —*v.,* **rid·dled**, **rid·dling**.

rid·dle[2] (rid′ əl) *v.,* **rid·dled**, **rid·dling**. **1.** to pierce in many places with holes: *The marksman riddled the target with bullets.* **2.** to sift through a coarse sieve.

ride (rīd) *v.,* **rode**, **rid·den**, **rid·ing**. **1.** to sit on and be carried by something in motion, such as a horse or vehicle, while controlling its movement: *He rides to school every day on his bicycle.* **2.** to travel or be carried on or in a vehicle or other conveyance: *We rode through the countryside on the train.* **3.** to proceed or be carried along, as if riding: *The ship rode over the waves.* **4.** to be carried or supported while moving: *The racing car rode on two wheels as it rounded the turn.* **5.** to carry or support a rider.

a bat, ā cake, ä father, är car, âr dare; e hen, ē mē, ėr term; i bib, ī kite, ir clear; o top, ō rope, ô saw, oi coin, ôr fork, ou out; u sun, ů book, ü moon, ū cute; ə about, taken

Remember that many words that end in *s, es, ed, er, est,* and *ing* are not listed as entry words. To find any of these words, you must look up the base word. For example, *riding* is not an entry word. To find it, you must look for its base word, *ride.*

ACTIVITY A Number your paper from 1 to 5. Write the answers to the questions on your paper.

1. Which word would appear first in a dictionary?
    a. brink   b. bright   c. bring

2. *Mouse* would appear on a dictionary page with which guide words?
    a. motor/mourn   b. maid/mice   c. mountain/mud

3. Which word would be found on a dictionary page with the guide words *flower/flurry*?
    a. fix   b. fluid   c. fly

4. What entry word would you look for to find out about *popping*?
    a. popper   b. pop   c. poppy

5. What entry word would you look for to find out about blueberries?
    a. blue   b. berry   c. blueberry

ACTIVITY B Number your paper from 1 to 6. Use the sample dictionary page to answer the questions below. Write the answers on your paper.

1. How many syllables does *rhythm* have? Which syllable is accented?
2. Which syllable in *ricochet* receives primary stress? Which receives secondary stress?
3. What word in the pronunciation key has the same vowel sound as the *i* in *ride*?
4. Write the meaning of each underlined word as it is used in the sentence.
   a. The little town was <u>rich</u> in history.
   b. Waldo was sorry he had eaten the <u>rich</u> dessert.

What can you do if you come across a word you don't know? You can sometimes get the meaning of a word from the other words and sentences around it. If you can't figure out the meaning of a word from context clues, you can always look it up in the dictionary. You'll find, as Waldo did, that the dictionary can be a very valuable book.

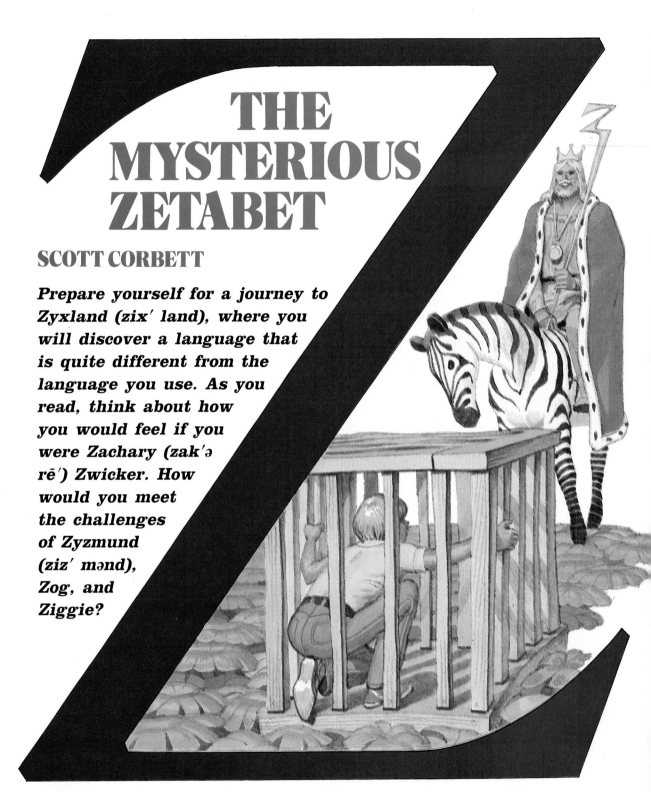

THE MYSTERIOUS ZETABET

SCOTT CORBETT

Prepare yourself for a journey to Zyxland (zix′ land), where you will discover a language that is quite different from the language you use. As you read, think about how you would feel if you were Zachary (zak′ə rē′) Zwicker. How would you meet the challenges of Zyzmund (ziz′ mənd), Zog, and Ziggie?

achary Zwicker sat in his backyard looking at his homework. It was a long list of words he was supposed to put into alphabetical order.

"The alphabet bores me!" said Zack.

The truth was, a lot of ordinary homework bored him. He liked to learn things, but in his own way. He liked to read books full of strange facts. He even liked looking through the dictionary for unusual words. His favorite were words that began with Z. With a name like his, this was not surprising.

Sighing, Zack leaned back against a tree. He closed his eyes and thought about his name and his initials. Z.Z. What wonderful initials for anyone to have. Z.Z. . . . . *Z-z-z-z* . . .

Zack felt himself drifting into space. Then he felt like he was rocking. Soon he saw that he was in a cage being carried along a crooked road.

Before he had time to do more than feel scared, a man in a uniform came galloping up on a zebra. He looked down at Zack.

"Zounds! You must be the boy we rescued from that place whose name begins with an A!"

Zack supposed he meant "America," but was too frightened to ask.

"I am the ruler of this nation, Zyzmund the Zeventh! What is your name?"

"Zachary Zwicker," said Zack.

"Zachary Zwicker?" asked Zyzmund. "With a name like that, you should go far here. Step out!"

When Zack stepped out of the cage he
started to fall sideways.

"The road twisted so much it
made me dizzy," he explained.

"All our roads are zigzag roads. We like
them that way. Welcome to Zyxland!"

"Where?"

"Zyxland. You are now in the land of the
zetabet."

"The what, sir?"

"The zetabet. You haven't learned your
ZYX's yet, but you will. Right now you only
know how to say the zetabet backwards. Soon you
will learn to recite it properly—z-y-x-w-v-u-t-s-r-q-
p-o-n-m-l-k-j-i-h-g-f-e-d-c-b-a—as fast as I just said
it myself.

"Be careful, young Zwicker," said Zyzmund
sternly. "You will be asked certain questions. If
you answer them correctly you may choose to
become a Zyxlander. If you fail, you will become
our prisoner.

"Of course, if you succeed, you may also
choose to return to the place where we found you.
However, you may do so only if you first do
something so impossible that I won't even waste
my time telling you," Zyzmund added with a
laugh. "Now listen closely to our rules."

"Yes, sir!"

"It is permissible for ordinary words to
begin with the last letters of the zetabet—l, k, j, i,
h, g, f, e, d, c, b, and even a. But important
names must begin with important letters. Above

all, A-names are forbidden! Do you understand?"

"Yes, sir!"

"Then go. From now on you will travel this road alone. I shall fly on ahead in my zeppelin and be waiting to meet you. If you succeed, we will meet at my palace, the Zenith Ziggurat."

"A ziggurat, sir? Isn't that one of those buildings shaped like a pyramid, only with zigzag sides?"

"*X-zack*-ly!" cried Zyzmund, pleased with Zack's description. "Now go, young Zwicker!"

Zigging left, zagging right, up the road went a nervous Zachary Zwicker. The first place he came to was a shop with flowers in the window and a sign that said, Phlower Shop.

"What a silly way to spell flower!" he thought. Then he remembered that "f" was at the wrong end of the zetabet.

A man came out of the shop and held up his hand. "Stop! Before you pass my shop you must tell me the name of our national phlower."

ack's mind went blank. For a moment he was too nervous to think. Then he made himself think of all the Z-words he had looked up in the dictionary. One of them came to his rescue.

"I know!" he said. "The zinnia."

"Pass!" said the man. Zack zigzagged on ahead.

Soon he came to a shop that had large maps in the window and a sign that said,

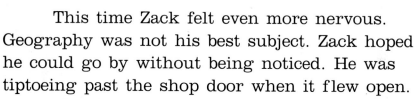

This time Zack felt even more nervous. Geography was not his best subject. Zack hoped he could go by without being noticed. He was tiptoeing past the shop door when it flew open.

"Stop!"

An important-looking man came out. He stood in front of Zack with his arms folded. Zack felt his legs turn to rubber.

"Before you pass my shop you must answer three questions."

"Y-yes, sir." A three-part question! He would never be able to handle that!

"I am Zog the Yeographer. Here is my first question. What are the three Yafrican nations we like best?"

ack brightened up. One thing he *was* interested in was Africa.

"I know!" he said. "Zaire, Zambia, and Zimbabwe!"

"Right! Now, for the second part, tell me the name of Zambia's great river."

"The Zambezi."

"Splendid! You must have gotten straight Z's in yeography in school. Now, here's the third part, but be careful. What are the two greatest rivers in the world?"

Zack knew he was in trouble now—and he couldn't see his way out. He knew the real answer, but if he gave it he would surely be made a prisoner.

"Well, there's the Mississippi. . ." he began.

"Yes, yes, but what about the other one?"

Suddenly Zack had it.

"The Yamazon!"

"Pass!"

As Zack went on, he realized how hungry he had become. "What's the point of trying to get to the Zenith Ziggurat if I starve to death first?" he said to himself. "I've just got to find something to eat!"

So far he had not seen any places to eat. Even if he came to one how could he buy something without any money?

Just as he was thinking about this, along came a man wearing a coat with a fur collar. He was carrying a large leather purse.

"Stop!" he said. "Before you pass me you must answer two questions."

He opened the leather purse and took out a large coin.

"I'll give you a hint," he said, winking. "We use the same name for our money that they use in Poland. Now tell me the name of our national coin."

That was all Zack needed.

"I know!" he said. "It's a zloty."

"Right! What kind of metal is it made of?"

"Zinc."

"Pass! Just for that you may have the coin, because I'm a very rich man. I have zillions of zinc zlotys."

"Thank you! Can I buy some food with this?"

"Yes! There's a place just a little farther up the road."

Zack walked on along the zigzag road. By now he felt almost faint. He had never been so hungry in all his life.

Then, just as he was turning the corner from a zig to a zag, he saw a huge wall ahead of him. The wall had a great pair of gates in it. Behind the wall he could see the Zenith Ziggurat. He was almost there!

In front of the wall stood a shop with a sign that said,

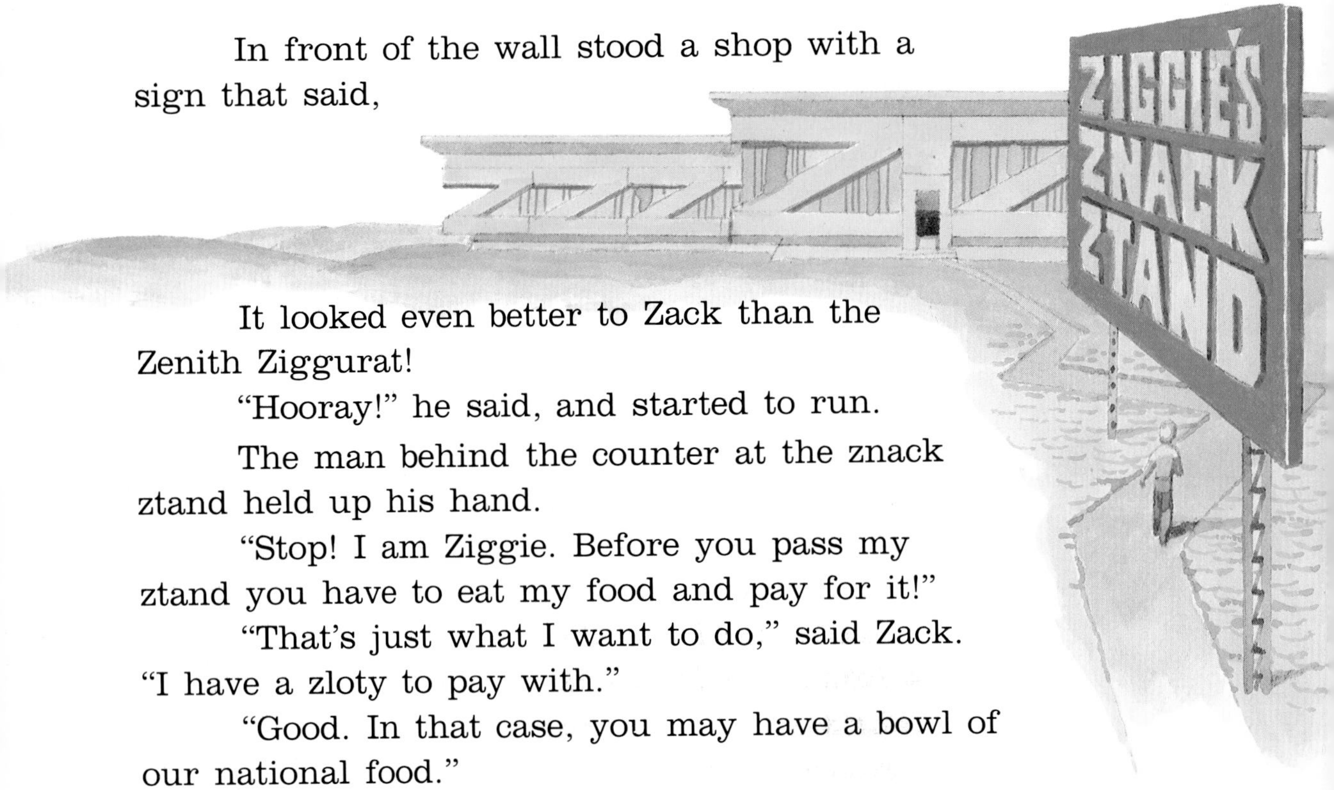

It looked even better to Zack than the Zenith Ziggurat!

"Hooray!" he said, and started to run.

The man behind the counter at the znack ztand held up his hand.

"Stop! I am Ziggie. Before you pass my ztand you have to eat my food and pay for it!"

"That's just what I want to do," said Zack. "I have a zloty to pay with."

"Good. In that case, you may have a bowl of our national food."

Zack stared at the bowl of stewed squash Ziggie set before him.

"Is that what I think it is?" asked Zack.

"What do you think it is?"

"Zucchini!"

"Right!"

"But I can't stand the stuff!"

"What? How dare you say such a thing! It's what we always eat here in Zyxland!"

Now the Zyxlanders had gone too far! Zack was so mad he stamped his feet and banged the counter with his fists.

"I came all this way and answered everyone's silly questions. Now I'm starving to death and I want a *hot dog*!"

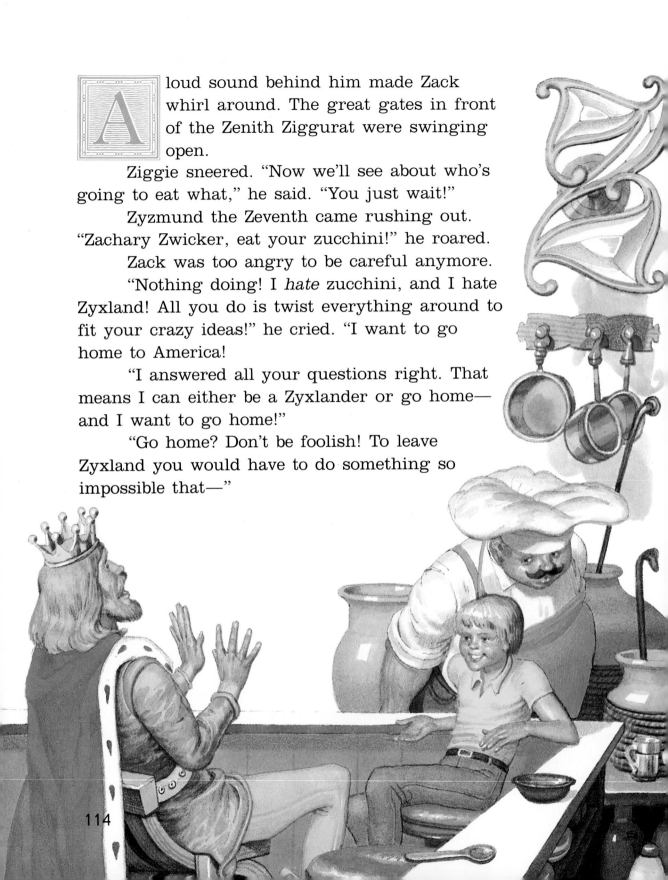

A loud sound behind him made Zack whirl around. The great gates in front of the Zenith Ziggurat were swinging open.

Ziggie sneered. "Now we'll see about who's going to eat what," he said. "You just wait!"

Zyzmund the Zeventh came rushing out. "Zachary Zwicker, eat your zucchini!" he roared.

Zack was too angry to be careful anymore.

"Nothing doing! I *hate* zucchini, and I hate Zyxland! All you do is twist everything around to fit your crazy ideas!" he cried. "I want to go home to America!

"I answered all your questions right. That means I can either be a Zyxlander or go home—and I want to go home!"

"Go home? Don't be foolish! To leave Zyxland you would have to do something so impossible that—"

"What is it? I'll do it!"

Zyzmund chuckled. "Now we've got you! You must ask a question about the zetabet that we can't answer! You have one minute to think of your question!"

Zack turned pale. What could he ask them about the zetabet that they wouldn't know? Why, the way Zyzmund had rattled it off, it was—

Zack snapped his fingers.

"I've got it!" he cried. "I've got my question!"

Everybody laughed.

"Very well, let us hear it," said Zyzmund.

"Here it is. Can you quickly recite the zetabet—"

"Why, of course!"

"*Backwards*?"

Now it was Zyzmund who turned pale.

"Backwards?"

"Backwards!"

"Oh. Well . . . of course I can!" he yelled.

"Then do it!"

Zyzmund cleared his throat.

"A-b-c-d-f—No, that's wrong! A-b-c-e-f-g—"

"Wrong again!" said Zack. "Well, I'll be going now."

"No, wait!" shouted Zyzmund. "A-b-c-d-e-f-g-h-i-m-l—Oh, drat!"

Zack's eyes popped open. Much to his surprise he was back home in his own yard. He was very glad to be there—on Appleton Avenue in Auburn, Alabama!

Thinking and Writing About the Selection

1. How did Zack get to Zyxland?
2. What were the rules of Zyxland?
3. What do you think was the hardest challenge Zack had to face in Zyxland?
4. Pretend you are a Zyxlander. Write two questions for Zack. Give the answers, too.

Applying the Key Skill
Figurative Language

Read each sentence about "The Mysterious Zetabet" below. Find the idiom in each. Then rewrite each sentence to show that you understand what the idiom means.

1. Zack's mind went blank when the man at the Phlower Shop asked him a question.
2. Zack felt his legs turn to rubber when the man at the Yeography Shop stood in front of him.
3. When Ziggie gave Zack some zucchini, Zack blew his top.
4. Zack got out of Zyxland by the skin of his teeth.

Scott Corbett

The settings Scott Corbett uses for his stories often come from his own life. His first book for children, *The Reluctant Landlord*, took place in Cape Cod where he was living. The story came from a true story involving his niece. Another story, *Diamonds Are Trouble*, is set in a country inn that is similar to a real inn on Cape Cod. His series of "Trick" books began with Kirby Maxwell who played in a park that is like the one the author played in when he was young.

Scott Corbett and his wife like to travel on freighters. Some of his books have been written on these trips. *The Turnabout Trick* was written during a trip around the world. "I started it in the Pacific Ocean, rewrote it in the Indian Ocean, and finished it in the Atlantic Ocean. *The Mystery Man* and *Steady Freddie!* were started during a three-month trip around South America. Oddly enough, though I have written several books that had a lot to do with the sea, I have never written a story while at sea that was not firmly based on land."

More to Read

The Lemonade Trick, The Great McGonigle's Gray Ghost, The Turnabout Trick

SPEAK OUT!

Susan Beth Pfeffer

When Reesa's composition "What I Like Best About America" won the school writing contest, she was thrilled. Then she found out that she would have to read her composition at the county contest. Reesa had always been afraid to speak in public. If she couldn't speak in her class of twenty-nine, how would she be able to make a speech in front of five hundred strangers? The contest is just two weeks away. That's not a long time to cure a lifelong fear, but Reesa is determined to try. A book she borrows, Stand Up and Speak Out! *may give Reesa the help she needs.*

When I got home from school, I took my composition and read it to myself silently a few times. *Stand Up and Speak Out!* recommended that, to let you get familiar with what you were going to say.

It was a pretty good composition. I felt proud knowing it was the best one at my school. After I'd read it five times, I was impatient to start reading it out loud.

I followed the book's directions again. First I read the composition out loud without trying to sound impressive, just to hear what the words sounded like. I did that a couple of times. Then I moved over to my full-length mirror and read the composition out loud in front of it a few times. At first I just read it. Then I practiced looking up and making eye contact. Of

course I was making eye contact with myself, and that felt pretty silly, but that was what the book said to do.

Then I went on to reading the composition to an audience. This consisted of my favorite teddy bear and Amanda, my best doll, the only one I couldn't bear to give up when I outgrew dolls last year. I sat them down on different chairs in my room and read the speech out loud again six times. By that point I was pretty sick of it, so I was almost glad when my sister Robby came in.

"I heard the silence," she said. "Are you through for the day?"

"For a while," I said. "Could you hear how I sounded?"

"I wasn't really listening," she said. "Why? Are

you ready now for a real live audience?"

"Oh, no," I said, and I was surprised how the thought of having a real live person hear me upset me.

"You'll have to be at some point," Robby said. "There won't be five hundred teddy bears out there, you know."

"I'm going to ask Heather over tomorrow," I said. "She can be my audience. *Stand Up and Speak Out!* says to read my speech out loud to people before I do it in public."

"She won't tell you what's wrong with you, though. Heather always thinks whatever you do is terrific."

"When I'm ready for serious criticism, I'll know who to ask. Right now all I want is someone who'll just listen and applaud."

After Robby left, I read my composition out loud to Teddy and Amanda two more times. The speech was sounding good. I was sure Heather would like it when I read it to her the next day.

Heather agreed to come over as soon as I asked her. We went home right after school. I was scared to have a human being to read it to, but it was only Heather, and I felt pretty good about how well I could read it. I'd read it a lot the day before, and I knew lots of good stuff about eye contact.

We went straight to my bedroom. I set up Teddy and Amanda in different corners, and put Heather in the center of the room. I figured since she was human, it was best to have her there. Then I read the composition to myself a couple of times. Finally, I started.

"I've always known I was lucky to be born an

American," I began. I knew I wasn't looking up. My eyes were glued to the paper. "I've got to start again," I told Heather. "I'm sorry."

"That's okay," she said. "Take your time."

I took a couple of minutes and read the essay to myself again. This time I was so familiar with it, I knew I'd be able to look up. I began again.

"I've always known I was lucky to be born an American," I said, looking straight ahead. Way over Heather's head, to the window behind her. If we'd been in the auditorium, I'd be looking at the doors, like all I wanted to do was get out.

"I'm not doing it right," I said. "I have to start again."

"It's hard to get it right the first time," Heather said. "That's why I'm here."

"I'll do it right this time," I said. "Just watch."

I looked down at the paper, and then started again. "I've always known I was lucky to be born an American," I said. I held my head up and looked at Heather, but it wasn't like a normal conversation. It was like she was in the audience somewhere, just the way she was supposed to be. I could see her smile at me, so I figured I should go on.

"Although my grandparents were born in the United States, their parents weren't, and they've told me many stories of how life was in the old country, and why it was so important for them to leave and seek a new life in the United States." Whew. That was a long one, and I managed just fine. Heather was still smiling, so I turned my head slightly and faced Teddy. "They didn't have much money, and they had to work very hard, but they never regretted leaving." I

was fine, but in the corner of my eye, I could see Heather was fighting off a giggle.

"What is it?" I asked. "Am I doing something wrong?"

"Nothing," she said. "Only you looked so sincere talking to the teddy bear, as if he really cared about your grandparents."

"Maybe this isn't such a good idea," I said.

"My being here?" asked Heather.

"No, all of it," I said. "Maybe I'm just kidding myself, and I will make a fool of myself. That would be so awful."

"You're not going to do that," Heather said. "You're going to be terrific."

"How do you know?" I asked.

"I know because I know what kind of person you are," Heather said. "You're not a quitter. You're going to read your composition

and you're going to win that contest. I know you will."

"Heather?" I asked. "What if I can't?"

"I don't even hear you," she said. "Now read me your speech, all right?"

"All right," I said, and I read it out loud. I didn't care about lifting my eyes off the paper, or addressing different parts of the audience. I just read it. When I finished,

Heather clapped, and demanded that I read it again.

I read it to her five times, and by the fifth time, I was hardly looking at the paper. I was looking around the room, talking to her and Teddy and Amanda like they were the world's biggest audience. At the end of each reading Heather clapped, and by the fifth reading, I felt like clapping, too.

Thinking and Writing About the Selection

1. What did Reesa do before reading her composition to an audience?
2. Why did Reesa want to read her composition to Heather and not to her sister?
3. Why should speakers try to have eye contact with their audiences?
4. Suppose you were asked to give a speech on any subject you like. What would you choose to talk about? What would you say?

Applying the Key Skill
Sequence of Events

Read the sentences about "Speak Out!" below.
Then write the sentences in the correct sequence.

Reesa read her composition all the way through, and Heather clapped.

Robby volunteered to listen to Reesa.

Heather came to Reesa's house to listen to her friend's composition.

Reesa's composition won the school contest.

Reesa read out loud in front of her mirror.

When Heather looked like she was ready to giggle, Reesa stopped reading.

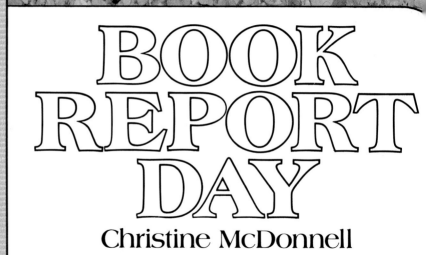

BOOK REPORT DAY

Christine McDonnell

*Have you ever had trouble
deciding what to do for a class assignment?
If you have, you are not alone.
The boy in this story,
Leo, doesn't know what he's going to do
for Book Report Day.
Will he think of something in time?*

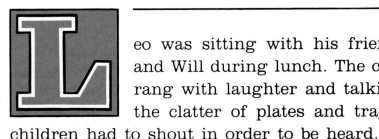

eo was sitting with his friends Ivy and Will during lunch. The cafeteria rang with laughter and talking and the clatter of plates and trays. The children had to shout in order to be heard.

"I'm going to be Pippi," Ivy said.

"What?" Leo was confused. He hadn't been listening to the conversation.

"I'm going to be Pippi Longstocking for Book Report Day," Ivy repeated. "I made a wig out of orange yarn."

Leo had forgotten all about Book Report Day.

"I'm coming as Willie Mays," said Will. "I got a biography out on him. You know, my dad named me after Willie Mays."

Leo nodded. Will had told him that at least ten times before. Even so, Will had a good idea. He could just wear his Little League uniform and carry a glove for his costume.

"When is Book Report Day?" Leo asked.

"Next Friday. Did you forget?"

Leo nodded glumly.

"I better go to the library this afternoon. Tell the guys I won't be able to play, okay, Will?"

After school Leo headed for the library before going home. He ran the whole way. At the top of the front stairs he leaned against a column and paused to catch his breath.

He thought about the assignment. Mrs. Wilson had announced it weeks ago, but he hadn't paid much attention. It had seemed so far away then. Now it was just next week. A book report in costume. Everyone had to come dressed as a character. You had to stand up and tell about your book dressed in a costume. Leo shuddered. He hated standing up in front of the class. Last year he hadn't minded. He liked being a clown last year. He used to say silly things and he didn't mind if people laughed. That was last year.

This year he was older. He wasn't a clown anymore. Or at least he didn't want to be one. Every time he had to stand up in front of the class, everyone laughed. Maybe they laughed because they were used to laughing last year. Whatever the reason, Leo wished they'd stop.

He pushed open the heavy wooden door and went inside. The library was warm and quiet. It smelled of floor polish and old books—a sweet, dry, lemony smell that made Leo feel calm and relaxed.

Mrs. Hutchins, the librarian, greeted Leo with a big smile. "Why, hello! I haven't seen you for some time. You must be busy playing football."

"How did you know?"

"Oh, it wasn't hard to guess. I haven't seen Will or Charley lately either, and football is the usual activity in the fall. What brings you in here on a bright afternoon?"

"I need a book for a book report," Leo answered.

Mrs. Hutchins led Leo over to the fiction shelves. "You're interested in space, aren't you, Leo?"

He nodded.

She handed him a book with a rocket ship on the cover and another showing two robots walking across a moonscape. They looked interesting, but Leo didn't want to go to school dressed like a spaceman or a robot. It would be too embarrassing to go in such a noticeable costume.

Mrs. Hutchins gave Leo some other books. "Thanks a lot, Mrs. Hutchins," he said finally. "I'll look these over."

He sat down at a table and went through the stack. Every single book would need a special costume. Some were impossible. How could he ever turn into a Borrower? They were only a few inches tall. He didn't want to go as a cat or a mouse  or a cricket. Cats and mice were babyish costumes, and a cricket would be too hard. A cricket would be one ugly costume, though, Leo thought. A giant cricket with a shiny black shell. Not bad. Pretty disgusting. It would be hard to make, though, and there wasn't much time. Besides, kids might laugh, even though it was ugly. If only he could think of a character that didn't need much of a costume.

The very best character, Leo decided, would be an ordinary kid. Maybe looking just a little bit different. Carrying or wearing something that identified him. Nothing too fancy.

Leo stacked the books carefully on the table and went back to Mrs. Hutchins' desk.

"Do you think you could show me a book about a regular person? A boy? Maybe a funny book? Not too long?"

"A thin funny book about a boy? I think we can find what you're looking for."

She walked briskly in front of the shelves, stopping three times to pick out a book. They didn't look especially thin to Leo. Mrs. Hutchins handed him the books and said, "Look these over and see what you think."

Over the next few days Leo looked carefully through all three books. The first was about a boy detective. He didn't wear anything special or carry anything unusual. In fact, there wasn't anything that Leo could think of that would make a costume.

The second book character was ordinary, too, but he had a dog. In one episode the boy carried his dog home in a box. Leo knew he couldn't take a dog to school.

The third book was also about a boy. He looked like a nice kid. Someone you would like to have for a friend. His name was Homer Price. That was the name of the book, too. Homer Price sauntered along with his hands in his pockets. He had a lot of adventures. One time he caught some thieves, and another time he made a mistake with his uncle's doughnut machine. Thousands of doughnuts came pouring out. That was Leo's favorite part. Poor Homer Price. Doughnuts everywhere.

How can I look like Homer Price? Leo wondered. He studied the illustrations in the book, but he couldn't decide what his costume should be. Book Report Day was only two days away.

It wasn't until Thursday afternoon that Leo finally figured out how he could be Homer Price. The idea came to him as he was walking home from school. While he was waiting for the light to change, Leo stopped to look in the window of Dee Dee's Bakery. Right in front was a tray of doughnuts. The doughnuts reminded him of Homer Price. Suddenly he knew just what to do!

He checked the price list. If he used all of his saved-up allowance, he could buy two dozen doughnuts. That would be enough for everyone in the class. He smiled at his reflection in the bakery window. His problem was solved. He stuck his hands in his pockets, just like Homer Price, and whistled all the way home.

On Friday, Book Report Day, Leo woke up and got dressed just the way he did every school day. The only thing he did differently was to tuck his savings safely into his back pocket. He also remembered to put *Homer Price* in his knapsack. He raced through breakfast so he would have plenty of time to stop at Dee Dee's. It was crowded in Dee Dee's, so even though he had started early, Leo reached school after the bell had rung.

Leo turned the corner at the end of the hall and pushed open the door to Room 16. Mrs. Wilson was sitting at her desk speaking to the class. She turned and paused as Leo came in, raising her eyebrows in disapproval.

I bet she thinks I don't have a costume, Leo thought as he walked to his desk.

Ivy gave him a welcoming poke as he passed by her seat. Her orange Pippi braids stuck out from her head at funny angles. From the other side of the room Will waved his glove a little. He was wearing his Little League uniform.

Leo carefully placed his boxes under his chair and listened to Mrs. Wilson.

"We are all going down to the auditorium," Mrs. Wilson announced. "We'll be using the stage for the book reports. I know that you are all very excited, but please remember that the other classes are busy with lessons and should not be disturbed. I want you to walk down to the auditorium as quietly as possible."

They did try to walk quietly, but one boy got the hiccups from excitement, and two other children got the giggles. Finally they reached the auditorium and everyone raced for the best seats.

"Everyone take a seat. That is, everyone who can sit down," Mrs. Wilson said, smiling at the enormous egg who could not fit on a chair in his costume. "I am handing out a slip of paper to each of you. After the reports are finished, we will vote for the best one."

Tommy Ryan gave the first report. It was about a boy in Colonial times who was apprenticed to Paul Revere. It sounded like an exciting book, but poor Tommy was all dressed up in knickers and a frilly shirt. He even had a three-cornered hat like the kind they sold at the historical museum, and fake metal buckles stuck onto his shoes. Tommy raced through his report as quickly as he could.

Next the enormous egg waddled onstage to loud applause. Being the egg was easier than being the dinosaur that hatches from it, Leo thought to himself. The other benefit of being an egg was that no one could see you inside the costume.

Emily Mott was next in line. Leo watched with interest. What is she? he wondered, looking at her costume.

Emily was covered with string. It was all tied together in a crisscross pattern and attached to her shoulders, arms, hands, knees, and feet. Maybe she's a fish caught in a net, thought Leo. I bet her book is *The Fisherman and His Wife*.

When Emily reached the center of the stage, she stood with her legs wide apart and stretched her arms out to each side. Suddenly everyone in the class gasped and laughed and clapped. The string across the front of Emily's costume was tied in such a way that it spelled *Some Pig*. Emily had come as the web in *Charlotte's Web!*

"Hey, Mott, how'd you do that?" Johnny Ringer called out from the back row.

Emily smiled and reached up to straighten her glasses. "I just tied lots of knots," she said. She seemed half proud and half embarrassed at all the attention. Leo liked her more than ever for not showing off. She never bragged about being smart.

139

"Excellent, Emily," said Mrs. Wilson. "Very imaginative."

The boy wearing his father's tuxedo jacket was supposed to be one of Mr. Popper's penguins. The tails of the coat dragged on the floor. The girl with the pinafore on was Laura in the "Little House" books. Ivy got a round of applause as Pippi Longstocking. Her braids stuck straight out, and one knee sock was up and the other was down. Everyone knew who she was right away.

Finally it was Leo's turn. He walked slowly up the steps and onto the stage carrying his book and the two boxes from Dee Dee's. No one laughed. Everyone sat quietly, watching.

First Leo stood the book up on the table in the center of the stage, so everyone could see the cover. Then he opened the boxes of doughnuts. All around the book he stacked the doughnuts, making towers of different heights.

"My name is Homer Price," Leo began. He told a little about Homer's adventures, and he told the story of the doughnut machine from beginning to end. When he finished, he said, "The only way to get rid of these doughnuts is for everyone to eat one."

With that, everyone in the class clapped. Leo went from seat to seat, giving out doughnuts. There was even one for Mrs. Wilson, who nodded as if to say, "Good job."

At the end of the book report presentations, the class voted. Mrs. Wilson collected the slips of paper and quickly counted them.

"Boys and girls, the prize for the best costume goes to Richard Wittaker for his enormous egg."

Everyone clapped. Richard waddled to the stage again for his prize. It looked, of course, like a book. Richard couldn't take it from Mrs. Wilson because his arms were trapped inside his giant shell.

"You may pick it up later, when you have taken off your costume," said the teacher.

"When you get hatched," called out Johnny Ringer. Everyone laughed.

"Second prize goes to Emily Mott for her web."

The class clapped again. Her prize was also shaped like a book.

"The third prize goes to Leo Nolan for his clever idea. Very original, Leo."

Leo was startled. His ears burned as the class clapped, and he knew they were turning red. He had to walk to the stage again with everyone watching. Mrs. Wilson handed him a package wrapped in green foil paper.

He said "Thank you," and gave the class an embarrassed smile as he walked back to his seat.

After school was dismissed for the day, Leo walked home slowly. He hadn't opened his prize yet. He was waiting to do that at home. It was a book, he knew. I hope it's funny, he thought. He remembered how surprised he had been when Mrs. Wilson had called out his name. He remembered his ears getting hot. But it was a nice memory. Nobody had laughed this time. Not once. They hadn't laughed, they'd clapped.

Leo stuck his hands in his pockets again and tried to walk like Homer Price, leaning back into the wind a little. He wasn't a clown anymore. He wasn't silly. He was clever, and original. Maybe next time he wouldn't even be embarrassed.

Discoveries

You make a discovery each time you learn something
new. Your discoveries may be about people, places, or
things. You also may make discoveries about yourself. In
Discoveries, you read about people who discovered new
interests and new ways of looking at things. You also read
about people who discovered that the words we use to
communicate can be mysterious and fun as well as useful.
The power and wonder of our language is something you
can discover over and over again.

Thinking and Writing About *Discoveries*

1. What discoveries did Steve make in "The Week Mom
   Unplugged the TVs"?
2. Jamie in "The Galumpagalooses" and Maria in "Maria's
   House" were both interested in art. How do you think
   each character would answer the question: "What
   should an artist try to show in a painting?"
3. What did Sequoyah learn about language as he worked
   on his syllabary?
4. What riddles might Waldo of "Four Riddles for a Fortune"
   have asked Zachary Zwicker in Zyxland?
5. What might Reesa of "Speak Out!" have told Leo of "Book
   Report Day" to help him present his book report?

 6. Write a paragraph about a discovery you have made.
   Tell what the discovery was and tell what you learned
   from it.

Introducing Level 10

MEMORIES

My childhood's home I see again,
   And sadden with the view;
And still, as memory crowds my brain,
   There's pleasure in it, too.

Abraham Lincoln

UNIT

Memories keep the past alive in our minds and in our hearts. In this unit, you will discover some of the ways memories are preserved. You will read about some of the people, places, and events of the past that make up the rich history of families, towns, states, and our country. What memories are special to you?

DAVY CROCKETT

Adrien Stoutenburg

Davy Crockett (1786–1836) lived in the Smoky Mountains of Tennessee during America's frontier days. He was an expert hunter and an officer in the Tennessee army. He served two terms in the Tennessee legislature and three terms as a representative in the United States Congress.

Davy enjoyed a good story. He also liked to stretch the truth a little. Some of Davy's stories stretched the truth so much that people said they were taller than he was. Stories that exaggerate, or stretch the facts, are called tall tales. As you read this tall tale, look for examples of how the facts have been stretched.

The state of Tennessee wasn't born too many years before Davy Crockett was. In a way, Tennessee and Davy grew up together. They both grew fast. Davy never became quite as tall as the Great Smoky Mountains, but by the time he was eight years old, he had a good start. All the Crockett family were on the large side. They had to be. Clearing out the wilderness by the Nolachucky River took grit and gumption. Davy had plenty of that, and more.

One of the most special things about Davy was his grin. He could grin from ear to ear. Since his ears were rather far apart, this made for a very big grin. He got his grin from his father. His father could

grin in the teeth of a blizzard and change it into a rainbow. For a long time Davy didn't know how powerful his own grin was. Then one day he grinned at a raccoon sitting up in a tree. The raccoon tumbled to the ground, dead right down to its striped tail.

From then on, Davy did most of his raccoon hunting that way. Davy still used his rifle now and then to keep in practice. One day, he saw a raccoon up in a cottonwood. It was a real, live raccoon, but it was so sad-looking that Davy had tears in his eyes as he raised his gun.

The raccoon said in a sad voice, "Pardon me, mister, but do you happen to be Davy Crockett?"

"I'm one and the same," said Davy.

"In that case," said the raccoon, "I'm as good as dead already. You might as well put your gun away." The raccoon crawled down from the tree. He stood with his head bowed as if he were already at his own funeral.

Davy had never met such a polite raccoon before. He stooped and patted the animal. "You've got such fine manners, little fellow," said Davy. "I want you to go home and raise up more raccoons like yourself."

The raccoon raced off. Then he remembered his manners. "Thank you, Mister Crockett," he called.

The time came for Davy to get married. He found a girl called Polly Finley Thunder Whirlwind. Polly had a good-sized grin, too. She could laugh the mud chinks out of a log cabin. She laughed so hard dancing with Davy one winter that the cabin was full of holes. The wind came through the holes until everyone nearly froze. They were all too busy shivering to have time for anything else. Davy brought home a wolf to lie in front of the coldest blast. It did the shivering for the whole family, which by then included several children.

Davy brought home another pet, a big bear. Davy had gotten caught in an earthquake crack and couldn't get free. A bear passed by. Davy hung on to him until the bear pulled him out of the crack. Davy was so thankful, he hugged the bear. The bear hugged Davy back and almost hugged him to death. Davy named the bear Death-Hug and told him that it would be safer if they just shook hands the next time.

Death-Hug grew tame enough to let Davy put a saddle on his back and ride him like a horse. They went all over Tennessee together.

Davy never lost his grin in all that time. It was his grin that made him decide to go into politics. Davy went into the woods and made speeches to his animal friends.

The animals figured life would be safer for them if Davy were elected to the state legislature. Then he would have to spend his time making laws instead of hunting. So they cheered and paraded, barking and howling. It sounded to Davy as if they were saying, "VOTE FOR CROCKETT." It sounded that way to his neighbors, too. So they went along with the animals and elected Davy to the Tennessee legislature.

Davy set out for Nashville. Some people laughed when they saw him, but Davy paid no attention. All his life he had lived by his motto—*Be sure you're right, then go ahead.* That's what he did then.

The Tennessee settlers liked what he did so well that they elected him to Congress.

Around that time, Davy moved his family to western Tennessee. The soil there was richer than a multimillionaire. Davy didn't bother to plant seeds in the regular way. Instead, he loaded his gun with the seeds and shot them into the ground. Pumpkin vines grew so fast that the pumpkins were worn out from being dragged across the soil. A man had to run fast just to pick one.

Things went along fine, until the time of the Big Freeze. The winter started out cold and grew colder. By January, it was so cold that smoke froze in fireplace chimneys. Davy's hair froze so stiff he didn't dare comb it. He was afraid it would crack. One morning, daybreak froze solid. When that happened, it became so cold that people didn't even dare think about it. If they did, their thoughts might freeze right inside their heads.

Davy told Polly, "I reckon I better amble around the country and see what the trouble is."

In the morning, he saw what the trouble was. The machinery that kept the earth turning was frozen. The gears and wheels couldn't move. The sun had been caught between two blocks of ice under the wheels. The sun had worked so hard to get loose that it had frozen in its own icy sweat.

Davy set the bear trap and caught a great fat bear. He took the bear and held him up over the earth's frozen machinery. Then Davy squeezed the bear until slippery, hot bear oil ran down over the wheels and gears. Next, he greased the sun's face until the oil melted the ice.

"Get moving!" Davy ordered. He gave one of the wheels a kick.

The earth began to turn again. The sun rolled over and flipped free. Davy stuck a piece of sunrise in his pocket and started for home.

Most people were grateful to Davy for breaking the cold snap. Some, however, began saying Davy wasted his time in Congress dancing, parading, and telling tall tales. When voting time came again, enough people voted against Davy for him not to get elected.

"Well, sir!" said Davy. "From now on, the people of Tennessee will get no help from me! Anyhow, the state's getting too crowded. I'm moving to Texas!"

Texas in those days was a part of Mexico. Davy and many of the other American settlers didn't like taking orders from the Mexican government. So Davy and his friends decided to make their own laws. When the President of Mexico heard this, he ordered his army to go after them.

The people who write history books say that Davy died fighting the Mexicans in San Antonio, Texas, at a fort called the Alamo. One thing is certain. The sun comes up in Texas and in Tennessee every day, summer or winter. The earth keeps turning smoothly, the way it's supposed to. If it ever does get frozen fast again, Davy Crockett may come along to squeeze some bear oil over the works and give the wheels a kick to start everything up again.

Thinking and Writing About the Selection

1. How did Davy get to have a bear for a pet?
2. How did the animals help Davy get elected to the Tennessee legislature?
3. What were two things that happened in the story that could have been true? What were two things that could not have happened?

 4. Davy's motto was "Be sure you're right, then go ahead." Make up a motto for yourself. Give an example of how you could do what the motto says.

Applying the Key Skill
Causes of an Event

Write sentences to explain what caused each of the following events in "Davy Crockett."

1. Davy Crockett brought a wolf home one winter.
2. Davy decided to find out what was causing the Big Freeze.
3. The machinery that kept the earth turning was frozen.
4. Davy got the earth turning again.
5. Davy decided to move to Texas.

THE BALLAD OF DAVY CROCKETT

TOM BLACKBURN

GEORGE BRUNS

1. Born on a moun-tain top in Ten - nes - see,
2. Off through the woods he's a - march-in' a - long,

Green - est state in the Land of the Free,
Mak - in' up yarns an' a - sing - in' a song,

Raised in the woods so's he knew ev - 'ry tree,
Itch - in' fer fight - in' an' right - in' a wrong; He's

Kilt him a b'ar when he was on - ly three.
ring - y as a b'ar an' twict as strong.

CHORUS

Da - vy, Da - vy Crock - ett,
Da - vy, Da - vy Crock - ett, the

1. through 19. | *20.*

King of the wild fron - tier!
buck - skin buc - ca - neer!

LEARNING ABOUT ❈ THE STATES ❈

A HISTORY MYSTERY

Richard Uhlich

The story of Davy Crockett told you something about the history of Tennessee and Texas. You can find out more about the history of these states, and the other 48, by reading this article. Before you begin reading, look through the article. Notice the headings and subheadings. They are clues to what the article is about.

What do people do when they study history? How do they figure out what happened in the past? The best way to find out is by studying some history yourself. Clues to the history mystery are not hard to find. There's history all around you—state history, for example.

You can start by thinking about names. What can a name tell you? Think about your own name. Is there a story behind it? Were you named after someone in your family? Was your name chosen because someone famous had the same name?

States have names, too.

Learning about state names is one way to learn about state history. The names of the states are clues to their history.

State symbols are other clues to study. Each state has its own flag, flower, and bird. These symbols were chosen to represent, or stand for, people and events from the past. The stories of these people and events are part of state history.

Other history clues can be found in places you might not think to look. Maps and dictionaries can tell you a lot about the states. As you read, you will learn about other places to look.

UNITED STATES OF AMERICA

CANADA

Alaska

Washington
Montana
North Dakota
Minnesota
Wisconsin
Michigan
Maine
Vermont
New Hampshire
Massachusetts
Rhode Island
New York
Connecticut

Oregon
Idaho
South Dakota
New Jersey
Pennsylvania
Delaware

Wyoming
Nebraska
Iowa
Illinois
Indiana
Ohio
West Virginia
Maryland
Virginia

Nevada
Utah
Colorado
Kansas
Missouri
Kentucky
Tennessee
North Carolina

California
Oklahoma
Arkansas
South Carolina

Pacific Ocean

Hawaii

Arizona
New Mexico
Mississippi
Alabama
Georgia

N

Texas
Louisiana

Atlantic Ocean

Florida

Gulf of Mexico

MEXICO

Can you name the 50 states? If you have trouble remembering them all, the map will help you. Just saying the names may give you some clues to their history. But if you want the whole story, try the dictionary. Maps and dictionaries are true guides to state history.

Old Names

Take a good look at the map. Study a few of the names. Some of the names are harder to pronounce and harder to spell than others. In the East, there are tongue-twisters such as Connecticut and Massachusetts. Have you ever wondered where those names came from, or what they mean?

If you look in your dictionary you will discover that they both come from the language of the people who first settled North America—the Indians. As a matter of fact, about half of our states have names that are of Indian origin.

The state of Massachusetts was named after the Indian tribe who lived around the hilly area near Boston. The name came from an Indian word meaning

Massachusetts

"at the big hill." Connecticut's name came from an Indian word which means "beside the long tidal river."

These state names remind us of how big a part the American Indians played in our history. Try to find out what other states have Indian names.

"New" Names

Take another look at the map. Focus your attention on the northeast coast. Notice that three of the state names begin with the word "New." One is *New* Hampshire, one is *New* York, and one is *New* Jersey.

Hampshire? York? Jersey? Do these names sound familiar? If you look them up in your dictionary, this is what you will find out: Two of them—New Hampshire and New Jersey—were named after places in England. The third—New York—was named after the English Duke of York.

What does that tell you? These states were settled and named by people who originally came from England.

159

Names in Names

Focus now on the southeastern part of the country. You may spot a few names that seem to have something in common: North Carolina, South Carolina, Georgia, and Louisiana.

You may have a hunch even before you look them up. Carolina? Georgia? Louisiana? What do they have in common? These state names have the names of people in them.

The Carolinas got their name from King Charles I of England. *Carolana* means "of Charles" in Latin. Georgia was named after King George II of England. Louisiana comes from the name a French explorer gave to the region in honor of Louis XIV, then the king of France.

Several other states were named after people. Can you find the one that was named after an American President?

CHARLES I

GEORGE II

Photos: By courtesy of the National Portrait Gallery, London.

Names from Spain

Now the pieces of the puzzle are coming together. You know that American Indian words are used as the names of some states. You know that other states were named after places or people. Take another look at your map. You will see a piece of land at the southernmost part of the east coast that sticks out into the ocean. Its name—Florida—does not seem to fit into the categories you know.

Georgia

Florida

What do you find out when you look it up in your dictionary? *Florida* is a Spanish word meaning "flowery." The Spanish explorer Ponce de Léon (pon' sə dā lā' ōn) chose this name for the region. He landed there during *Pascua florida* (päs' kwä flō rē' dä)—the Spanish festival of flowers, which takes place at Easter.

In the western part of the country, there are several states that also have Spanish names. For example, Colorado comes from a Spanish word meaning "reddish." The name was first given to the Colorado River by Spanish explorers. They chose the name because of the reddish appearance of the water.

Another state name of Spanish origin is Nevada. It was named after a great mountain range in the region, the Sierra Nevada. *Nevada* means "snow-covered" in Spanish.

STATE FLAGS

Looking at state flags is another way to learn about the history of the states. The colors and symbols on state flags have stories behind them.

A Lone Star

Texas is known as the "Lone Star State." The single star on its flag shows where this nickname came from. But why is the star there?

Texas was once a part of Mexico. Then it became an independent republic. The star is a reminder of the independence Texas had before it became part of the United States in 1845.

A Grizzly Bear

California's flag tells a similar tale. It has a single star in the left-hand corner, a grizzly bear in the center, and the words "California Republic." This flag was first raised in 1846 by American settlers who were fighting Mexico for their freedom.

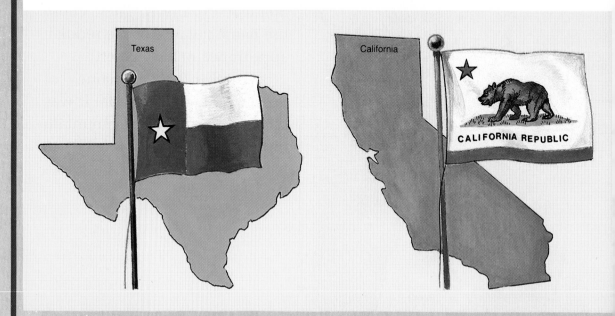

A Battle Star

The flags of some southern states, like Mississippi, remind us of the Civil War. In 1860 and 1861, a group of states withdrew from the Union. They formed a new government known as the Confederacy. The Confederate battle star still appears in the upper left corner of Mississippi's flag.

A Pattern of Stars

Alaska's flag was designed by a 13-year-old Indian boy named Benny Benson. A contest was held to choose a design for the flag.

Benny's design had a blue background. On it were seven gold stars in the shape of the Big Dipper. This constellation is also known as the Great Bear. A single gold star stood for the North Star.

Here is what Benny wrote about his design: "The blue field is for the Alaska sky and the forget-me-not, an Alaska flower. The North Star is for the future of the state of Alaska, the most northerly of the Union. The dipper is for the Great Bear—symbolizing strength."

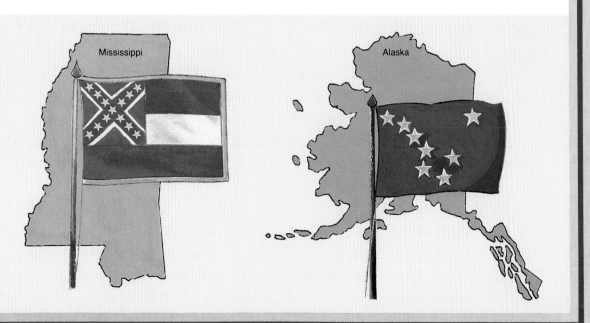

Mississippi

Alaska

STATE BIRDS AND FLOWERS

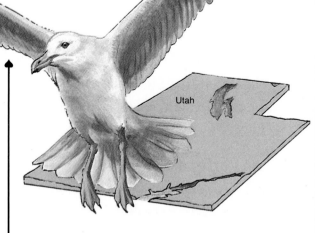

Utah

There are official birds and flowers for each state. These symbols provide more clues about state history.

Sea Gulls and Lilies in Utah

The state bird and state flower of Utah once saved the early pioneers who settled there. The settlers were members of a religious group called the Mormons. They arrived in Utah in 1847 and began to plant crops and build towns. In 1848, swarms of grasshoppers came to the area. They began eating the crops. The Mormons had no way to stop them. Then, a large number of sea gulls from the Great Salt Lake flew in. They ate

Utah
USA 20c

California Gull & Sego Lily

the grasshoppers! Many of the crops were saved. However, many had been destroyed.

The Mormons began to run out of food. This time friendly Indians came to the rescue. They showed the Mormons how to dig up and eat the root, or bulb, of the sego (sē′ gō) lily. That saved them from starving.

Without the sea gulls and the sego lily, the Mormon pioneers might not have survived.

Fighting Bird of Delaware

One of the proudest and toughest state birds is the blue hen chicken of Delaware. The story of this bird goes all the way back to the late 1770s, the time of the American Revolution. When a troop of soldiers left Delaware to fight in the war, they took some blue hen chickens with them. These birds were known to be good fighters.

Before long, the soldiers became famous for their fighting. They were nicknamed "Blue Hen's Chickens." When Delaware adopted a state bird, it chose the blue hen chicken.

Ohio's Red Carnation

Ohio's state flower was chosen in honor of our 25th President, William McKinley from Ohio. The red carnation did not grow in the United States. The flower was brought here from Europe just after the Civil War. McKinley was one of the first to wear a red carnation in the buttonhole of his suit jacket. It became his symbol of good luck. He would often give carnations to friends.

The last person to receive a carnation from the President was a small girl he met at a fair in Buffalo, New York. The date was September 6, 1901. A few minutes later, McKinley was shot. He died about a week later.

In 1904, Ohio voted to adopt the red carnation as its state flower in honor of President McKinley.

Ohio
USA 20c

Cardinal & Red Carnation

Looking at a map or flag, or noticing birds and flowers, may remind you of some of the facts you have learned about the states. If you keep on the lookout, you may find out even more. Your search could take you to places like libraries or museums. Post offices and parking lots are other places to look.

The United States Postal Service has issued a series of stamps that features the bird and flower of each state. Another series has the state flags. Stamps show important people, places, and events from history. There's a lot of information on a little stamp!

Looking at license plates is another way to find out about the states. Some license plates show the products states are famous for. One example is the Kansas license plate, which has wheat on it. Other license plates tell about the natural beauties of the states. The Rocky Mountains appear on the Colorado plate. Michigan's nickname, "Great Lakes State," appears on its license plate.

Keep on the lookout. Who knows what you'll find out about the 50 great states that make up our country!

Thinking and Writing About the Selection

1. What three symbols do all the states have?
2. What can you learn about a state by finding out about its name? Give an example to support your answer.
3. Are state symbols important today? Why or why not?
4. If you were asked to design a flag for your school, what symbols would you choose? What would the symbols represent?

Applying the Key Skill
Main Idea and Supporting Details

Reread the paragraphs from "Learning About the States" listed below. Then copy the diagrams and fill in the missing supporting details.

1. fourth paragraph under "Names from Spain"

Nevada is a state name of Spanish origin.	MAIN IDEA

	SUPPORTING DETAILS

2. second paragraph under "On the Lookout"

There's a lot of information on a little stamp!	MAIN IDEA

	SUPPORTING DETAILS

On The Map

Most of our states take their names from other languages, from other places, or from people. Does it surprise you that nearly half the states have American Indian names? You may recognize these names by the way they sound. Say, *Arizona*, *Minnesota*, *Nebraska*, and *Tennessee*. Can you think of three other states whose names might be Native American? Check in a dictionary or an encyclopedia to see if you are right.

Two states might fool you. One state name means "land of the Indians," but the name is not American Indian. Can you name the state? *Idaho* may sound Indian, but it isn't. *Idaho* is a mystery name. No one is sure where it came from.

Try these: What state was named for William Penn? For Lord De La Warr? What state takes its name from the French words *vert* and *mont*, meaning "green mountain"? Cities, towns, and rivers get their names the same way states do. Below are a few examples.

	NAME	ORIGIN
cities	Pittsburgh	for William Pitt
	Santa Fe	Spanish for "holy faith"
rivers	Hudson	for Henry Hudson
	Susquehanna	American Indian for "crooked water"

What place name in your state can you think of that comes from another language?

MAIN IDEA AND SUPPORTING DETAILS

Writers use sentences to build paragraphs. Good writers put their paragraphs together in an orderly way. This helps readers understand a writer's information and ideas.

Most sentences in a paragraph tell about one subject or topic. The most important information about the topic of a paragraph is called the **main idea**. Often the main idea is stated in a sentence. Many times this sentence is the first or the last in a paragraph.

Other sentences explain the main idea by giving examples or other related information. These sentences are **supporting details** for the main idea.

ACTIVITY A Read the paragraph below. Then copy the diagram and fill in the missing supporting details.

Davy Crockett first became known as an expert hunter and frontiersman. He also served as an officer in the Tennessee army. Later, he was elected to the Tennessee legislature. After that, he served three terms as a representative in Congress. In 1835, Crockett went to Texas, where he died in the famous defense of the Alamo. Today, Davy Crockett is remembered for the many things he did during his lifetime.

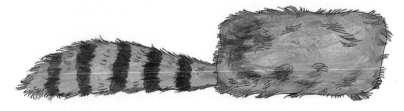

Davy Crockett was an expert hunter and frontiersman.	
	Supporting Details
He was elected to the Tennessee legislature.	
Davy Crockett is remembered for the many things he did during his lifetime.	Main Idea

ACTIVITY B Read the paragraph below. Then make a diagram to show the main idea and supporting details.

The state of Hawaii is special in several ways. It became a state on August 21, 1959. That makes it the youngest state in the Union. It is an island state—the only state that is not on the mainland of North America. Hawaii is also the southernmost state. The island of Oahu (ō ä′ hü) is as far south as central Mexico.

THE LEGEND OF THE BLUEBONNET

TOMIE dePAOLA

The state flower of Texas is a bright blue blossom that covers the Texas hills every spring. These wild flowers, called bluebonnets, were named by the settlers who came to Texas. The settlers thought the bluebonnets looked like the sunbonnets worn by pioneer women.

The story of how the bluebonnets came to Texas is a Comanche (kə man' chē) Indian legend. A legend is a story passed down through the years. It is usually based on some facts, but the story is more important. As you read, you will see that the legend of the bluebonnet is not only a tale about the origin of a flower. It is also the story of the courage and sacrifice of a young girl.

173

"Great Spirits, the land is dying. Your People are dying, too," the long line of dancers sang. "Tell us what we have done to anger you. End this drought. Save your People. Tell us what we must do so you will send the rain that will bring back life."

For three days, the dancers danced to the sound of the drums, and for three days, the People called Comanche watched and waited. Even though the hard winter was over, no healing rains came.

Drought and famine are hardest on the very young and the very old. Among the few children left was a small girl named She-Who-Is-Alone. She sat by herself watching the dancers. In her lap was a doll made from buckskin—a warrior doll. The eyes, nose, and mouth were painted on with the juice of berries. It wore beaded leggings and a belt of polished bone. On its head were brilliant blue feathers from the bird who cries "Jay-jay-jay." She loved her doll very much.

"Soon," She-Who-Is-Alone said to her doll, "the shaman will go off alone to the top of the hill to listen for the words of the Great Spirits. Then, we will know what to do so that once more the rains will come and the Earth will be green and alive. The buffalo will be plentiful and the People will be rich again."

As she talked, she thought of the mother who made the doll, of the father who brought the blue feathers. She thought of the grandfather and the grandmother she had never known. They were all like shadows. It seemed long ago that they had died from the famine. The People had named her and cared for her. The warrior doll was the only thing she had left from those distant days.

175

"The sun is setting," the runner called as he ran through the camp. "The shaman is returning." The People gathered in a circle and the shaman spoke.

"I have heard the words of the Great Spirits," he said. "The People have become selfish. For years, they have taken from the Earth without giving anything back. The Great Spirits say the People must sacrifice. We must make a burnt offering of the most valued possession among us. The ashes of this offering shall then be scattered to the four points of the Earth, the Home of the Winds. When this sacrifice is made, drought and famine will cease. Life will be restored to the Earth and to the People!"

The People sang a song of thanks to the Great Spirits for telling them what they must do.

"I'm sure it is not my new bow that the Great Spirits want," a warrior said.

"Or my special blanket," a woman added, as everyone went to their tipis to talk and think over what the Great Spirits had asked.

Everyone, that is, except She-Who-Is-Alone. She held her doll tightly to her heart. "You," she said, looking at the doll. "You are my most valued possession. It is you the Great Spirits want." She knew what she must do.

As the council fires died out and the tipi flaps began to close, the small girl returned to the tipi where she slept, to wait.

The night outside was still except for the distant sound of the night bird with the red wings. Soon everyone in the tipi was asleep, except She-Who-Is-Alone. Under the ashes of the tipi fire one stick still glowed. She took it and quietly crept out into the night.

She ran to the place on the hill where the Great Spirits had spoken to the shaman. Stars filled the sky, but there was no moon. "O Great Spirits," She-Who-Is-Alone said, "here is my warrior doll. It is the only thing I have from my family who died in this famine. It is my most valued possession. Please accept it."

Then, gathering twigs, she started a fire with the glowing firestick. The small girl watched as the twigs began to catch and burn. She thought of her grandmother and grandfather, her mother and father, and all the People—their suffering, their hunger. Before she could change her mind, she thrust the doll into the fire.

She watched until the flames died down and the ashes had grown cold. Then, scooping up a handful, She-Who-Is-Alone scattered the ashes to the Home of the Winds, the North and the East, the South and the West. There she fell asleep until the first light of the morning sun woke her.

She looked out over the hill, and stretching out from all sides, where the ashes had fallen, the ground was covered with flowers—beautiful flowers, as blue as the feathers in the hair of the doll, as blue as the feathers of the bird who cries "Jay-jay-jay."

When the People came out of their tipis, they could scarcely believe their eyes. They gathered on the hill with She-Who-Is-Alone to look at the miraculous sight. There was no doubt about it, the flowers were a sign of forgiveness from the Great Spirits.

As the People sang and danced their thanks to the Great Spirits, a warm rain began to fall and the land began to live again. From that day on, the little girl was known by another name—"One-Who-Dearly-Loved-Her-People."

Every spring, the Great Spirits remember the sacrifice of a little girl and fill the hills and valleys of the land, now called Texas, with the beautiful blue flowers.

Even to this very day.

Thinking and Writing About the Selection

1. How did She-Who-Is-Alone get that name?
2. Why did the shaman go off alone to the top of a hill?
3. Name one event in the legend of the bluebonnet that could have been based on facts.

 4. What is your most valued possession? Why is it valuable to you?

Applying the Key Skill
Causes of an Event

Write sentences to explain what caused each of the following events in "The Legend of the Bluebonnet."

1. The settlers who came to Texas decided to call a wildflower the bluebonnet.
2. The warrior doll that belonged to She-Who-Is-Alone reminded her of her parents.
3. The People knew that the Great Spirits had forgiven them.
4. She-Who-Is-Alone became known as "One-Who-Dearly-Loved-Her-People."

CELEBRATION

Alonzo Lopez
Papago Indian

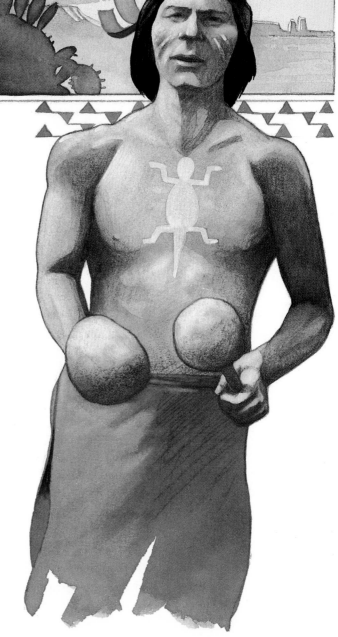

I shall dance tonight.
When the dusk comes crawling,
There will be dancing
    and feasting.
I shall dance with the others
    in circles,
      in leaps,
        in stomps.
Laughter and talk
    will weave into the night,
Among the fires
    of my people.
Games will be played
And I shall be
    a part of it.

REFERENCE SOURCES

Where can you look when you need information? Two good **reference sources** are the encyclopedia and the almanac.

An **encyclopedia** contains information about important people, places, things, and ideas. An encyclopedia is usually a set of books. Each book is called a volume.

An **almanac** is a single volume that gives information about the events of the past year. It lists records and achievements of people, and gives facts about places. It includes many charts and tables, and often has maps.

Key words or terms are important in finding information in an almanac or an encyclopedia. Key words are the most important words in a question or topic. For example, the key words in the question "When did the bluebonnet become the state flower of Texas?" are *bluebonnet* and *Texas*.

Once you know the key words, you can refer to the index or contents in an almanac.

ACTIVITY A Number your paper from 1 to 4. On your paper, write the key word or words you would use to find where to look for the following information in an almanac.

1. the names of the governors of the states
2. records set in different events of the Olympic games
3. the major rivers of the world
4. the highest and lowest temperatures ever recorded

ACTIVITY B Number your paper from 1 to 10. Read each question below. If you would look in an encyclopedia to find the answer, write **Encyclopedia** beside the number. If you would use an almanac, write **Almanac**. If you would use both reference sources, write **Both**.

1. What is the population of Chicago?
2. What are the important products made or grown in Idaho?
3. When and where was poet Emily Dickinson born?
4. What baseball team has won the World Series the greatest number of times?
5. How do bees make honey?
6. Who won the Nobel Prize for Medicine last year?
7. Who was the first President to live in the White House?
8. When did Franklin Delano Roosevelt become President?
9. What is the state flower of Minnesota?
10. Who was given the Academy Award for best actress one year ago?

ACTIVITY C Write the key word or words you would use to find the answers to the questions in **ACTIVITY B**.

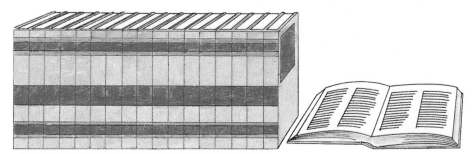

WHERE THERE'S A WILL, THERE'S A WAY

Alberta Wilson Constant

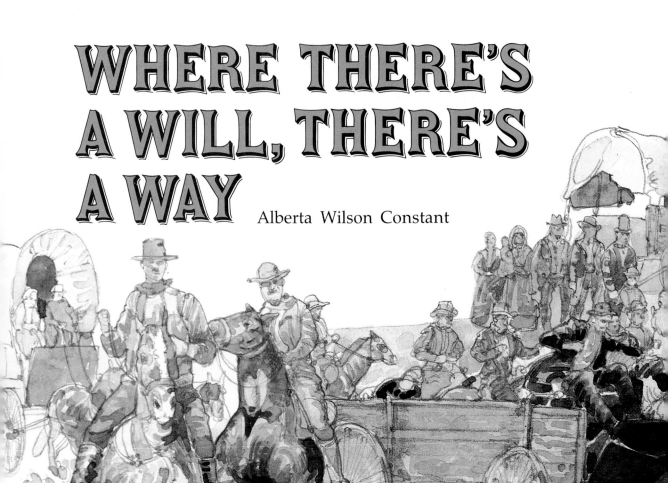

In 1862, the United States government passed the first of the Homestead Acts. These acts provided free land for settlers who agreed to farm the land and live on it. In 1893, many people came to Oklahoma when the Cherokee Outlet was offered for homesteading. They were so eager for land that they raced to make their claims. In this story, a girl named Betsy remembers the day of the race.

I never in this world would have thought about writing a book if it hadn't been for Miss Charity. She said that all of us in Skiprock School were part of history. She said that any of us who came to the Cherokee Strip for the big run for land should put down all that we could remember. Some day it would be important, she said. That set me to thinking.

Our whole family came down from Kansas when the Cherokee Strip was opened for homestead claims in 1893. Some folks called it the Cherokee Outlet. But most of those who lived there called it the Strip. The Strip is that long, straight part of Oklahoma Territory that lies right south of the Kansas line. It belonged to the Cherokee Indians, but they leased it to cattle ranchers. Finally the government bought it to open for settlement. The land was for anyone who was fast enough to get a claim and tough enough to live on it and prove up. (That last is really from Papa. I've heard him say it so often that I thought I thought of it.)

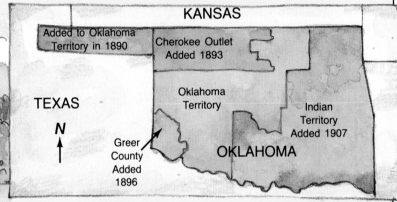

A lot of folks we knew in Kansas came down for the Run. Men came alone mostly, but Mama said that the Richardsons were all in this together. It was a case of "united we stand or divided we fall." We weren't even to talk about falling! Papa was the only one to ride in the Run. A person had to be twenty-one or the head of a family. Nell and Tom and I stayed in the wagon with Mama.

I wish I'd paid more attention to the way things were the day of the Run. I guess I was too excited. The riders lined up as far as you could see. Out in front of the line was a soldier, holding a gun. We could tell which rider was Papa by the red handkerchief he tied around the crown of his hat. Watching the line, it seemed like an awful long time ago that he'd kissed Mama and Nell and me, and shaken hands with Tom and told him to look after us. If anything happened to Papa. . . .

There was a terrible roaring noise and the ground shook under me. It was the Run! All I could see was a long, long cloud of dust, going faster and faster. Rex was barking, and I was jumping up and down, screaming. Not that I knew it! Nell told me later. Sometimes a wagon would lock wheels with another and turn over and spill people out. In a few minutes the men on horseback began to pull away from the rest. I saw a flash of red going out of sight and I knew it was Papa. I *knew* it was. Quicker than I can tell about it, the big wide prairie swallowed the riders. Only the heavy wagons, the men on foot, and the folks like us who were waiting were left.

187

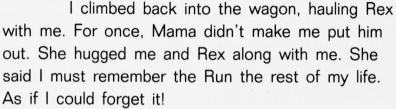

I climbed back into the wagon, hauling Rex with me. For once, Mama didn't make me put him out. She hugged me and Rex along with me. She said I must remember the Run the rest of my life. As if I could forget it!

It was about a year after the Run that we got our school. Miss Charity came down to be the teacher. The things that happened at the Run were dim and dusty in my mind. After Miss Charity started talking about how it was really history, I got excited remembering. I raised my hand and asked her what, besides just the Run, was history, because I'd decided to write a book. She said for me to put down how things began.

That was how I got started to writing this book. The things I put in it may not be *real* history, but they're going to be true.

Right off I found out one thing. It's hard to know where to start a book. Authors don't have an easy time. We have a card game of *Authors* and most of them have worried-looking faces.

Hard or not, I'm going ahead. Our copybook says, "Where there's a will, there's a way." That means I've got a head start, because Papa says I'm the most willful child he's ever seen.

Still, I didn't have any place to start my book. I thought and thought about it. When Rex and I went out to bring in Old Blue, it was on my mind. In the Strip you can't just turn a cow out to graze, because there aren't any fences yet, and the coyotes might chase her. We didn't have feed enough to keep her up. Every morning it was my chore to lead Old Blue to some good grass, and hobble her. Then I'd go get her in the evening. Even with a hobble she could get quite a ways away and I'd hear her bell before I saw her. I went toward the bell sound, calling "Soooooo boss, Soooooooo."

Old Blue was down in a hollow where the grass was thick. There she stood, chewing her cud. She was laughing at me, watching me hunt her. I sicked Rex onto her, but before he got started, he scooped up the trail of a rabbit and took off north. I had to run about a mile to round him up. Then I had to go back and get Old Blue and take off the hobble and put on her halter before I could start home. I was sure winded! Halfway home I topped a little rise and sat down to rest.

Rex came and sat beside me. I get put out at Rex, but I love him just the same. I leaned against him, and I could hear his heart going thum . . . thum . . . thum . . . thum. The sun was slipping down the side of the sky. The shadows had turned blue. The wind that never stops in the Strip sighed past my ears. Rex's heartbeat and mine and the sigh of the wind were all part of the same thing . . . thum . . . thum . . . thum. I put my hand on the ground and felt the prairie throbbing, too.

There was a hawk riding the wind above us. He dived and came winging up in a curve so high he went out of sight. He was a part of the prairie. The mouse, or whatever he dived for, that squeaked off to a safe place in the grass was, too. "Everything's part of everything," I whispered into Rex's ear. It was too big an idea to hold onto, though, and it slipped away, even before I said it. All that stayed was the thum . . . thum . . . thum.

Straight ahead of us was our house. Papa and Tom were coming back from the field. They'd been working with the plow to get the ground into shape for a wheat crop. Our team, Puss and Bess, walked ahead. The sound of the harness came in little jingles on the wind. Tom and Papa walked side by each, and even this far off a person could see they belonged together. They walked the same way; they pushed their hats back the same way. Mama came out to the well. The sun flashed on the tin bucket. I couldn't really hear the well rope creak as the bucket came up full, but I could *feel* it. Nell was out by the wire pen feeding the hens. She came over by Mama, and then they both went back into the soddy.

A soddy is what you call a sod-house in the Strip. It's made of sod "bricks." We had a sod roof, too, with the grass side up. From a ways off, the way I was, it wasn't like a separate thing at all . . . just a part of the prairie, a part of the wind and the whole wide world. All of a sudden I loved it so hard that I couldn't stand it! I jumped up and began to run. Rex ran alongside, barking like he was crazy, and Old Blue began to trot. I knew, I knew, I knew where to start my book! Right with the soddy! That was the place!

Thinking and Writing About the Selection

1. Why was Papa the only one to ride in the run?
2. Why did Betsy decide to write a book?
3. What does "Where there's a will, there's a way" mean?
4. If you were going to write a book, what would you write about? Why?

Applying the Key Skill
Maps

Use the map in "Where There's a Will, There's a Way" to answer the questions below.

1. What state borders Oklahoma to the south and west?
2. When was Greer County added to Oklahoma?
3. What land was added to Oklahoma in 1893?
4. What was the name of the largest area added to Oklahoma?
5. If you were in the Cherokee Outlet and wanted to travel to Greer County, in what direction would you go?
6. If you traveled from the Indian Territory to Greer County, in what direction would you have gone?

CAUSES OF AN EVENT

As you read, you find out about things that have happened. You are often told why a particular event occurred, or took place. In the introduction to "Where There's a Will, There's a Way," you learned:

> Many people went to Oklahoma in 1893
> because they were eager for free land.

The two parts of this sentence are related in a cause-and-effect relationship.

EFFECT: Many people went to Oklahoma in 1893
CAUSE: because they were eager for free land.

Figuring out cause-and-effect relationships is one way to understand what you read. A **cause** is the reason something happens. An **effect** is the result, or the thing that happens. The words *because*, *in order to*, *since*, and *so* often signal a cause-and-effect relationship.

There is often more than one cause for an effect, or event. Read the following paragraph.

> Many people claimed land in Oklahoma under the Homestead Act of 1893. Some were eager to get free land. Others felt that the land there was better than the land they had. Still others were drawn by the spirit of adventure.

In the paragraph, three causes are given for an event. The following diagram shows how the sentences in the paragraph are related.

CAUSES

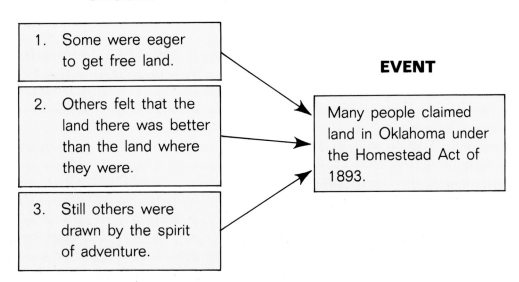

1. Some were eager to get free land.

2. Others felt that the land there was better than the land where they were.

3. Still others were drawn by the spirit of adventure.

EVENT

Many people claimed land in Oklahoma under the Homestead Act of 1893.

ACTIVITY Find the sentence in the paragraph below that states an effect. Write the sentence on your paper and label it **effect**. Find the three sentences that tell the causes of the effect. Write each sentence on your paper and label it **cause**.

Mount Girard is a high mountain near the little town of Merton. The path to the top is long and, in many places, steep. Although Sarah, Maria, and Ellen had lived in Merton all their lives, they had never been to the top of Mount Girard. Because they all liked to hike and climb, the girls decided to go to the top of the mountain one day. They also wanted to see the view from the top, which was said to be quite beautiful. The hike would help them earn points toward the Girl Scout merit badges they were working for, too. The day of the hike turned out to be a day of great adventure for everyone.

THIS IS WHAT I KNOW

Denise Gosliner Orenstein

*What would it be like to move from your state
to a state that is very far away? In this story,
Shawn finds out what a long move means. Will Shawn
learn a new way of life, as her mother says?
How will learning about the past help Shawn?*

I haven't always lived here. My mother is a teacher. Last summer, we moved from New York City to live in Klawock (klä' wäk), a town on an island in Alaska. This island only has small buildings. My mother says we will learn a new way of life. I don't know about that.

My name is Shawn. My hair is red and curly. When we first moved to this island, everyone stared. I thought they stared because my hair is red.

I guess you know what an island is like. It's a piece of land with water all around. This island kind of sits in the middle of the ocean. My mother says I shouldn't say "kind of." It's not good English.

I learned a bunch of other things when I
moved here, too. Like how to clean a fish without
feeling funny and slimy. And how to find salmon-
berries in the spring. My friend Vesta taught me that.

I want to tell you about my friend Vesta. Her
hair is short and dark. She knows how to tie three
different kinds of rope knots with her eyes closed,
and she can hop backward on ice without slipping.
Vesta is a Tlingit (kling' ət) Indian.

This is what I know: there are five kinds of
native people living in Alaska. "Native" means people
who have always lived in a place. The five kinds of
native people are Eskimo, Athabaskan (ath' ə bas'
kən), Haida (hī' də), Aleut (ə lüt'), and Tlingit.

My friend Vesta has a grandfather who loves
me. It wasn't always like that. I used to be scared of

196

Vesta's grandfather because he was so old and quiet, and sometimes his hands shook. When I visited Vesta's house, her grandfather would stare at me. I thought he didn't like me because my hair was red. This is how I felt when I first moved to Klawock and met Vesta's grandfather: I was sad. I missed New York City and my friends from my New York school.

Vesta was the only one at school who was nice to me. She sat next to me in class and lent me her red pen. One day, she invited me to visit her house after school. That made me feel better.

We were drinking tea when Vesta's grandfather came in. He was carrying a walking stick and wore a brown parka. He walked slowly, looked at me, but didn't speak. My hair started to feel very red. I decided to go home.

The next time I saw Vesta's grandfather, I was in John Petrovitch's store. Mr. Petrovitch has a Russian name. Maybe he is related to some Russians who used to live here.

I nodded to Vesta's grandfather when I came in the store, and pulled up my jacket hood to cover my red hair. Vesta's grandfather looked at me but didn't move.

"Hello, Shawn," Mr. Petrovitch said. "What can I do for you?" Somehow I felt strange in front of Vesta's grandfather. Mr. Petrovitch and Vesta's grandfather were looking at me. I pulled on the strings of my jacket hood. "Shawn?" Mr. Petrovitch said.

I knew I had to speak. "Mr. Petrovitch," I said, looking down, "my mother needs some lettuce and powdered milk."

This is what I know: no one in Klawock drinks regular milk from a carton. Milk comes from cows, and there are no cows in Klawock. If the people in Klawock had milk sent from the lower states, the milk would go sour on the long, long trip. There's a kind of milk that is all dried up. It looks like soap flakes. This is powdered milk. It never goes sour. When you mix it with water, it almost tastes like fresh milk.

"Well, Shawn," Mr. Petrovitch said, "I'll be happy to sell you some milk, but the lettuce is no good. It froze on the way up from Seattle."

Sometimes the weather in Alaska is so cold, things freeze quickly. Since the Klawock soil doesn't have the right minerals for vegetables to grow, we order lettuce and things like that from a city called Seattle. Seattle is in a state called Washington. When the weather is real cold, the vegetables we get from

Seattle freeze before we can eat them. We eat canned food a lot because it never freezes or goes bad.

"Okay, Mr. Petrovitch," I said, looking down at my boots, "I'll just take the milk."

All this time, Vesta's grandfather was quiet, but I could feel him looking at me. I figured he didn't like me much. All the way home, I wondered why.

Now, this is the part that gets surprising. At least, I didn't expect what happened to happen. Vesta moved away to another town. Her father got a job in a cannery in a place called Ketchikan (kech' i kan'). Vesta and her mother had to go to Ketchikan, too.

This is what I know: there are a lot of fish in Alaska. Many people all over the state go fishing for a living. That's their regular job. All the fish that are caught are sent to places across the United States. A cannery is a place where fish are cleaned and put into cans to be sent away. Vesta's father went to work in one of those canneries.

After Vesta left, nothing was the same. No one in school whispered with me or passed me notes and funny drawings. No one invited me over after school. No one gave me tea.

One day, when I came home from school, my mother called me into the kitchen. She was making deer stew. Sometimes people call it "venison." I don't know why.

"Shawn," my mother said, stirring the stew with a big wooden spoon, "I made some stew for Vesta's grandfather. With the family away, he needs a little looking after."

I didn't say anything. Vesta's grandfather seemed old enough to look after himself. My mother put the spoon down.

"I'd like to give some of this stew to Vesta's grandfather for dinner. I think he would appreciate a hot meal."

I looked away. I knew what was coming.

"Shawn," my mother continued, "would you please take a bowl of the stew over to Vesta's grandfather's house after school tomorrow?"

"Why do I have to?" I asked.

"I just finished telling you, Shawn," Mother said very slowly. "Vesta's grandfather is living all alone. It seems to me that you would want to do something for your friend's grandfather."

I didn't want to, but I guess I had to. The next day, after school, I poured a bunch of deer stew into a bowl. I wondered whether the bowl was big enough. Vesta's grandfather might eat a lot. Next I covered the bowl with tinfoil so the stew wouldn't fall out while I was walking. I sat down and stared at the bowl of deer stew for a long while. I might have felt a little scared.

When I knocked on Vesta's grandfather's door, no one answered. I knocked again, then pushed the door gently. It opened halfway.

"Hello," I said softly. "Hello," I said again, louder. I looked inside. Vesta's grandfather was sitting at the kitchen table, cutting a piece of wood with a knife. He didn't look up. I walked into the house and put the bowl of stew on the table for Vesta's grandfather.

"My mother and I thought you might like some deer stew," I said. "My mother made it."

Vesta's grandfather reached out and touched the bowl with his fingertips. And then he looked up.

    This is what I know: Vesta's grandfather's face
is different from any other face I've ever seen. His
skin is the color of wood, the lines on his face like
the grain of wood. The eyes are very dark, very
large, and very still. I held my breath.

    Vesta's grandfather put one hand on my arm
and pointed to a chair. "Sit down," he said. Vesta's
grandfather had never spoken to me before. I sat
down next to him. He picked up the piece of wood
again and began cutting it with a knife. I had seen
other men in Klawock cut wood like that. It's called

carving. It's a kind of artwork. Vesta's grandfather began to talk as he carved. This is what he said:

"This wood is like the pulse of a wrist. It's full of motion and warm inside the hand. What I am carving is alive." I watched the piece of wood change shape as Vesta's grandfather carved. It looked like magic. All at once, I could see the shape of a small, curved paddle. Suddenly, I wasn't scared of Vesta's grandfather any more.

"Are you carving a paddle?" I asked Vesta's grandfather.

He nodded and said: "This is a paddle like those from long ago. All we had in those days were paddles to move our boats. We had no engines. Even then, we carved our paddles like pieces of art. When I was small, like you, my uncle taught me to carve as I am carving now. He handed down what he knew. My uncle was an artist from way back, and taught me not to do anything halfway. The Tlingit people treat art as something to be respected."

"Have you ever carved a totem pole?" I asked Vesta's grandfather.

This is what I know: a totem pole is a tree without any branches. The wood is carved with all kinds of animals and painted all different colors. There are a lot of totem poles in Klawock. Vesta's grandfather nodded. "The totem pole here in Klawock," he said, "the one with the fox on top? I carved that."

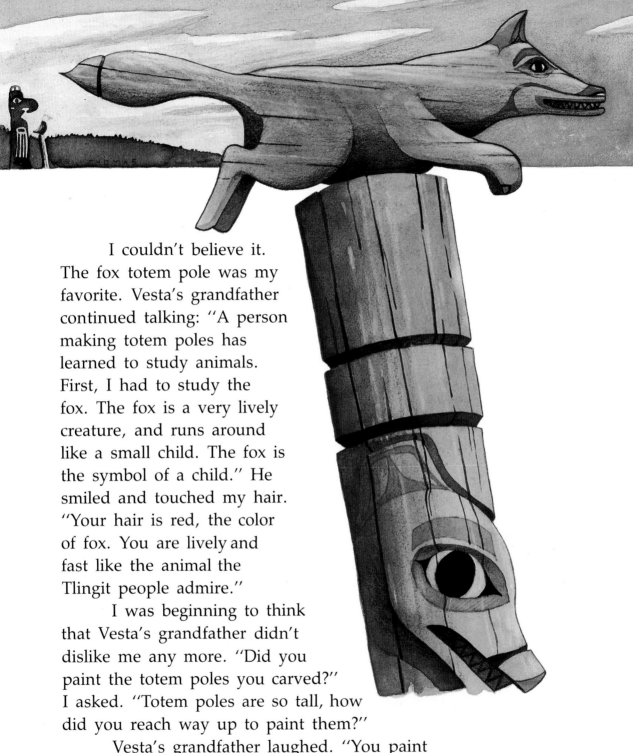

I couldn't believe it. The fox totem pole was my favorite. Vesta's grandfather continued talking: "A person making totem poles has learned to study animals. First, I had to study the fox. The fox is a very lively creature, and runs around like a small child. The fox is the symbol of a child." He smiled and touched my hair. "Your hair is red, the color of fox. You are lively and fast like the animal the Tlingit people admire."

I was beginning to think that Vesta's grandfather didn't dislike me any more. "Did you paint the totem poles you carved?" I asked. "Totem poles are so tall, how did you reach way up to paint them?"

Vesta's grandfather laughed. "You paint the totems when they are lying down across the ground," he said, "before they are placed upright to stand in the sky. Long ago, we used paintbrushes made from wild bushes, and made all different kinds of paints from nature around us. Some paints were made from tree bark, some from blueberries and blackberries. These old Indian paints last for hundreds of years. They never fade in the sun. Now, these paints from long ago are gone. Very few people remember them."

Vesta's grandfather put the paddle on the table next to the bowl of deer stew. It was finished. Vesta's grandfather looked at me.

"This paddle is for you," he said. "Take it home."

I felt funny. The paddle was so beautiful. I didn't feel right taking Vesta's grandfather's paddle home. He picked up the paddle and handed it to me. It felt warm, warm from the heat of his hands.

Vesta's grandfather looked at me. "The Tlingit does not turn down any gift," he said, "but accepts it with open arms."

That is when Grandfather and I became friends. Now I bring Grandfather his dinner every Friday afternoon. Sometimes he tells me stories from the time that he was young. Sometimes we carve animals out of warm, soft wood. Sometimes we eat Tlingit candy made from green seaweed and sugar.

This is what I know: in the late afternoon, the Klawock sky turns pink. If you walk up the hill behind the school yard, you can see totem poles shine in the moving light. Stand under the one with the red fox on top. Hold your breath. Hear the sounds from long ago.

Thinking and Writing About the Selection

1. How did Shawn feel when she first moved to Klawak? Why did her feelings change?
2. Why didn't Shawn want to bring the stew to Vesta's grandfather?
3. Why do you think Vesta's grandfather gave Shawn the paddle he carved? Do you think Shawn should have accepted the paddle?
4. What do you know about Alaska and its people now that you have read this story? Write a list of the facts you have learned.

Applying the Key Skill
Draw Conclusions

Use complete sentences to answer the following questions about "This Is What I Know."

1. Why did Shawn conclude that Vesta's grandfather did not like her?
2. What information in the story supports the conclusion below?
   Tlingit traditions were important to Vesta's grandfather.
3. Why did Shawn conclude that Vesta's grandfather really loved her?

Good Ole What's-His-Name

You have learned that many place names come from people's last names. But where did people's last names come from? Long ago, people had only first names. Imagine how confusing this may have been if a lot of people named Tom, Dick, and Harry lived near one another. Last names came about so that people could be told apart.

Suppose that there were several Toms, Dicks, and Harrys living in one village. You might distinguish them by telling whose son each is. There might be Tom, Dick's son; Tom, Harry's son; and Tom, Tom's son. To say this in a shorter way, you might say Tom Dickson, Tom Harrison, and Tom Tomson (Thomson).

There are other ways of saying "son of" in other languages. In "This is What I Know," Shawn says, "Mr. Petrovitch has a Russian name." In Russian, *vitch* means "son of," and *Petro* means "Peter." *Petrovitch* means "son of Peter." In Spanish "son of Peter" is *Pérez*.

Mac and *Mc* mean "son of," too. Can you tell what the Irish or Scottish names McDougal, Macdonald, McAdam, MacArthur, and MacNeill mean?

From *fitz*, a form of the French word *fils* ("son"), we have Fitzpatrick, Fitzgerald, and Fitzsimmons.

Some last names tell how people looked [Short, White, Longfellow, Redman, Klein (*klein* means "small" in German)] or what work they did [Baker, Cook, Cooper (barrelmaker), Fisher, Chávez ("key maker" in Spanish), Singer, and Cartwright (cartmaker)].

Is your last name among those mentioned above? If not, try to find out what it means.

REPORT

Prewrite

In "This Is What I Know," Shawn learned many facts about Alaska. Other stories in this unit presented facts about other states. Suppose you have been invited to take part in a state writing contest. To enter the contest, you must write a report called "This Is What I Know About My State." The rules say that the report must be two paragraphs. The first paragraph must give general information. The second paragraph may be on a topic of your choice.

The state has sent a list to help you plan your report. Part I of the list gives the information that must be included in the first paragraph of the report. Part II gives you a choice of topics that might be used for the second paragraph.

Part I	Part II
State capital	Geography of state
State flower and bird	History of state
State flag	Famous people
Number of people in state	Popular sports teams
Largest city	Vacation places

Before you write, decide which topic you will write about in your second paragraph. Next, think about where you can find information for your report. Last, read and make notes.

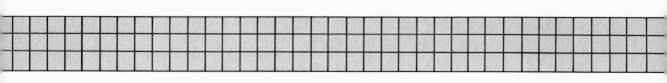

Write

1. Write the sentences for the first paragraph in the order given in Part I of the list. Write a main idea sentence to begin your paragraph.
2. The main idea sentence of your second paragraph should state the topic. The detail sentences should tell facts about the topic. Try to make the paragraph more interesting by using personal examples. If your topic is Vacation Places, for example, tell about a trip you may have made to one of the places.
3. Try to use Vocabulary Treasures in your report.
4. Now write the first draft of your report.

VOCABULARY TREASURES

official	appreciate
represents	citizens

Revise

Read your report. Have a friend read it, too. Think about this checklist as you revise.

1. Did your first paragraph tell about all the information from Part I of the list?
2. Did the main idea of the second paragraph state the topic, and the detail sentences give facts about that topic?
3. Did you use vocabulary that would catch your reader's attention? Use Vocabulary Treasures and your Glossary for help.
4. Did you proofread your report for correct use of capital letters and spelling?
5. Now rewrite your report to share.

FROM THE HILLS OF GEORGIA

Mattie Lou O'Kelley

This selection
is from an autobiography, or book a
person writes about his or her own
life. Artist Mattie Lou O'Kelley uses
her paintings and her own words to
describe what it was like to live on
a farm in Maysville, Georgia, during
the early 1900s. As she shares her
childhood memories, you will learn
about a way of life from the not too
distant past.

210

EMILY
MATTIE
ARRIVES

I remember Mama talking about when I was born, March 30, 1908. There were three brothers and three sisters waiting for me: Willie, Lillie, Gertrude, Ruth, Tom, and Ben. Mama had a doctor for the first time. I don't know how many women friends were there to help, but I did survive the name they gave me—Emily Mattie Lou.

W hat a fuss. Talking, talking, talking. Then they tell me to go out to the woodpile to play. Finally Papa comes outside to tell me that I have a new baby brother. John Tyler has come into the family. Soon Mama will take him out in the fields with us while she works, hanging a quilt to shade him. From now on I'll have a playmate and companion.

PAPA'S WORKSHOP

Willie, Tom, and Ben shoe the mules, sharpen the field plows, and keep the farm tools in shape here in Papa's shop. It's my job to turn the grindstone and blow the bellows to make the fire red. Johnnie helps me. Next to the road is the potato bank, where Papa stores his sweet potatoes.

It's a mile from our house to the three-room schoolhouse. We always walk unless it's raining, and then we get to ride in the buggy or surrey. We go seven months in the winter and two in the summer. I wish I could stay home like Johnnie does. In the summer I like to carry pomegranates in my pocket. They smell so warm and good. I like to keep one on my desk top.

THE CROSSROADS SCHOOLHOUSE ON A SNOWY DAY

SPRINGTIME IN GEORGIA

Outdoors and barefoot after the long cooped-up winter. The peach trees and apple trees are blooming, but my favorite is the wild plum—soft as baby lace. We make playhouses and leaf hats down behind the poplars until the bees come out. Mama hurries us away to the field, where Papa's plowing, shouting, "Come hive the bees! They're swarming!" Ready with his winter-made hives, Papa leads the bees to their new homes.

215

The branch that runs in the pasture below the house is one of my favorite spots. On hot summer days Johnnie and I build a dam so we can go wading. We look for crawfish, minnows, and little green snakes. Sometimes we climb the big apple tree and eat the new green apples with salt.

PLAYING IN THE BRANCH

COTTON GINNING TIME

September, and the hills are white with opening cotton bolls. Now that I'm six, Mama fixes me my own cotton-picking sack. This year I'll pick on her row, and next year I can have a row all my own. Johnnie and I like to play on the huge bales of cotton Papa brings back from the gin and dumps in the yard until it's time to haul them off to market.

THANKSGIVING

Time for everyone to come home. Willie and his wife, Ethel Mae, and their two girls, Mary Helen and Sister, and Ruth and Loney with their son, Sosebee. Papa, Tom, and Ben go to Maysville to meet Lillie's train from Atlanta. Lillie's now a city girl, and her arms are filled with packages for the rest of us—toys and dolls, candy for the whole family, and watercolor paints and pastels, specially for me.

Thinking and Writing About the Selection

1. Who is the man with the red tie in *John Tyler Comes*? How do you know?
2. What are some signs of spring in *Springtime in Georgia*?
3. How would you describe Mattie Lou O'Kelley's paintings? What kinds of colors does she use? What kinds of scenes does she like to paint?
4. Mattie Lou O'Kelley used words and paintings to save her memories. What are some other things people can do to keep their memories?

Applying the Key Skill
Draw Conclusions

Read each conclusion below. Then write two or three sentences that give information found in "From the Hills of Georgia" to support the conclusion.

1. The O'Kelley farm was a very busy place.
2. During the summer, Mattie Lou and her brother Johnnie were never bored.
3. Mattie Lou and her brothers helped with the work on the farm.

A TRUNK FULL OF HISTORY

Susan Nanus

Sometimes you do not have to go far to learn about the past. In this play, Charlie and Katie find out about the history of their family and their town. Their discoveries about the past begin right in their own attic.

CHARACTERS

Charlie Watson, *a boy in the fourth grade*
Katie, *his younger sister*
Charles From the Past, *a boy from 1905*

Other characters from 1905:

Willie	The Banker
The Ice Man	The Drummer
Emily	Man #1
Maryann	Man #2
A Messenger	Woman #1
Dr. Johnson	Woman #2
The Mayor	Townspeople
The Editor-in-Chief	

TIME

The Present and the Past

SETTING

An attic in Middlebury and then . . .

(*A large old trunk sits in the middle of a bare stage. Suddenly, a loud thumping is heard from inside. The trunk begins to rock back and forth as if someone is trying very hard to get out. After a moment, the trunk is quiet again. Charlie and Katie enter the attic. They look around.*)

CHARLIE: See? There's no one here.

KATIE: But I heard a noise. A loud noise.

CHARLIE: Well, there's nothing up here but this old trunk, and trunks don't make noise. Let's go back downstairs.

KATIE: Okay. (*As they turn to go, the top of the trunk flies open. Out pops Charles From the Past.*)

CHARLES FROM THE PAST: Well, that does it! I am sick and tired of waiting! Sick and tired, do you hear? (*Charlie and Katie jump back in amazement.*) What's the matter with you? Don't you have any curiosity?

CHARLIE: Who are you?

KATIE: How did you get in that trunk?

CHARLES FROM THE PAST: (*stepping out of the trunk*) Why, in my day, if there were an old trunk in the attic, *every* kid in town would be wanting to have a look inside!

KATIE: Look at the funny way he's dressed, Charlie.

CHARLIE: Where did you come from?

KATIE: Did you find those clothes in the trunk?

CHARLES FROM THE PAST: There's a lot more than clothes in there. There's a whole world! It's just waiting to be discovered, if you know where to look for it.

CHARLIE: (*suspiciously*) What kind of world?

CHARLES FROM THE PAST: The special world of your very own history—full of stories and . . .

CHARLIE: Stories?

KATIE: You mean like secrets?

CHARLES FROM THE PAST: Could be.

(*Suddenly, Willie comes running in.*)

WILLIE: Hey, Charles, did you hear the news? They're putting up a nickelodeon on Main Street!

KATIE: What's a nickelodeon?

223

WILLIE: It's a picture show that lasts about ten minutes and costs a nickel.

(*The Ice Man appears. He walks bent over, as if he is carrying a heavy load on his back.*)

ICE MAN: Ice for sale! Ice for sale!

KATIE: Charlie, look!

ICE MAN: I've got 40, 60, 80 pounds of ice all cut and ready for the ice box.

KATIE: Ice box? Is that like a refrigerator?

ICE MAN: Never heard of that before. I'm talking about a big wooden box with two compartments. You put your food in the top one, and the ice in the bottom to keep it cool.

CHARLIE: Excuse me, but how did you get here?

ICE MAN: Just walked across the street. Got my horse and wagon hitched over there, see? (*He points. Charlie stares offstage.*)

(*The Ice Man exits as Emily and Maryann enter from either side of the stage. Maryann makes the motions of ringing up an old telephone box on the wall.*)

MARYANN: Ring, ring! Ring, ring! Hello, Emily?

EMILY: (*picking up an imaginary receiver and speaking into an imaginary mouthpiece on the wall*) Is that you, Maryann?

CHARLIE: Who are all these people?

KATIE: Who cares? This is fun.

CHARLIE: But it doesn't make any sense. And the more I ask, the less I understand.

CHARLES FROM THE PAST: Maybe you're asking the wrong questions.

EMILY: (*continuing her conversation*) Speak up, Maryann! I can hardly hear you.

MARYANN: (*shouting into the mouthpiece*) I'M SO PROUD! YOU HAVE THE FIRST TELEPHONE IN TOWN AND I HAVE THE SECOND!

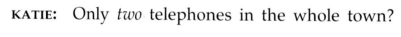

KATIE: Only *two* telephones in the whole town?

CHARLES FROM THE PAST: Only two private telephones. Certain businesses like the bank or the railroad office have them, but very few people have one in their own home.

KATIE: Then how do you tell each other things?

CHARLES FROM THE PAST: We visit, we write letters, or . . .

(*The Messenger enters.*)

MESSENGER: Message for Dr. Johnson!

CHARLES FROM THE PAST: . . . we send messages.

(*Dr. Johnson runs in.*)

DR. JOHNSON: Over here, young man! (*The Messenger hands Dr. Johnson the message. He opens it and reads it. Then he looks up and makes an announcement.*) Ladies and gentlemen, boys and girls, the Mayor and the Dedication Parade are on the way! (*Suddenly, the sound of a drum is heard.*)

WILLIE: Here they come!

(*A noisy procession of men, women, and children march in. At the head is the Mayor, followed by the Editor-in-Chief, the Banker, and the Drummer.*)

EMILY, MARYANN, THE ICE MAN, DR. JOHNSON, AND WILLIE:
(*clapping and cheering*) Hooray! Hooray!

(*The Mayor finally stops the parade and steps forward.*)

MAYOR: Thank you, thank you! Now quiet down, folks, so we can get on with our dedication.

CHARLIE: (*to Charles From the Past*) What town is this supposed to be anyway?

MAYOR: You back there, I said quiet! (*He composes himself.*) Dear ladies and gentlemen! As Mayor of Middlebury, I am proud to announce the construction of the first department store in our fair town. Until now, all we've had is the general store and the mail-order catalog, but we will soon have our very own department store right here on Main Street.

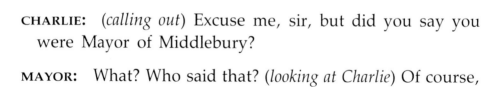

CHARLIE: (*calling out*) Excuse me, sir, but did you say you were Mayor of Middlebury?

MAYOR: What? Who said that? (*looking at Charlie*) Of course, I'm the Mayor. Are you new in town?

CHARLIE: I was born and raised in Middlebury.

MAYOR: Then stop asking ridiculous questions. (*Everyone laughs.*) Now, as I was saying . . .

CHARLIE: You don't look like the picture of the Mayor in the newspaper.

MAYOR: Newspaper editor is my brother-in-law, son. He's always trying to make me look bad.

(*Everyone laughs again.*)

MAYOR: (*continuing his speech*) Yes sir, folks, 1905 will be a great year for us all.

CHARLIE: 1905?

MAYOR: (*annoyed at the interruption*) Of course it's 1905. What's the matter with you?

CHARLIE: You mean this is Middlebury in 1905?

EDITOR-IN-CHIEF: Say, sonny, have you been to school lately?

CHARLIE: Of course. I go to John F. Kennedy Elementary School on Dairy Road.

TOWNSPEOPLE: Who? What was that name?

MAN #1: Never heard of it.

MAN #2: Only thing on Dairy Road is the dairy!

KATIE: Really? What about Saw Mill Road? Is there a saw mill over there?

MAN #1: Sure is. My grandfather built it in 1875. We've got a big factory down there.

KATIE: I never saw any factory.

MAN #2: It's right next to the river. You can't miss it.

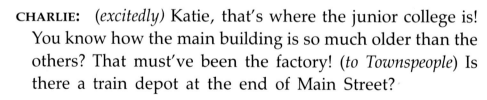

CHARLIE: (*excitedly*) Katie, that's where the junior college is! You know how the main building is so much older than the others? That must've been the factory! (*to Townspeople*) Is there a train depot at the end of Main Street?

WOMAN #1: Sure is. Brand new ticket office, too. Built in 1903. We even have one of those new typewriting machines.

CHARLIE: I always thought that diner looked like an old railroad depot.

KATIE: You mean Joe's Diner where we always buy hot chocolate?

CHARLIE: Sure. You know those old wooden benches in there? They must have been in the waiting room of the station. (*to Townspeople*) May I ask another question?

MAYOR: You sure have a lot of questions!

ICE MAN: Keep asking, young fella. It's a sight more entertaining than listening to the Mayor's speech.

EDITOR-IN-CHIEF: True, true.

MAYOR: Now hold on here!

CHARLIE: What else are you going to build? What are your other plans for this town?

MAYOR: Well, we plan to install brand new gaslight street lamps on Main Street, so folks can see where they're going at night.

CHARLIE: Katie, he's talking about those old street lamps near the supermarket!

MAYOR: We've also got plans for a new shoe factory out on the edge of town.

CHARLES FROM THE PAST: I thought we were going to have a park.

MAYOR: A park?

CHARLES FROM THE PAST: When you were elected you promised this town a park, Mr. Mayor.

MARYANN: You certainly did, Mr. Mayor!

KATIE: You mean there are no parks in this town?

ICE MAN: Not a single one. It sure would be nice, though.

CHARLES FROM THE PAST: Greenway Park sure has a nice ring to it.

MAYOR: What did you say?

KATIE: Charlie! Greenway Park is right near our house.

CHARLES FROM THE PAST: Well, if Mayor Greenway builds the park, I think it should be named after him, don't you?

TOWNSPEOPLE: (*shouting*) Hear! Hear!

MAYOR: (*to himself*) Hmmm . . . Greenway Park . . . that's not a bad idea . . .

WILLIE: We need a place for baseball . . .

WOMAN: And flowers . . .

MAN #2: A place for some quiet . . .

MAYOR: Ladies and gentlemen! I have an announcement. As your Mayor, I must bow to the will of the people. If you want a park, then you will have one. We will start on Greenway Park this very day.

TOWNSPEOPLE: (*cheering*) Hooray for the Mayor! Hooray for Greenway Park! (*They begin to sing.*) "For he's a jolly good fellow, for he's a jolly good fellow, for he's a jolly good fellow—that nobody can deny!"

(*As they sing, they begin to move off stage. Katie and Charlie are busy talking and do not notice.*)

CHARLIE: So that's how Greenway Park got its name. I wonder what else . . . (*He turns around and sees that everyone is gone. Only the trunk remains on stage.*) Hey! Where'd everyone go?

KATIE: The whole town's gone! (*She goes over to the trunk, opens it, and looks in.*) Charlie, look! (*Katie pulls out the cap, vest, knickers, and shoes that Charles From the Past was wearing.*)

CHARLIE: Those are his clothes, all right. But who *was* he? (*He pulls out an old album from the trunk.*) Wait a minute. What's this? (*He reads the cover.*) "Private Property of Charles Watson."

KATIE: Charles Watson? That's *your* name, Charlie.

CHARLIE: (*reading*) "Age 12, 1905." (*He opens the album and finds a photograph.*) Katie, look! It's a picture of that boy in these same clothes. Do you know who this is? Our great-grandfather! The man that I was named after. (*He turns the page.*) Look, here's a map of Middlebury that he must have made.

KATIE: (*looking at the map and pointing*) There's Greenway Park! (*pointing to another place on the map*) But what's this?

CHARLIE: (*reading the map*) Middlebury Shoe Factory. I guess it was built after all. Look, it's on Dairy Road. It must have been near where our school is. Come on, Katie. Let's go! Maybe there's a sign left or something.

KATIE: You know what? I'll bet Grandma knows something about it. Why don't we ask her?

CHARLIE: Okay! Who knows what stories she might have to tell.

KATIE: (*teasingly*) Stories? You mean like secrets?

CHARLIE: A whole world, Katie. If we know where to look for it. Let's go!

(*They run off. The curtain closes.*)

Thinking and Writing About the Selection

1. Name two things used by people in 1905 that people today do not usually use. Name two things used in 1905 that are still used today.
2. Why were the people of Middlebury having a Dedication Parade?
3. What made the Mayor change his mind about building a park in Middlebury?
4. Make a list of some street names in your town or city. Choose one, and explain how you think it got its name. If you can, find out if you were right.

Applying the Key Skill
Maps

Draw a map of your neighborhood.

Be sure to include a north arrow on your map.

N
↑

Use colors and other symbols on your map. Explain each symbol in the map key. Look at the map key below.

KEY			
house	⌂	library	▦
store	⌂	park	▲▲
school	⌂	bridge	⋈
hospital	⊞	railroad	╫

Label the streets in your neighborhood. Show your house on the map. Then trace the route you follow from your house to a place in your neighborhood.

MAPS

In the story "A Trunk Full of History," Charlie found an old map of Middlebury. It might have looked like the street map on the next page.

A street **map** can help you find your way around a city or town. It shows where the streets are and gives their names. It also shows the location of parks, lakes and rivers, important buildings, and interesting places.

All maps are smaller than the area they represent. There is not room on a map to show everything exactly as it is. For this reason, much of the information on a map is shown by symbols. A **symbol** is something that stands for something else. Symbols can be small drawings or certain kinds of lines. Color is a special symbol used on maps. The symbols used on a map are explained in the **key**. Look at the key for the map of Middlebury. What does the color green stand for on the map? What symbol does the map use to show a school?

Most maps have a **north arrow** to show you which way north is. Find the arrow pointing toward the letter N on the map. The N stands for "north." If you know which way north is, you can easily figure out the other directions. When you face north, east is to your right, west is to your left, and south is behind you.

By using the north arrow, you can see that Main Street in Middlebury runs east and west. In what direction from First Street is Second Street?

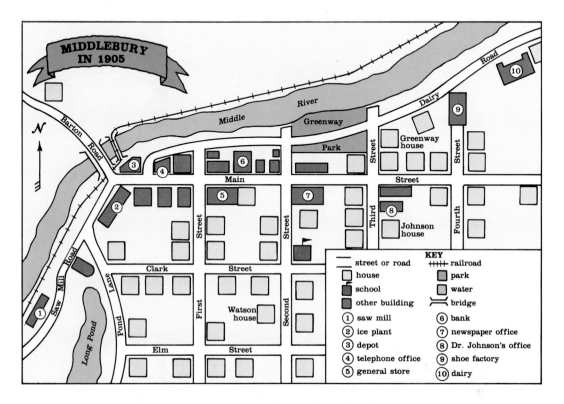

MIDDLEBURY IN 1905

KEY

—	street or road	┼┼┼┼	railroad
▢	house	◼	park
◼	school	▢	water
◼	other building	⤫	bridge
①	saw mill	⑥	bank
②	ice plant	⑦	newspaper office
③	depot	⑧	Dr. Johnson's office
④	telephone office	⑨	shoe factory
⑤	general store	⑩	dairy

ACTIVITY Number your paper from 1 to 5. Use the map above to answer the questions. Write the answers on your paper.

1. How many bridges are shown on the map?
2. What borders Greenway Park on the north? On the west? On the east?
3. In what direction is the Johnson house from Dr. Johnson's office?
4. What building is located at the north end of Fourth Street?
5. Is the Watson house closer to the school or the general store?

CHILDTIMES

*In "A Trunk Full of History," Charlie and
Katie learned about the history of their town
through a magical adventure.
In this selection, you will learn about the
history of a real town.
Three women wrote about their childtimes,
or the times in which they grew up.
They are from three different generations
of the same family: grandmother,
mother, and daughter.*

Pattie Frances Ridley Jones
Born in Bertie County, North Carolina
December 15, 1884

It's been a good long time since my childtime. Yours is now, you're living your childtime right this minute, but I've got to go way, way back to remember mine.

Memory is a funny thing. You never know how it's going to act. A lot of things that I saw and heard, and heard about, when I was a girl, I can't call to mind at all now. My memory just hop-skips right over them. Some other things, I can almost remember, but when I try to catch hold of them, they get mixed up with something else, or disappear. But then, there are the things that keep coming back, keep coming back just as plain, just as clear. . . .

Towns build up around work, you know. People go and live where they can find jobs. That's how Parmele got started.

At first, it was just a junction, a place where two railroads crossed. Two Atlantic Coast Line railroads, one running between Rocky Mount and Plymouth, and one running between Kinston and Weldon. Not too many people lived around there then, and those that did were pretty much spread out.

Well, around 1888, a man named Mr. Parmele came down from New York and looked the place over, and he saw all those big trees and decided to start a lumber company. Everybody knew what that meant. There were going to be jobs! People came from everywhere to get work. I was right little at that time, too little to know what was going on, but everybody says it was something to see how fast that town grew. All those people moving in and houses going up. They named the town after the man who made the jobs, and they called it *Pomma-lee*.

The lumber company hired a whole lot of people. They hired workers to lay track for those little railroads they call tram roads that they were going to run back and forth between the town and the woods. They hired lumberjacks to chop the trees down and cut them up into logs, and load them on the tram cars. They hired men to build the mill and put the machinery in, and millworkers to run the machines that would cut the logs into different sizes and dry them and make them nice and smooth.

Mr. Parmele had so many people working for him that he had this special store built just for them, a commissary, where they could buy what they needed—groceries, and medicine, and shoes, and yard goods—just about anything they needed.

We were living in a place called Robersonville, about three miles from Parmele, when Papa heard about the mill going up. Early one morning he took the train to go see about getting a job. They hired Papa, and that's when we moved to Parmele.

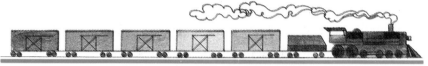

Lessie Blanche Jones Little
Born in Parmele, North Carolina
October 1, 1906

I used to hear Papa and Mama and their friends talking about the lumber mill that had been the center of life in Parmele before I was born, but there wasn't any mill when I was growing up. The only thing left of it was the sawdust from all the wood they had sawed there. The sawdust was about a foot thick on the land where the mill had been. I used to love to walk on it. It was spongy, and it made me feel like I was made of rubber. I'd take my shoes off and kind of bounce along on top of it. But that was all that was left of the mill.

My Parmele was a train town. The life of my town moved around the trains that came in and out all day long. About three hundred people lived in Parmele, most of them black. Most of the men and women in Parmele earned their living by farming. They worked on the farms that were all around in the area. When I was a little girl, they earned fifty cents a day, a farm day, sunup to sundown, plus meals. After they got home, they had all their own work to do, cooking and cleaning, laundry, chopping wood for the woodstove, and shopping.

I used to love to go shopping with Mama. There was so much to see downtown. When people started getting cars, the only gasoline pump in town was down there. There were stores, four or five stores, where you could buy clothes, or yard goods, or groceries, or hardware, and the post office was in the corner of one store. The water tank and the coal chute where the trains got refills were downtown, and so was the train station.

Twice I lived in houses that the trains had to pass right by on their way to the station. I'd hear that whistle blow, and I'd run out on the porch just in time to see the train come twisting around the curve like a long black worm. I'd wave at the people sitting at the windows, and they'd wave back at me.

Parmele had trains coming in and going out all day long. Passenger trains and freight trains. There was always so much going on at the station that I wouldn't know what to watch. People were changing trains and going in and out of the cafe and the restaurant. They came from big cities like New York and Chicago and Boston, and they were all wearing the latest styles. Things were being unloaded, like furniture and trunks and plows and cases of fruit.

The train station was a gathering place, too. A lot of people went there to relax after they had finished their work for the day. They'd come downtown to pick up their mail, or buy a newspaper, and then they'd just stand around laughing and talking to their friends. And on Sundays people would come all the way from other towns, just to spend the afternoon at the Parmele train station.

Eloise Glynn Little Greenfield
Born in Parmele, North Carolina
May 17, 1929

I grew up in Washington, D.C. Every summer we took a trip down home. Down home was Parmele.

To get ready for our trip, Daddy would spend days working on our old car, putting it in shape to go on the road, and Mama would wash and iron all of our clothes. Then everything would be packed in the tan leather suitcase and the black cardboard suitcase, and we'd be ready to go.

Mama and Daddy would sit in the front with Vedie in Mama's lap, and Wilbur, Gerald, and I sat in the back with our legs on top of the suitcases. This was before cars had trunks. Or radios. Or air conditioners or heaters. And there were no superhighways. The speed limit was forty-five miles an hour, and we went thirty-five to keep from straining the car.

It was an eight-hour trip to Norfolk, Virginia, where we always went first. Grandma Pattie Ridley Jones and Grandpa had moved there by that time, and we'd spend about a week with them, then go on to Parmele for another week.

By the time of my visits there, only a few trains were still passing through. My Parmele wasn't a train town or a mill town. It was a quiet town. Chinaberry trees and pump water and tree swings and figs and fat, juicy grapes on the vine. Parmele was me running from the chickens when I was little, riding around the yard in a goat-pulled cart, sitting on the porch and letting people going by in their cars wave at me, reading in the rocking chair, taking long walks with the children of Mama's and Daddy's childtime friends. Parmele was uncles and aunts and cousins. And Granny. And Pa.

Thinking and Writing About the Selection

1. How did Parmele get its name?
2. What became the center of life in Parmele after the lumber mill closed down?
3. Why was Parmele "home" to Eloise Greenfield?
4. Think of a place where you once lived or visited. Write a description of the place as you remember it.

Applying the Key Skill
Main Idea and Supporting Details

Reread the paragraphs in "Childtimes" listed below. Then copy the diagrams and fill in the missing main idea and/or supporting details.

1. sixth paragraph under "Pattie Frances Ridley Jones"

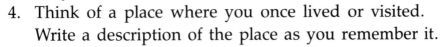

| The lumber company hired a whole lot of people. | MAIN IDEA |

| |
| | SUPPORTING DETAILS |
| |

2. third paragraph under "Lessie Blanche Jones Little"

| | MAIN IDEA |

| There were stores where you could buy things. | SUPPORTING DETAILS |
| |
| |

Eloise Greenfield

"I want to give children words to love, to grow on."

Eloise Greenfield was born in Parmele, North Carolina. Her family moved to Washington, D.C., when she was very small. She, her husband, and two children still live there.

When she was a teenager, Eloise Greenfield played the piano and had a singing group with three friends. She loved to read but did not decide to write until she was an adult.

As a writer, she wanted to provide black children with good books about themselves and their heritage. "I wanted my young Brothers and Sisters to have books that would remind them of the strength they had inherited," she has said. This author likes to write biographies and fiction. But she has also written short stories and magazine articles.

Two of her most recent books were written with her mother, Lessie Jones Little. One is a picture book called *I Can Do It By Myself.* The other, *Childtimes*, contains memories of the childhoods of her grandmother, her mother, and herself. The selection you have just read comes from that book.

More to Read *Mary McLeod Bethune, Rosa Parks*

KNOXVILLE, TENNESSEE

Nikki Giovanni

I always like summer
  best
    you can eat fresh corn
    from daddy's garden
      and okra
        and greens
          and cabbage
          and lots of
            barbecue
              and buttermilk
                and homemade ice-cream
                  at the church picnic
                  and listen to
                    gospel music
                      outside
                        at the church
                          homecoming
                            and go to the mountains with
                            your grandmother
                              and go barefooted
                                and be warm
                                  all the time
                                    not only when you go to bed
                                      and sleep

SYNONYMS AND ANTONYMS

Suppose your younger brother or sister came up to you and asked you what the word *huge* meant. You might give the words *big*, *large*, and *enormous* as examples.

A good way to define a word is by using another word that has the same or nearly the same meaning. *Enormous* and *huge* are synonyms. **Synonyms** are words that have the same or nearly the same meaning.

ACTIVITY A Number your paper from 1 to 5. Write the word that is a synonym of the key word.

1.	**rock**	horse	stone	field
2.	**make**	construct	play	work
3.	**city**	country	town	state
4.	**angry**	bad	mad	mean
5.	**quick**	slow	often	fast

ACTIVITY B Number your paper from 1 to 5. Write the two words in each row that are synonyms.

1.	country	continent	nation	county
2.	continue	start	complete	begin
3.	form	sign	signal	warning
4.	often	soon	later	frequently
5.	near	over	below	beneath

248

What word could you use in place of the underlined word to change the meaning of the sentence below to its opposite?

I <u>have</u> a story to tell you.

If you said "haven't," you were correct. *Have* and *haven't* are antonyms. **Antonyms** are words that have opposite meanings. You have probably played a game in which you are given a word and asked to give its opposite. Here are some common antonyms: *good, bad; tall, short; first, last; up, down.*

ACTIVITY C Number your paper from 1 to 5. Write the word that is an antonym of the key word.

1. **there**	where	here	near
2. **take**	get	buy	give
3. **all**	none	some	few
4. **kind**	friendly	cruel	good
5. **hard**	soft	rough	difficult

ACTIVITY D Number your paper from 1 to 5. Write the two words in each row that are antonyms.

1. sometimes	never	always	often
2. add	connect	plan	disconnect
3. sad	friendly	joyful	lost
4. special	best	most	worst
5. allow	go	forbid	do

PICTURE THE PAST

Hannah Lyons Johnson

In this selection, a photo-essay, you will learn about the ways people enjoyed themselves in the early part of this century. The photographs and descriptions will help you to picture the past.

Playmate, Come Out and Play With Me!

Children had fewer toys in the early 1900s than they do today. Many toys were homemade, like kites. Store-bought toys were often made of heavy iron. There were model trains, circus wagons, ice wagons, police wagons, and fire engines. Stuffed toy bears called Teddy Bears were given to many children. They were named after President Theodore (Teddy) Roosevelt who was a great outdoorsman.

Baseball and basketball were popular sports. Most towns had their own teams. Football was a lot rougher than it is today. The players wore thin leather helmets and pads that didn't protect them very well. In 1905, President Teddy Roosevelt asked for a new set of rules to protect the players. The forward pass was started to move the players away from each other more.

Then, as now, children loved bicycles and riding toys. Bicycle races for children and adults were part of Fourth of July and Labor Day celebrations.

Winter was a time when adults as well as children enjoyed skating. Races were held, with events like the 100-yard dash and the one-mile race for the county championship. Iceboats also whizzed along on frozen lakes and rivers. At winter carnivals, iceboat, skating, and horse and sleigh races were enjoyed by all.

That's Entertainment

Children at the turn of the century entertained themselves. There was no television or radio but there was plenty to do. Reading was a favorite pastime. Books about a clever boy named Tom Swift, who invented many things including a diamond-making machine, were popular.

In the fall, children went on straw rides (hay rides). Sometimes a group of children would get

together at someone's house for a taffy pull. Two children pulled a lump of just-cooked and cooled candy back and forth between them. After a while, it became taffy.

In the summer, traveling tent shows were set up in town. There were many things to see and hear. Bands, magicians, singers, and storytellers entertained one and all.

The circus train came to the larger towns in summer. Many boys and girls watched the workers and elephants set up the main tent. Everyone saw the circus parade that went up the main street.

County fairs had fun for all the family, too. There were horse races, auto races, and bicycle races. Prizes were given for the best pies, cakes, quilts, squashes, bulls, colts, and jams. There was usually an art show or a car show. There were wonderful things to eat and drink and smell and hear.

Everyone loved parades and there were plenty of them. Often the houses along the street where the parade went were decorated with flags. There were Fourth of July parades, Thanksgiving parades, Easter parades, and bicycle parades. Children spent hours decorating their bikes, hoping to win prizes.

People used to go to theaters to see live shows. Groups of actors traveled from town to town. A person could see six acts for a nickel. Fancier shows cost up to a dollar. The acts might include dogs, acrobats, dancers, singers, and comedy teams.

Music was an important part of entertainment. Most homes had a musical instrument in the parlor or living room. Pianos were the most common. Some families had phonographs. The first ones were powered by hand cranks. If the phonograph wasn't cranked up enough, the recording would stop in the middle of a song.

Cameras also began to appear in the home. In 1900, the Kodak Brownie camera came on the market at the cost of one dollar. Photograph albums filled up with snapshots.

Around 1903 a new kind of entertainment appeared in America. The MOVIES! Storefronts were made into small movie theaters called nickelodeons. For a nickel people could see black and white silent movies like the exciting *Great Train Robbery*. Piano or organ players accompanying these early films provided the only sound.

Every Saturday afternoon, children paid their nickels to see the marvelous, magical movies.

Thinking and Writing About the Selection

1. What were many store-bought toys in the early 1900s made of?
2. Why did President Roosevelt want new rules for football games?
3. How were the first movies different from the movies of today?
4. If you had lived in the early 1900s, what would have been your favorite form of entertainment? Explain your answer.

Applying the Key Skill
Synonyms and Antonyms

Read each sentence from "Picture the Past" below. Write each underlined word. Then write the synonym or antonym the author used.

1. Iceboats glided along on frozen lakes and rivers.
2. Every Saturday afternoon, children paid their nickels to see the wonderful, magical movies.
3. Football was a lot safer than it is today.
4. Pianos were an unusual musical instrument in homes.

THE ONCE-IN-A-LIFETIME MOVIE

Carol Snyder

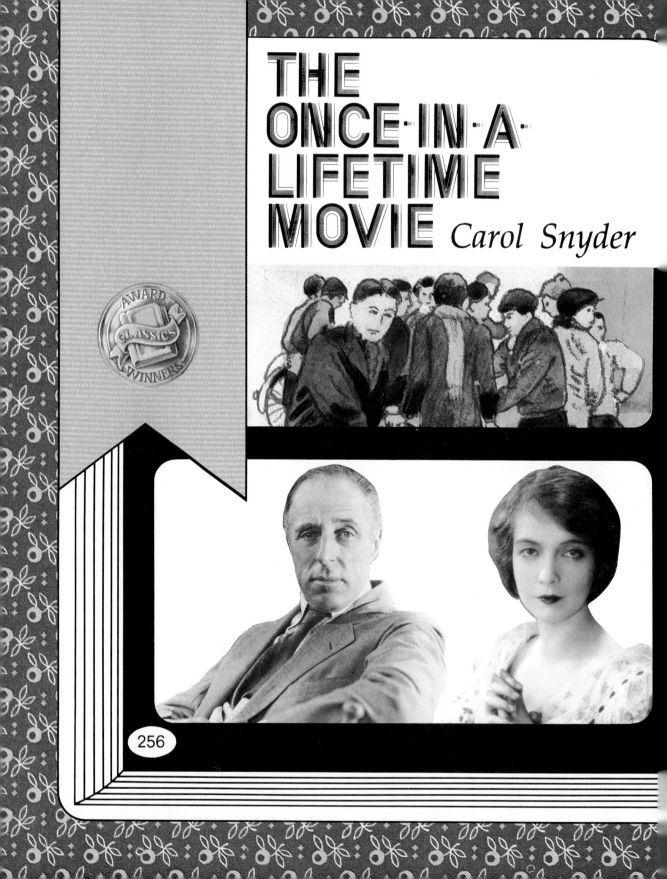

It is 1920, in a section of New York called the Bronx. Ike and his friends are in a movie theater, eager for the show to begin. The lights dim, and an announcement appears on the screen:

MOVIE INDUSTRY RETURNS TO NEW YORK!
THE FAMOUS D.W. GRIFFITH
LEAVES HOLLYWOOD FOR MAMARONECK.
NEW MOVIE STARRING LILLIAN GISH NOW BEING FILMED
AT THE GRIFFITH ESTATE.
EXTRAS NEEDED. WILL PAY A DOLLAR-FIFTY A DAY.

It was the chance of a lifetime, and the boys just couldn't pass it up. Mamaroneck was just north of the Bronx. They would be extras in the new D.W. Griffith movie!

ke dragged his half rust, half blue bike out from under the stairs and bumped it down the outside stone steps. What a perfect day this would be!

Morton Weinstein, James Higgins, Herbie and Joey, Robert, Patrick, Jack, Dave, Sammy, Danny, Tony, Bernie, and Sol were all ready. They watched as Ike stuffed his lunch into a leftover World War I canvas pack strapped to the back of his bike.

"My father drew the directions," Patrick said, handing Ike a wrinkled piece of newspaper. "He said it doesn't take him long to ride there. We have to take the Boston Post Road all the way." Mr. Murphy delivered furniture on a truck, so everyone in the neighborhood always asked him how to get anywhere.

With a wave from Ike, who was in the lead position, the army of bike riders were on their way, pedaling up East 136th Street to the end of Brook Avenue, caps, hair, and scarves flying in the breeze.

The parade of bicycles whizzed past four-story apartment houses with bedding airing out on each fire escape. Past the firehouse, where Ike's friend the fire chief waved and Ike waved back.

A jog right, and the boys were on Third Avenue. A few blocks more, another right turn, and they were on the Boston Post Road at last. It was a great day. Everything was going to be terrific. They were off to a nice easy start. There would be plenty of time to get to Mamaroneck by noon, stay a while, and ride back before it got dark.

The army of fourteen boys continued pedaling out of the South Bronx. Up the Boston Post Road they went. On . . . and on . . . and on, riding through Bronx Park with its duck pond and cages of wild animals.

"I'm getting tired," said Bernie. "Let's watch the bears at the zoo."

Of course they could stop for a while, to eat, rest, and make plans, Ike figured. There was plenty of time to get to Mamaroneck. The boys quickly parked their bikes on the dirt path near the wooden arrow marked BEAR PITS. They sat down on the hard March ground and munched sandwiches, and planned some more. Between bites, the boys discussed.

After a while, Ike got up and brushed the dirt from his pants. "It's eleven o'clock," he announced. "Let's get on our way." The time was going fast. The boys kicked up their U-shaped kickstands, mounted their bikes, and rode on . . . and on . . . and on.

The scenery was changing now as the boys traveled north. No more cars or horses. No more fancy apartments. In fact, there were no apartments at all. No stores or schools or anything. Ike took a deep breath. The air smelled sweet. They were in the country. Wide open fields. Cows and sheep relaxing on the crisp brown winter grass mooed and baaed as the trail of bikes passed.

The boys rode . . . and rode . . . and rode. Muscles aching. Bikes squeaking. Mamaroneck couldn't be much farther . . . or could it? Ike wondered.

"I never knew the Bronx was so big," Ike shouted. Then he stopped and pulled Mr. Murphy's black-lined directions out of his pocket. It didn't *look* far, as a line drawn on paper. It only looked like an inch to Mamaroneck. Then Ike realized Mr. Murphy must have meant it wasn't a long ride by motor truck, not pedal bikes. "Hurry up you guys," Ike said, finally admitting there might be a problem. "We may be too late already."

"What do you mean?" Bernie and Sol asked.

But Ike did not stop to answer. For now there was yet another problem: Not only were they late, but now to make matters worse, the weather was definitely changing. A wind stirred the trees, and a cold feeling crept through the soles of Ike's shoes. The sun disappeared behind a very big, swollen cloud, a cloud that might be swollen with snow.

"Come on!" With these words, Ike led the others on their way north . . . and farther north. The wind got colder and colder, biting at their faces. The boys rode out

259

of the Bronx and into Pelham. Soon they saw the gentle hills of New Rochelle.

As Ike and the boys entered the bustling village of New Rochelle, a trolley squealed along on its tracks, and the clanging bell sent the boys pedaling fast this way and that to get out of the way.

When they passed a big corner store with a sign that said BAUMER PIANO CO. VICTROLAS, the boys wanted to stop, rest, and look at the window display. Ike, too, felt like stopping. His muscles felt ready to pop like a dried-out rubber band, but he kept going.

Then, just as thirteen weak voices called, "When, Ike? When, already?" Ike spotted a sign, and felt like the soldiers must have felt when they came home from the war, as he read: WELCOME TO MAMARONECK. "At last," he sighed.

A gull flew overhead and there it was . . . a glimpse of shoreline. ORIENTA POINT, the arrow directed. Ike looked around as he rode. There was another sign: THE GRIFFITH ESTATE.

Ike had never seen such a big house before, and on so much land! The boys laid down their bikes behind the bushes and followed Ike as he raced down this path and up that one.

"That Griffith's got as many paths as the Bronx Gardens," Tony Golida shouted.

"Our whole block of apartments could fit on all this land," Ike said. "There's so much room." Then he pointed to the sweeping tree branches. "Look!" he yelled. "These tree branches are chained together."

260

"Have they got a tree thief around here?" Patrick Murphy asked.

"Must be because of the wind," Ike suggested, hanging on to his cap.

He kept the boys busy . . . so busy, he hoped they wouldn't notice the awful silence. The silence of plans that did not work out! The silence of no movie actors, no cameras, no scenery, and no money. The boys tried the locked doors of one building and peered in the dark windows of another. The only sign of life Ike saw was a car way off in the distance.

Danny Mantussi was the first to say something.

"Some plans you make, Ike!" Danny grumbled. "How are we going to make money here? There's not even anyone to pay us! And how will we get home in this snow? Huh?"

"Yeah," shouted Sammy. "We rode all this way for nothing!"

Ike felt as if his mouth would never smile again. Not only were all the boys tired and cold, but the snow was sticking to the ground. Ike was saved only by the fact that with the flurry of snow there came a flurry of activity. In one building, dark window shades were pulled up and faces peered out. Suddenly, doors opened and cameras and crews seemed to come out of nowhere. Busy people, still buttoning their coats, poured out of the next building.

"Snow!" they shouted. "Snow! At last we can shoot the snow scene." Men wearing heavy overcoats came out carrying something big that rested on three tall legs.

Ike almost gave them all away with a shriek of joy when he saw what was sitting on the three tall wooden legs. It looked like three boxes sitting one on top of the other, with a big, thick rubber band stretched along the side. Ike knew it was the movie camera. His heart beat with excitement. At least he'd gotten to see a real camera. One dream had come true.

He'd worry about getting home in this snow a little later. It couldn't hurt to watch for a little while. Maybe they could still be extras and earn a dollar-fifty each. That was a lot of money. A dollar and fifty cents could buy 600 pounds of potatoes, even, Ike figured. What would make Mr. Griffith choose *them*? Ike wondered, waiting for an idea.

Morton Weinstein poked Ike and pointed. "Look at that beautiful lady," he gasped. "Isn't that the one from the movie, *Busted Flowers*?"

"You mean Lillian Gish, the star of *Broken Blossoms*?" Ike had barely said the words when he realized Morton was right. It was Lillian Gish, and next to her, standing at the doorway, was a man Ike knew must be "a somebody of importance" because even Miss Gish listened to him, saying, "Yes, Boss."

"That's got to be Mr. Griffith," Ike whispered to James Higgins. Ike's mouth stayed open. He couldn't believe he was really seeing the famous Mr. Griffith, the man in charge, the man with the money . . . and Lillian Gish, yet, a real live movie star. Wow!

Then, Ike noticed that other people had walked from that distant car he'd seen and now stood near the camera.

263

They were not filming and they were not acting. They, too, were watching, and they were kids, too.

"Hey, guys," Ike said, pointing to some other boys. "Looks like we're not the only ones who want to be extras. How are we going to get Mr. Griffith to ask *us*?"

Mr. Griffith did notice the boys, but he did not ask them to be extras. He asked them to be quiet. Then he smiled and waved at the other onlookers as if he knew them. They waved back.

Ike figured he and his friends didn't have a chance to be extras. Mr. Griffith would surely choose the people he knew. He shivered and took out the scarf Mama had stuffed in his pocket. He wrapped it around his neck, waiting for an idea.

"Now!" Mr. Griffith got everyone's attention with one word . . . just like Mama, Ike thought. "In the next scene, remember Miss Gish, you're shopping for the barn dance party. Swing your basket," he instructed, "and hop around."

Mr. Griffith was watching Lillian Gish. "That's a DARB!" he said, and laughed, raising his arm and making a circular O.K. sign with his thumb and finger.

"What's a darb?" Danny whispered.

"It must mean something is O.K.," answered Morton. "Look at Mr. Griffith's fingers."

"It must mean something is even better than O.K.," Ike said. "Look at his smile. To me this snow is a darb!" he added, enjoying the word as he lifted a handful of snow and licked it. This was going to be a real snow. They hadn't had one all winter. They hadn't had a single snowball fight either. As they watched the cameras and

264

the actors, Ike made a snowball, but he didn't throw it. He put it down next to him. The snow was getting deep very fast, he noticed. How would they get home? But he decided they would stay just a little longer.

Then Mr. Griffith was pointing at him. "What's your name?" he said to Ike.

Ike coughed to clear his throat. "Ike Greenberg," he said finally.

"Well, Ike Greenberg. . . . You want to earn some money?"

Ike almost choked with excitement. This was the big moment. They'd be extras for sure. "Yes," Ike said, looking up at Mr. Griffith, "I'd like to earn money." Then he looked at his friends.

"Come here," Mr. Griffith said, starting to walk.

He didn't stop walking, so Ike walked fast to catch up with him. Ike's heart thumped. He wanted to ask Mr. Griffith if the other boys could be in the movie, too, but what if Mr. Griffith got mad? Finally Ike got the words out nice and loud. "Can my friends earn money, too, Mr. Griffith?" he said, feeling very brave—and very generous at including his friends as extras in the movie.

"Of course they can help," Mr. Griffith said. He looked up at the sky and said, "Looks like there will be a lot to do."

Ike couldn't understand what the sky had to do with it, but he was very happy as he called his friends. The boys crowded around and Ike told them the good news. They slapped him on the back, their way of thanking him for including them.

Then, Mr. Griffith signaled to his crew, and much to Ike's surprise there were . . . no cameras . . . no action . . . just three men handing out shovels to Ike and his friends as Mr. Griffith shouted to the boys, "Clear a path so we can put the camera on the platform with wheels. I'll pay you each a nickel."

"Shovels!" Danny Mantussi muttered, giving Ike a dirty look. "We rode all the way to Mamaroneck to shovel snow?" This time Danny didn't give Ike a thank-you slap on the shoulders. He gave him a swat!

Ike felt terrible. He was sure he'd figured out how to get to be an extra. "Well, anyway, we'll still earn money," he said, looking on the brighter side. "Five cents is not a dollar-fifty but it's something." That's all he could think of to say. He felt so disappointed. Shoveling they could do on East 136th Street. The sanitation department always hired them to shovel the snow so the streets would be clear for traffic. And they paid a lot of money—twenty-five cents an hour.

Ike pushed the shovel in. This was not what the boys had dreamed they'd be doing in the first big snow. They'd waited all winter to have the East 136th Street snowball fight. A lump the size of a snowball grew in Ike's stomach as he and the boys shoveled the path clean. He ached to bend down, put the shovel aside, and take a handful of that glistening white miracle and make the most perfect snowball. He forced himself to finish the job. But after the last shovelful, unable to stop himself, Ike dropped the shovel, grabbed a handful of snow, rolled it, patted it and then—as if the snowball had a

269

mind of its own—it flew out of his hand and zoomed right at Danny Mantussi.

Okay, so they wouldn't be in the movies, Ike thought, but they wouldn't miss the fun of the first snowball fight. At least they would have a good time.

Before anyone knew what was happening, snowballs were flying left and right. Sammy threw one at Ike, and as it slid down his neck, Ike shivered and pulled his scarf tighter. Tony Golida's black jacket had white marks all over the back, where snowballs hit as he hid his face. Morton was screaming his usual, "Watch out for my glasses," and James Higgins threw the biggest snowball of them all.

The boys were too busy to notice the whirr of the movie camera and Mr. Griffith shouting orders. "Billy, don't miss the kid with the snow down his neck. Quick! Get the kid with the glasses. Get them all, Billy. That's it! Get them all. What a darb! What an absolute DARB of a snowball-fight scene!"

Finally the boys were satisfied and snow covered. They looked up.

"Now that's what I call acting!" Mr. Griffith said. "Here's a dollar-fifty for each of you." He reached into his pocket and paid each very snow-covered and surprised boy. Then he gave them each another nickel for shoveling.

At first Ike was speechless. He'd never seen so much money! The boys yelled "Thanks" and patted Ike on the back, a friendly pat. "What a good idea you had."

"See, I told you I'd think of something," Ike said.

The story you just read is fiction, but it was based on real people and real events. D.W. Griffith really was a famous moviemaker in the early 1900s. He was called the father of American films. Way Down East was a real movie, and Lillian Gish was a real actress who starred in it. Many of the scenes in the movie were filmed at the Griffith Estate in Mamaroneck, New York, including a scene with children throwing snowballs! It is also true that children from the Bronx would ride their bikes north, hoping for that once-in-a-lifetime chance of being in a movie. It is possible that boys very much like Ike and his friends could have been the ones in the movie!

Memories

Memories are a link to the past. Because memories have been preserved, we can find out about the people and events of long ago. Stories, ballads, legends, paintings, photographs, and even maps tell us about the past. These things help us to understand history. In *Memories*, you read about state and local history. You also read about the memories of a painter who grew up in Georgia and of a writer who was born in North Carolina. Your study of history can enrich your own memories about our country and your state, town, and family.

Thinking and Writing About *Memories*

1. People still remember Davy Crockett who lived in the early 1800s. In what ways have memories of Davy Crockett been preserved?

2. What do maps such as those in "Learning About the States" and "Where There's a Will, There's a Way" tell about history?

3. Use information from "Learning About the States" and "A Trunk Full of History" to write some guidelines for people who want to find out about state and local history.

4. Compare the paintings in "From the Hills of Georgia" and the photographs in "Picture the Past." Which gave you a better picture of how things were in the past? Why?

5. If you could make a movie about your town, what would you show? What people would you interview?

 6. Make a list of things you would put into a time capsule that people will open one hundred years from now. Then write a letter to the people of the future. Tell them about your life in the present.

Introducing Level 10

GIFTS

When we give, we share something of ourselves. We let someone know that we care. In this unit, you will meet people (and a moose!) who share the special gifts of friendship and understanding. You will read about people who give happiness to others by sharing their talents or by finding just the right gift. What are some special gifts you could share?

Not what we give, but what we share—
For the gift without the giver is bare.

James Russell Lowell

273

BLUE MOOSE

Manus Pinkwater

What would you do if a blue moose appeared on your doorstep? Mr. Breton must decide what he will do. As you read this fantasy, think about the things that happen. Could they really have taken place?

Mr. Breton had a little restaurant on the edge of the big woods. When winter came, the north wind blew through the trees and froze everything solid. Then it snowed. Mr. Breton didn't like it.

Mr. Breton was a very good cook. Every day people from the town came to his restaurant. They ate gallons of his special clam chowder. They ate plates of his special beef stew. They ate fish stew and special homemade bread. The people from the town never talked much, and they never said anything about Mr. Breton's cooking.

"Did you like your clam chowder?" Mr. Breton would ask.

"Yup," the people would say.

Mr. Breton wished the people would say, "Delicious!" or "Good chowder, Breton!" All they ever said was, "Yup." In winter they came on skis and snow-shoes.

Every morning Mr. Breton went out behind his house to get firewood. He wore three sweaters, a scarf, galoshes, a woolen hat, a big checkered coat, and mittens. He still felt cold. Sometimes raccoons and rabbits came out of the woods to watch Mr. Breton. The cold didn't bother them. It bothered Mr. Breton even more when they watched him.

One morning there was a moose in Mr. Breton's yard. It was a blue moose. When Mr. Breton went out his back door, the moose was there, looking at him.

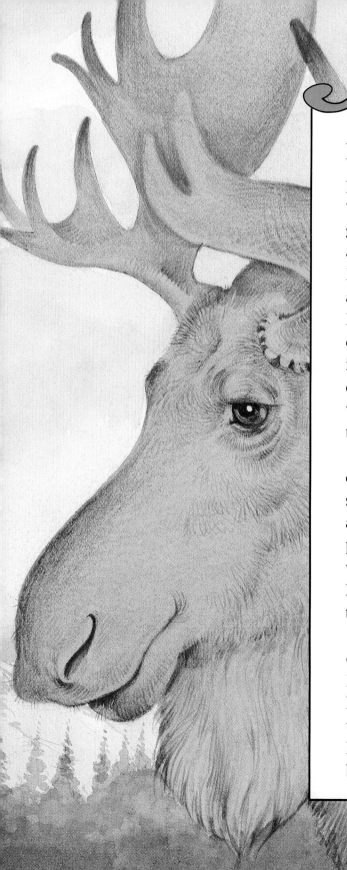

After a while Mr. Breton went back in and made a pot of coffee while he waited for the moose to go away. It didn't go away; it just stood in Mr. Breton's yard, looking at his back door. Mr. Breton drank a cup of coffee. The moose stood in the yard. Mr. Breton opened the door again. "Shoo! Go away!" he said to the moose.

"Do you mind if I come in and get warm?" said the moose. "I'm just about frozen." He brushed past Mr. Breton and walked into the kitchen. His antlers almost touched the ceiling.

The moose sat down on the floor next to Mr. Breton's stove. He closed his eyes and sat leaning toward the stove for a long time. Wisps of steam began to rise from his blue fur. After a long time the moose sighed. It sounded like a foghorn.

"Can I get you a cup of coffee?" Mr. Breton asked the moose. "Or some clam chowder?"

"Clam chowder," said the moose.

Mr. Breton filled a bowl with creamy clam chowder and set it on the floor. The moose dipped his big nose into the bowl and snuffled up the chowder. He made a sort of slurping, whistling noise.

"Sir," the moose said, "this is wonderful clam chowder."

Mr. Breton blushed a very deep red. "Do you really mean that?"

"Sir," the moose said, "I have eaten some very good chowder in my time, but yours is the very best."

"Oh my," said Mr. Breton, blushing even redder. "Oh my. Would you like some more?"

"Yes, with crackers," said the moose.

The moose ate seventeen bowls of chowder with crackers. Then he had twelve pieces of hot gingerbread and forty-eight cups of coffee. While the moose slurped and whistled, Mr. Breton sat in a chair. Every now and then he said to himself, "Oh my. The best he's ever eaten. Oh my."

Later, when some people from the town came to Mr. Breton's house, the moose met them at the door. "How many in your party?" the moose asked. "I have a table for you; please follow me."

The people from the town were surprised to

see the moose. They felt like running away, but they were too surprised. The moose led them to a table, brought them menus, looked at each person, snorted, and clumped into the kitchen. "There are some people outside; I'll take care of them," he told Mr. Breton.

The people were whispering to one another about the moose when he clumped back to the table. "Are you ready to order?" he asked.

"Yup," said the people from the town. They waited for the moose to ask them if they would like some chowder, the way Mr. Breton always did. But the moose just stared at them as though they were very foolish. The people felt uncomfortable. "We'll have the clam chowder."

"*Chaudière de* clam (shō dyer′ də klam′); very good," the moose said. "Do you desire crackers or bread?"

"We will have the crackers," said the people from the town.

"I suggest you have the bread; it is hot," said the moose.

"We will have the bread," said the people from the town.

"And for dessert," said the moose, "will you have gingerbread or apple *jacquette* (zhä ket′)?"

"What do you recommend?" they asked.

"After the *chaudière de* clam, the gingerbread is best."

"Thank you," said the people from the town.

"It is my pleasure to serve you," said the moose. He balanced the bowls of chowder on his antlers.

At the end of the meal, the moose clumped to the table. "Has everything been to your satisfaction?"

"Yup," said the people from the town, their mouths full of gingerbread.

"I beg your pardon?" said the moose. "What did you say?"

"It was very good," said the people from the town. "It was the best we've ever eaten."

"I will tell the chef," said the moose.

The moose clumped into the kitchen and told Mr. Breton what the people from the town had said. Mr. Breton rushed out of the kitchen and out of the house. The people from the town were sitting on the porch, putting on their snow-shoes. "Did you tell the moose that my clam chowder was the best you've ever eaten?" Mr. Breton asked.

"Yup," said the people from the town. "We think that you are the best cook in the world; we have always thought so."

"Always?" asked Mr. Breton.

"Of course," the people from the town said. "Why do you think we walk seven miles on snowshoes just to eat here?"

The people from the town walked away on their snowshoes. Mr. Breton sat on the edge of the porch and thought it over. When the moose came out to see why Mr. Breton was sitting outside

without his coat on, Mr. Breton said, "Do you know, those people think I am the best cook in the whole world?"

"Of course they do," the moose said. "By the way, aren't you cold out here?"

"No, I'm not the least bit cold," Mr. Breton said. "This is turning out to be a very mild winter."

*   *   *

When spring finally came, the moose became moody. He spent a lot of time staring out the back door. Flocks of geese flew overhead, returning to lakes in the north, and the moose always stirred when he heard their honking.

"Chef," said the moose one morning, "I will be going tomorrow. I wonder if you would pack some gingerbread for me to take along."

Mr. Breton baked a special batch of gingerbread, packed it in parcels, and tied the parcels with string so the moose could hang them from his antlers. When the moose came downstairs, Mr. Breton was sitting in the kitchen, drinking coffee. The parcels of gingerbread were on the table.

"Do you want a bowl of coffee before you go?" Mr. Breton asked.

"Thank you," said the moose.

"I shall certainly miss you," Mr. Breton said. "You are the best friend I have."

"Thank you," said the moose.

"Do you suppose you'll ever come back?" asked Mr. Breton.

"Not before Thursday or Friday," said the moose. "It would be impolite to visit my uncle for less than a week." The moose hooked his antlers into the loops of string on the parcels of gingerbread. "My uncle will like this." He stood up and turned toward the door.

"Wait!" Mr. Breton shouted. "Do you mean that you are not leaving forever? I thought you were lonely for the life of a wild moose. I thought you wanted to go back to the wild free places."

"Chef, do you have any idea how cold it gets in the wild free places?" the moose said. "And the food! Terrible!"

"Have a nice time at your uncle's," said Mr. Breton.

"I'll send you a post-card," said the moose.

Thinking and Writing About the Selection

1. What did Mr. Breton wish the people from the town would do?
2. Why do you think the moose started to help Mr. Breton in his restaurant?
3. Why do you think the people never told Mr. Breton that he was the best cook in the world?
4. What do you think the blue moose told his uncle about Mr. Breton? How would the blue moose have described his new life at the restaurant?

Applying the Key Skill
Realism and Fantasy

Write these headings on your paper:

Could Happen   Could Only Happen in a Fantasy

Then write each of the following sentences from "Blue Moose" under the proper heading.

Mr. Breton had a little restaurant on the edge of the big woods.

The people from the town ate gallons of his special clam chowder.

To help Mr. Breton, the blue moose waited on tables in the restaurant.

The blue moose carried bowls of chowder on his antlers.

Mr. Breton was sad to see the blue moose go.

The blue moose promised to send Mr. Breton a postcard.

Word Stew

In the story "Blue Moose," the moose called clam chowder *chaudière de clam*. The English word *chowder* comes from the French word *chaudière*, which means "stew pot." Chowder is a thick soup or stew, usually cooked in a pot. The name of the pot came to be used for its contents.

When you look at a *menu* (a French word we have borrowed), you will recognize many words from other languages.

German	Chinese	Dutch
sauerkraut	tea	waffle
hamburger	chop suey	cookie

Italian	French	American Indian
macaroni	meringue	succotash
spaghetti	omelette	squash (short for askutusquash)

Food names, like other names, have stories behind them. Seeds from an Asian melon were first planted and grown in Europe at Castle Cantaloupo in Italy. Today we call the melons *cantaloupe*.

Peach Melba is a delicious desert made of peaches, ice cream, and raspberry syrup. This dish was invented for and named in honor of Nellie Melba, a famous opera singer.

Find out what languages these food names come from: ketchup, vanilla, chocolate. See if you can discover how Parker House rolls, Cheddar cheese, and Brunswick stew got their names.

285

PREFIXES

Prefixes are word parts that are added to the beginning of base words. A prefix may be a single letter or a group of letters. A new word is made when a prefix is added to a base word.

Recognizing prefixes and knowing their meanings can help you understand the meanings of many words. Below are some common prefixes and their meanings.

im-, in- = not; without	
non-	= not; lack of; the opposite of
un-	= not; the opposite of

In "Blue Moose," you read, "The people felt <u>uncomfortable</u>" when the moose stood staring at them. Do you recognize the prefix *un* in the underlined word? You should be able to figure out that *uncomfortable* means "not comfortable."

Later the moose says, "It would be <u>impolite</u> to visit my uncle for less than a week." The base word in the underlined word is *polite* and the prefix is *im*. The meaning of *impolite* is "not polite."

The prefixes in the box above all have the meaning "not." When one of these prefixes is added to a base word, the new word is an antonym of the base word. You know that antonyms are words with opposite meanings.

ACTIVITY A Write an antonym of each base word below by adding one of the prefixes in the box. Then write a definition of the new word.

1. kind
2. fiction
3. easy
4. possible
5. known
6. important

> **mis-** = bad or wrong; badly; wrongly; lack of

Another common prefix and its meanings are in the box above.

How do you know which meaning to use to define a word with the prefix *mis*? The way the word is used in a sentence will help you. Read the definitions of the underlined words below.

1. The player <u>misunderstood</u> the signal. (understood wrongly)
2. The dog showed his <u>mistrust</u> by growling. (lack of trust)
3. The child was scolded for its <u>misbehavior</u>. (bad behavior)

ACTIVITY B Number your paper from 1 to 4. Write a definition for each underlined word below.

1. The reporter <u>misquoted</u> the mayor's statement.
2. Ted's <u>misplay</u> cost the Eagles the game.
3. It is wrong to <u>mistreat</u> animals.
4. José and Maria arrived at the depot at different times because of a <u>misunderstanding</u> about when they were to meet.

Beezus and Her Little Sister

Beverly Cleary

Do you have a little sister, brother, cousin, or neighbor? If you do, you might understand how Beezus sometimes feels about her little sister, Ramona.

One day, for example, Beezus was trying to finish her sewing project, but Ramona was being impossible. She kept riding her tricycle around the table, blowing on a harmonica. What could Beezus do?

Ramona loved to listen to Beezus read The Littlest Steam Shovel. *That would calm her down. But Beezus must have read about Scoopy the Steam Shovel and his clunk-clunking more than a hundred times. There had to be some other way to deal with Ramona, but what could it be?*

Beezus watched her little sister pedal furiously around the living room, inhaling and exhaling. Why did she have to like a book about a steam shovel anyway? Why couldn't she like something quiet, like *Peter Rabbit*?

Plainly something had to be done and it was up to Beezus to do it. The best thing to do with Ramona, Beezus had learned, was to think up something to take the place of whatever her mind was fixed upon. And what could take the place of *The Littlest Steam Shovel*? Another book, of course, a better book, and the place to find it was certainly the library.

"Ramona, how would you like me to take you to the library to find a different book?" Beezus asked.

For a moment Ramona was undecided. She was torn between wanting *The Littlest Steam Shovel* read aloud again and the pleasure of going out with Beezus. "O.K.," she agreed at last.

"Get your sweater while I tell Mother," said Beezus.

"Clunk! Clunk!" shouted Ramona happily.

When they reached the library, Beezus hurried Ramona into the children's section and seated her on a little chair in front of the picture books. "See, Ramona," she whispered, "here's a book about a duck. Wouldn't you like that?"

"No," said Ramona in a loud voice.

Beezus's face turned red in embarrassment when everyone in the library looked at Ramona. "Sh-h," she whispered, as Miss Greever, the grownups' librarian, looked in their direction. "You're supposed to speak quietly in the library."

Beezus selected another book. "Look, Ramona. Here's a funny story about a kitten that falls into the goldfish bowl. Wouldn't you like that?"

"No," said Ramona in a loud whisper. "I want to find my own book."

If only Miss Evans, the children's librarian, were there! She would know how to select a book for Ramona. "All right, you can look," Beezus agreed, to keep Ramona quiet. "I'll go find a book for myself."

When Beezus had selected her book, she returned to the picture-book section. She found Ramona sitting on the bench with both arms wrapped around a big flat book. "I found my book," she said, and held it up for Beezus to see. On the cover was a picture of a steam shovel with its jaws full of rocks. The title was *Big Steve the Steam Shovel*.

"Oh, Ramona," whispered Beezus. "You don't want that book."

"I do, too," insisted Ramona, forgetting to whisper. "You told me I could pick out my own book."

Beezus gave up. Ramona was right. At least it would be due in two weeks, but Beezus did not feel very happy at the thought of two more weeks of steam shovels.

Beezus took her book and Ramona's book up to Miss Greever's desk.

"Is this where you pay for the books?" asked Ramona.

"We don't have to pay for the books," said Beezus.

Beezus pulled her library card out of her sweater pocket. "I show this card to the lady and she lets us keep the books for two weeks. A library isn't like a store, where you buy things."

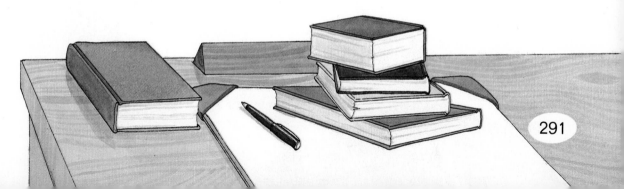

Ramona looked as if she did not understand. "I want a card," she said.

"You have to be able to write your own name before you can have a library card," Beezus explained.

"I can write my name," said Ramona.

"Oh, Ramona," said Beezus, "you can't, either."

"Perhaps she really does know how to write her name," said Miss Greever, as she took a card out of her desk. "Write your name on this line," she told Ramona.

Ramona grasped the pencil in her fist and began to write. She pressed down so hard that the tip snapped off, but she wrote on. When she laid down the pencil, Beezus picked up the card to see what she had written. The line on the card was filled with

"That's my name," said Ramona proudly.

"That's just scribbling," Beezus told her.

"It is too my name," insisted Ramona, while Miss Greever quietly dropped the card into the wastebasket. "I've watched you write and I know how."

"Here, Ramona, you can hold my card." Beezus tried to be comforting. "You can pretend it's yours."

Ramona brightened at this, and Miss Greever checked out the books on Beezus's card. As soon as they got home, Ramona demanded, "Read my new book to me."

And so Beezus began. "Big Steve was a steam shovel. He was the biggest steam shovel in the whole city. . . . " When she finished the book she had to admit she liked Big Steve better than Scoopy. His only sound effects were tooting and growling, and by the end of the book Beezus had learned a lot about steam shovels. Unfortunately, she did not want to learn about steam shovels. Oh, well, she guessed she could stand two weeks of Big Steve.

"Read it again," said Ramona. "I like Big Steve. He's better than Scoopy."

"How would you like me to show you how to really write your name?" Beezus asked, hoping to divert Ramona from steam shovels.

"O.K.," agreed Ramona.

Beezus found pencil and paper and wrote *Ramona* in large, careful letters.

Ramona studied the paper. "I don't like it," she said.

"But that's the way your name is spelled," Beezus explained.

"You didn't make dots and lines," said Ramona. Grabbing the pencil, she wrote,

"But, Ramona, you don't understand." Beezus took the pencil and wrote her own name on the paper. "You've seen me write *Beatrice*, which has an *i* and a *t* in it. See, like that. You don't have an *i* or a *t* in your name, because it isn't spelled that way."

Ramona looked doubtful. She grabbed the pencil again and wrote with a flourish,

"That's my name, because I like it," she announced. "I like to make dots and lines." Lying flat on her stomach on the floor she began to fill the paper with *i*'s and *t*'s.

The next two weeks were fairly peaceful. Mother and Father soon tired of tooting and growling and, like Beezus, they looked forward to the day *Big Steve* was due at the library.

As for Ramona, she was perfectly happy. She had three people to read aloud a book she liked, and she spent much of her time covering sheets of paper with *i*'s and *t*'s.

Finally, to the relief of the rest of the family, the day came when *Big Steve* had to be returned. "Come on, Ramona," said Beezus. "It's time to go to the library for another book."

"I have a book," said Ramona, who was lying on her stomach writing her version of her name on a piece of paper with purple crayon.

"No, it belongs to the library," Beezus explained, glad that for once Ramona couldn't possibly get her own way.

"It's my book," said Ramona, crossing several *t's* with a flourish.

"Beezus is right, dear," said Mother. "Run along and get *Big Steve*."

Ramona looked sulky, but she went into the bedroom. In a few minutes she appeared with *Big Steve* in her hand and a satisfied expression on her face. "It's my book," she announced. "I wrote my name in it."

Mother looked alarmed. "What do you mean, Ramona? Let me see." She took the book and opened it. Every page in the book was covered with enormous purple *i*'s and *t*'s in Ramona's very best handwriting.

"Mother!" cried Beezus. "Look what she's done! And in crayon so it won't erase."

"Ramona Quimby," said Mother. "you're a very naughty girl! Why did you do a thing like that?"

"It's my book," said Ramona stubbornly. "I like it."

"Mother, what am I going to do?" Beezus demanded. "It's checked out on my card and I'm responsible. They won't let me take any more books out of the library, and I won't have anything to read, and it will all be Ramona's fault. She's always spoiling my fun and it isn't fair!"

"I do *not* spoil your fun," stormed Ramona. "You have all the fun. I can't read and it isn't fair." Ramona's words ended in a howl as she buried her face in her mother's skirt.

"I couldn't read when I was your age and I didn't have someone to read to me all the time, so it is too fair," argued Beezus.

"Children!" cried Mother. "Stop it, both of you! Ramona, you were a very naughty girl!" A loud sniff came from Ramona. "And, Beezus," her mother continued, "the library won't take your card away from you. If you'll get my purse I'll give you some money to pay for the damage to the book. Take Ramona along with you, explain what happened, and the librarian will tell you how much to pay."

This made Beezus feel better. Ramona sulked all the way to the library, but when they got there Beezus was pleased to see that Miss Evans, the children's librarian, was sitting behind the desk.

"Hello, Beatrice," said Miss Evans. "Is this your little sister I've heard so much about?"

Beezus wondered what Miss Evans had heard about Ramona. "Yes, this is Ramona," she said and went on hesitantly, "and, Miss Evans, she—"

"I'm a bad girl," interrupted Ramona, smiling at the librarian.

"Oh, you are?" said Miss Evans. "What did you do?"

"I wrote in a book," said Ramona, not the least ashamed. "I wrote in purple crayon and it will never, never erase. Never, never, never."

Embarrassed, Beezus handed Miss Evans *Big Steve the Steam Shovel.* "Mother gave me the money to pay for the damage," she explained.

The librarian turned the pages of the book. "Well, you didn't miss a page, did you?" she finally said to Ramona.

"No," said Ramona, pleased with herself. "And it will never, never—"

"I'm awfully sorry," interrupted Beezus. "After this I'll try to keep our library books where she can't reach them."

Miss Evans looked through a file of little cards in a drawer. "Since every page in the book was damaged and the library can no longer use it, I'll have to ask you to pay for the whole book. I'm sorry, but this is the rule. It will cost two dollars and fifty cents."

Two dollars and fifty cents! What a lot of things that would have bought, Beezus thought, as she pulled three folded dollar bills out of her pocket and handed them to the librarian. Miss Evans put the money in a drawer and gave Beezus fifty cents in change.

Then Miss Evans took a rubber stamp and stamped something inside the book. By twisting her head around, Beezus could see that the word was *Discarded*. "There!" Miss Evans said, pushing the book across the desk. "You have paid for it, so now it's yours."

Beezus stared at the librarian. "You mean . . . to keep?"

"That's right," answered Miss Evans.

Ramona grabbed the book. "It's mine. I told you it was mine!" Then she turned to Beezus and said triumphantly, "You said people didn't buy books at the library and now you just bought one!"

"Buying a book and paying for damage are not the same thing," Miss Evans pointed out to Ramona.

Beezus could see that Ramona didn't care. The book was hers, wasn't it? It was paid for and she could keep it. And that's not fair, thought Beezus. Ramona shouldn't get her own way when she had been naughty.

"But, Miss Evans," protested Beezus, "if she spoils a book she shouldn't get to keep it. Now every time she finds a book she likes she will . . . " Beezus did not go on. She knew very well what Ramona would do, but she wasn't going to say it out loud in front of her.

"I see what you mean." Miss Evans looked thoughtful. "Give me the book, Ramona," she said.

Doubtfully Ramona handed her the book.

"Ramona, do you have a library card?" Miss Evans asked.

Ramona shook her head.

"Then Beezus must have taken the book out on her card," said Miss Evans. "So the book belongs to Beezus."

Why, of course! Why hadn't she thought of that before? It was her book, not Ramona's. "Oh, thank you," said Beezus gratefully, as Miss Evans handed the book to her. She could do anything she wanted with it.

For once Ramona didn't know what to say. She scowled and looked as if she were building up to a tantrum. "You've got to read it to me," she said at last.

"Not unless I feel like it," said Beezus. "After all, it's my book," she couldn't help adding.

"That's not fair!" Ramona looked as if she were about to howl.

"It is too fair," said Beezus calmly. "And if you have a tantrum I won't read to you at all."

Suddenly, as if she had decided Beezus meant what she said, Ramona stopped scowling. "O.K.," she said very cheerfully.

Beezus watched her carefully for a minute. Yes, she really was being agreeable, thought Beezus with a great feeling of relief. And now that she did not have to read *Big Steve* unless she wanted to, Beezus felt she would not mind reading it once in a while. "Come on, Ramona," she said. "Maybe I'll have time to read to you before Father comes home."

"O.K.," said Ramona happily as she reached for Beezus's hand.

Thinking and Writing About the Selection

1. What kind of books did Ramona like best?
2. Do you think Ramona had been to the library before? Why or why not?
3. Why was it a good idea to give Beezus the discarded library book and not Ramona?

 4. Think about your favorite book. Write a letter to the author telling him or her why you enjoyed reading the book.

Applying the Key Skill
Character's Motives or Feelings

Use complete sentences to answer the questions about "Beezus and Her Little Sister" below.

1. Why did Beezus take Ramona to the library?
2. How did Ramona feel when Beezus tried to choose a book for her?
3. Why did Beezus try to teach Ramona how to write her name?
4. How did the family feel when it was time to return *Big Steve* to the library?
5. Why did Ramona write in the library book?
6. Why didn't Ramona throw a tantrum when Miss Evans said the library book belonged to Beezus?

Beverly Cleary

When Beverly Cleary was a little girl, there was no public library in the small town of Yamhill, Oregon. Her mother arranged for books to be sent to the town from the state library. Beverly Cleary looked forward to each weekly shipment. It was the beginning of a lifelong love of literature that has made her one of the most popular authors of books for children.

Her mother encouraged her writing. She also warned, however, that writing was not the most reliable way to make a living. So Beverly Cleary decided to become a children's librarian, "the next best thing to a writer."

During World War II, she worked as a librarian in an army hospital. It was then that she wrote her first book, *Henry Huggins.* It became a bestseller.

Where does this author get her ideas? Not just from her life but from her readers. *Dear Mr. Henshaw* began after she got several letters from boys requesting a story about a boy whose parents are divorced.

As a child, Beverly Cleary remembers "the great feeling I got when I discovered I was reading and enjoying what I read." Now you can experience that same feeling by reading stories like *Beezus and Ramona.*

More to Read *Henry Huggins, Dear Mr. Henshaw, The Mouse and the Motorcycle*

THE LIBRARY

Barbara A. Huff

It looks like any building
When you pass it on the street,
Made of stone and glass and marble,
Made of iron and concrete.

But once inside you can ride
A camel or a train,
Visit Rome, Siam, or Nome,
Feel a hurricane,
Meet a king, learn to sing,
How to bake a pie,
Go to sea, plant a tree,
Find how airplanes fly,
Train a horse, and of course
Have all the dogs you'd like,
See the moon, a sandy dune,
Or catch a whopping pike.
Everything that books can bring
You'll find inside those walls.
A world is there for you to share
When adventure calls.

You cannot tell its magic
By the way the building looks,
But there's wonderment within it,
The wonderment of books.

BOOK REVIEW

Prewrite

Ramona found a book she liked to read. You probably have a favorite book, too. Part of the fun of having a favorite book is sharing it with someone. Imagine that you work for a magazine that has a section called FAVORITE STORIES. In this section, people write reviews of their favorite books. You have been asked to write a review of your favorite book or story for this month's magazine.

First you choose your favorite book or story. Then you decide to do something a little different from the usual book review. You decide to write a review of the story as if you were the main character. For example, if you wrote about the story "Blue Moose," you would be the blue moose. If you wrote about "Beezus and Her Little Sister," you might be Beezus or Ramona.

Before you begin to write your review, make notes about the parts of the book you will include in your review. Use this list to help organize your thinking.

1. Give the title, author, and illustrator.
2. Name the main characters. Choose the character you will be. How will you describe your character?
3. Describe the setting, where the story takes place.
4. Explain the plot by telling about two or three things that happen to the character you have chosen. Don't give away the end of the story.

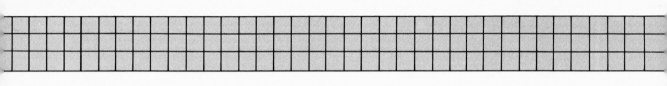

Write

1. You will write your review in first person. That means you will use pronouns such as *I*, *me*, and *my*. For example:

    I am an unusual animal called a blue moose.

2. Your first paragraph may describe you as the main character as well as other main characters in the story. Other paragraphs can describe the setting and the plot.

3. Give the title, author, and illustrator at the beginning or end of the review.

4. Try to use Vocabulary Treasures in your review.

5. Now write the first draft of your review.

VOCABULARY TREASURES

criticism	original
exasperating	character

Revise

Read your review. Have a friend read it, too. Think about this checklist as you revise.

1. Would your review interest someone in reading the book? Did you tell too much or too little?

2. Did you include the title, author, and illustrator of the book?

3. Did you choose adjectives that help your reader "see" how the character looks and acts. Use Vocabulary Treasures and the Glossary for help.

4. Did you proofread for complete sentences? Are your sentences short, or have you used too many *ands*?

5. Did you proofread for spelling and punctuation?

6. Now rewrite your book review to share.

CHARACTER'S MOTIVES OR FEELINGS

Think of the last time you met someone new. It may have been a new student in your class or a new neighbor. At first, you didn't know the person very well, but with time you grew to know that person better.

The people you meet in a story are called **characters**. When you begin reading a story, the characters are like people you have just met. As you read, you learn more and more about each character.

You learn about characters by what they do and what they say. How they do and say things is also important. Read the examples below.

1. Ellen went to her room and began to look for her sweater. She hummed a song as she opened the closet door.
2. Ellen rushed to her room and frantically began searching for her sweater. She pulled so hard on the closet door that it banged against the wall.

Ellen seems calm in the first sentence. She seems just the opposite in the second sentence. What words helped you to know?

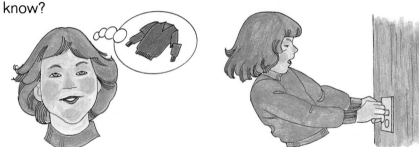

Writers give other clues about a character's feelings by describing how they look, or their appearance. How might a character who is trembling be feeling? How might a character who is shaking his head be feeling?

ACTIVITY Number your paper from 1 to 6. Read the sentences below. Write the word from the box that best describes the feeling of the character.

happy	determined	embarrassed
puzzled	angry	undecided

1. Ramona was torn between wanting her book read aloud again and the pleasure of going out with Beezus.
2. Beezus's face turned red when everyone in the library looked at Ramona.
3. "No," said Ramona in a loud whisper. "I want to find my own book."
4. "Mother!" cried Beezus. "Look what she's done! And in crayon so it won't erase."
5. "Ramona Quimby," said Mother. "You're a very naughty girl! Why did you do a thing like that?"
6. After they returned the book, Ramona skipped along beside Beezus.

Felita

Nicholasa Mohr

The school year had started so well. For the first time, Felita was in the same class as her best friend, Gigi, and her other friends Consuela (kōn swā' lə) and Paquito (pä kē' tō). Then, in October, Miss Lovett announced that their class was going to put on a play for Thanksgiving. Felita and Paquito volunteered to help with the sets. Consuela agreed to work on makeup. Gigi did not volunteer to do anything. Then, when Miss Lovett said that everyone could try out for the different parts in the play, Felita set her heart on being Priscilla, the heroine. She told all her friends how much she wanted the part. Everyone said she would be perfect. It was strange, but Gigi wouldn't even talk about the play. Felita can tell you the rest of the story.

Finally the day came for the girls to read for the part of Priscilla. I was so excited I could hardly wait. Miss Lovett had given us some lines to study. I had practiced real hard. She called out all the names of those who were going to read.

I was surprised when I heard her call out "Georgina Mercado." I didn't even know Gigi wanted to try out for Priscilla. I looked at Gigi, but she ignored me. We began reading. It was my turn. I was very nervous and kept forgetting my lines. I had to look down at the script a whole lot. Several other girls were almost as nervous as I was.

Then it was Gigi's turn. She recited the part almost by heart. She hardly looked at the script. I noticed that she was wearing one of her best dresses. She had never looked that good in school before. When she finished, everybody clapped. It was obvious that she was the best one. Miss Lovett made a fuss.

"You were just wonderful, Georgina," she said, "made for the part!" Boy, would I have liked another chance. I bet I could have done better than Gigi.

Why hadn't she told me she wanted the part? It's a free country, after all. She could read for the same part as me. I wasn't going to stop her! I was really angry at Gigi.

Just before all the casting was completed, Miss Lovett offered me a part as one of the Pilgrim women. All I had to do was stand in the background.

"I don't get to say one word," I protested.

"Felita, you are designing the stage sets and you are assistant stage manager. I think that's quite a bit. Besides, all the speaking parts are taken."

"I'm not interested, thank you," I answered. Then I turned and left. I didn't need to play any part at all. Who cared?

Gigi came over to me the next day with a great big smile all over her face. I just turned away and made believe she wasn't there.

"Felita, are you taking the part of the Pilgrim woman?" she asked me in her sweetest voice, just like nothing had happened.

"No," I said, still not looking at her.

"Oh," was all she said, and walked away. Good, I thought. I don't need her one bit!

The play was going to be performed on the day before Thanksgiving. I made the drawings for most of the scenery. I made a barn, a church, trees and grass, cows, and a horse. Paquito made a wonderful fence out of cardboard.

311

By the time we set up the stage, everything looked beautiful. Gigi had tried to talk to me a few times. I just couldn't be nice back to her. She acted like nothing had happened, like I was supposed to forget she hadn't told me she was going to read for the part! I wasn't going to forget that just because she was now Miss Popularity. She could go and stay with all her newfound friends for all I cared!

The play was a tremendous hit. No doubt about it, Gigi was perfect as Priscilla. Even though the kids clapped and cheered for the entire cast, Gigi got more applause than anybody else. She just kept on taking a whole lot of bows. After it was finally all over, Gigi came over and spoke to me.

"Your sets were really great. Everybody said the stage looked wonderful."

"Thanks." I looked away.

"Felita, are you mad at me?"

"Why should I be mad at you?"

"Well, I did get the leading part, but . . . "

"Big deal," I said. "I really don't care."

"You don't? But . . . I . . . "

"Look," I said, interrupting her, "I have to go. I promised my mother I'd get home early. We have to go someplace."

I rushed all the way home. I didn't know why, but I was still furious at Gigi. What was worse was that I was unhappy about having those feelings. Gigi and I had been real close for as far back as I could remember. Not being able to share things with her really bothered me.

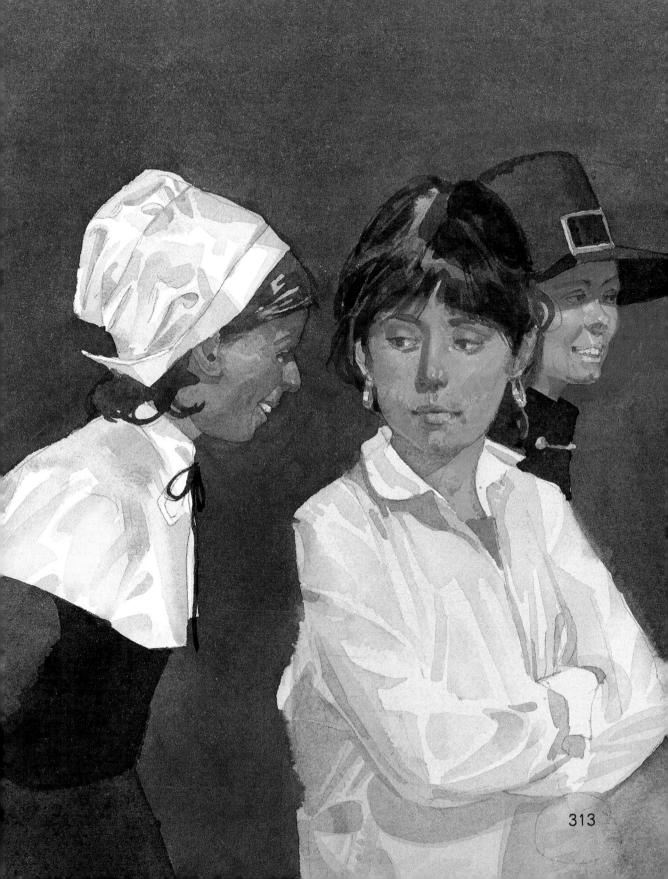

We had a great Thanksgiving. The dinner was just delicious. Abuelita (ä' bwā lē' tä) said I could go home with her that evening. It felt good to be with my grandmother in her apartment. We sat quietly for a while, and then Abuelita spoke.

"Tell me, Felita, how have you been? It seems like a long time since we were together like this." She smiled her wonderful smile at me.

"I'm okay, Abuelita."

"Tell me about your play at school. Rosa tells me you worked on the stage sets. Was the play a success?"

"It was. It was great. The stage looked beautiful. My drawings stood out really well. I never made such big drawings in my life."

"I'm so proud of you. Tell me about the play. Did you act in it?"

"No." I paused. "I didn't want to."

"I see. Tell me a little about the story."

I told Abuelita all about it.

"Who played the parts? Any of your friends?"

"Some."

"Who?"

"Well, this boy Charlie Martinez played John Alden. Louie Collins played Captain Miles Standish. You don't know them. Mary Jackson played the narrator. That's the person who tells the story. You really don't know any of them."

I was hoping she wouldn't ask, but she did.

"Who played the part of the girl both men love?"

"Oh, her? Gigi."

"Gigi Mercado, your best friend?" I nodded. "Was she good?"

"Yes, she was. Very good."

"You don't sound too happy about that."

"I don't care." I shrugged.

"But if she is your best friend, I should think you would care."

"I . . . I don't know if she is my friend anymore, Abuelita."

"Why do you say that?"

I hadn't spoken about it before. Now with Abuelita it was easy to talk about it.

"Well, we all tried out for the different parts. Everybody knew what everybody was trying out for. But Gigi never told anybody she was going to try out for Priscilla. She kept it a great big secret. Even after I told her that I wanted to try for the part, she kept quiet about it. She just wanted the part for herself, so she was mysterious about the whole thing."

"Are you angry because Gigi got the part?"

It was hard for me to answer. I thought about it for a little while. "Abuelita, I don't think so. She was really good in the part."

"Then maybe you are not angry at Gigi at all."

"What do you mean?"

"Well, maybe you are a little bit . . . hurt?"

"Hurt?" I felt confused.

"Do you know what I think? I think you are hurt because your best friend didn't trust you. From what you tell me, you trusted her, but she didn't have faith in you. What do you think?"

"Yes." I nodded. "Abuelita, yes. I don't know why. Gigi and I always tell each other everything. Why did she act like that to me?"

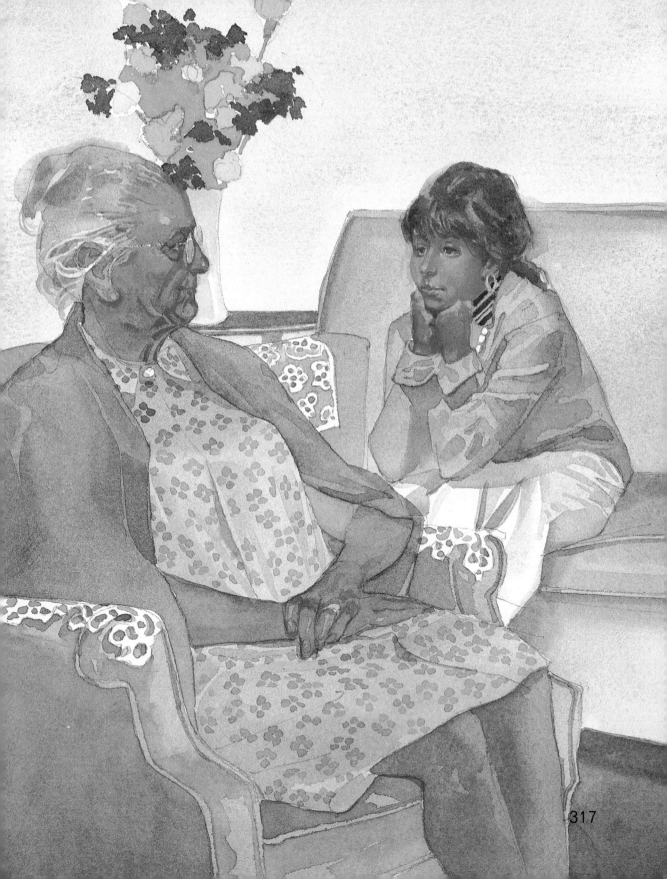

"Have you asked her?"

"No."

"Why not? Aren't you two speaking to each other?"

"We're speaking. Gigi tried to be friendly a few times."

"Don't you want to stay her friend?"

"I do. Only she came over to me acting like . . . like nothing ever happened. Something did happen! What does she think? Does she think she can go around being sneaky and I'm going to fall all over her? Just because she got the best part, she thinks she's special."

"You should give her a chance. Perhaps Gigi acted in a strange way for a reason."

"She wasn't nice to me, Abuelita. She wasn't."

"I'm not saying she was. Or even that she was right. Listen, Felita, friendship is one of the best things in this whole world. It's one of the few things you can't go out and buy. You can buy clothes, food, even luxuries, but there's no place I know of where you can buy a real friend. Do you?"

I shook my head. Abuelita smiled at me and waited. We were both silent for a long moment. I wondered if maybe I shouldn't have a talk with Gigi. After all, she had tried to talk to me first.

"Abuelita, do you think it's a good idea for me to . . . maybe talk to Gigi?"

"You know, that's a very good idea," Abuelita nodded.

"I feel better already, Abuelita."

"Good," Abuelita said. "Now let's you and I get to sleep. Abuelita is tired."

I kept thinking of what Abuelita had said, and on Monday I waited for Gigi after school. It was as if she knew I wanted to talk. She came over to me.

"Hello, Gigi," I said. "How are you?"

"Fine." Gigi smiled. "Want to walk home together?"

"Let's take the long way so we can be by ourselves," I said.

We walked without saying anything for a couple of blocks. Finally, I spoke.

"I wanted to tell you, Gigi, you were really great as Priscilla."

"Did you really like me? Oh, Felita, I'm so glad. I wanted you to like me, more than anybody else. Of course, it was nothing compared to the sets you did. They were something special. Everybody loved them.

"Look." Gigi stopped walking and looked at me. "I'm sorry about . . . about the way I acted. I'm sorry I didn't say anything to you or the others. I was scared you all would think I was silly or something. I mean, you wanted the part, too. I figured I'd better not say anything."

"I wouldn't have cared, Gigi. Honest."

"Felita . . . it's just that you are so good at a lot of things. You draw just fantastic. You beat everybody at hopscotch and kick-the-can. You know about nature and animals, much more than the rest of us. Everything you do is always better than . . . what I do! I just wanted this part for me. I wanted to be better than you this time. For once I didn't want to worry about you. Felita, I'm sorry."

I was shocked. I didn't know Gigi felt that way. I didn't feel better than anybody about anything I did. She looked so upset, like she was about to cry any minute. I could see she was miserable and I wanted to comfort her. I had never had this kind of feeling before.

"Well, you didn't have to worry. I was terrible." We both laughed with relief. "I think I was the worst one!"

"Oh, no, you weren't." Gigi laughed. "Jenny Fuentes was the most awful."

"Worse that me?"

"Much worse."

"And how about Louie Collins? I didn't think he read better than Paquito."

"Right," Gigi agreed. "I don't know how he got through the play. He was shaking so much that I was scared the sets would fall right on his head."

It was so much fun, Gigi and I talking about the play and how we felt about everybody and everything. It was just like before, only better.

Thinking and Writing About the Selection

1. What happened when Felita read for the part of Priscilla?
2. How had Gigi prepared herself to try out for the part of Priscilla?
3. How did Abuelita help Felita?
4. Why do you think Felita felt that her friendship with Gigi was "just like before, only better" at the end of the story?

Applying the Key Skill
Character's Motives or Feelings

Use complete sentences to answer the questions about "Felita" below.

1. Why didn't Felita take the part of the Pilgrim woman?
2. Why didn't Gigi tell Felita that she was trying out for the part of Priscilla?
3. How did Felita feel when Gigi got the part?
4. Why was Felita shocked when Gigi explained why she wanted the part in the play?

Secret Talk

Eve Merriam

I have a friend
and sometimes we meet
and greet each other
without a word.

We walk through a field
and stalk a bird
and chew a blade of
pungent grass.

We let times pass
for a golden hour
while we twirl a flower
of Queen Ann's lace

or find a lion's face
shaped in a cloud
that's drifting, sifting
across the sky.

There's no need to say,
"It's been a fine day"
when we say goodbye:
when we say goodbye
we just wave a hand
and we understand.

323

THE DANCING MAN

Ruth Bornstein

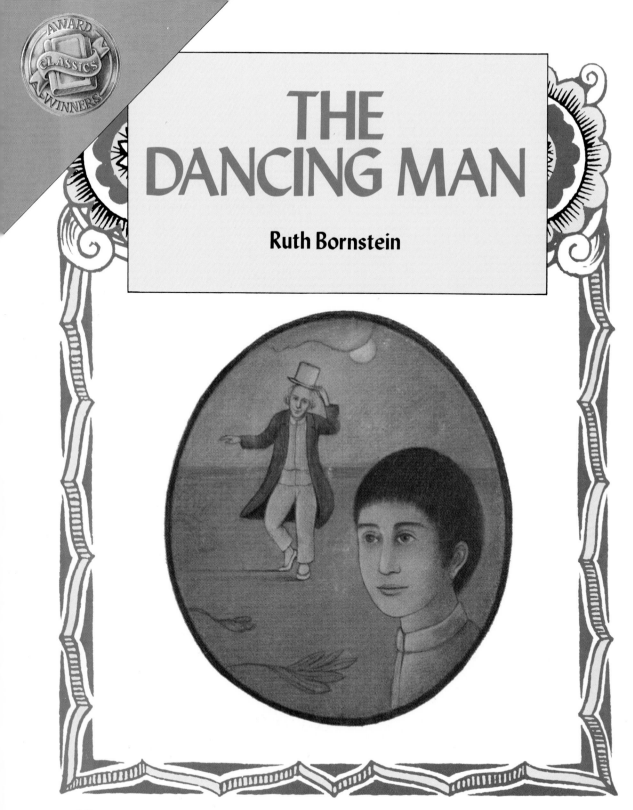

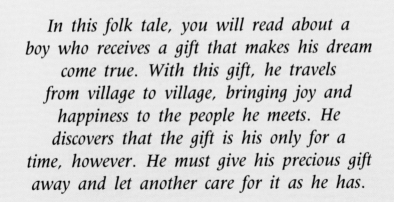

In this folk tale, you will read about a boy who receives a gift that makes his dream come true. With this gift, he travels from village to village, bringing joy and happiness to the people he meets. He discovers that the gift is his only for a time, however. He must give his precious gift away and let another care for it as he has.

Once, in a poor village by the Baltic Sea, there lived an orphan boy named Joseph. When he was still very small, Joseph knew that life in the village was dreary and hard. No one laughed. No one danced. But Joseph saw that all around him the world danced.

Fire danced in the hearth. Trees swayed with the wind. Clouds danced in the sky. Even the sun and moon moved across the heavens. When his work was done, Joseph ran to the shore and felt in his bones how the waves danced in the sea. And Joseph longed to move, to sway, to dance with the world. He dreamed that, one day, he would dance down the road from village to village, even as far as the south-ernmost sea. But he told no one. No one would understand.

One evening, when the wind blew and silver

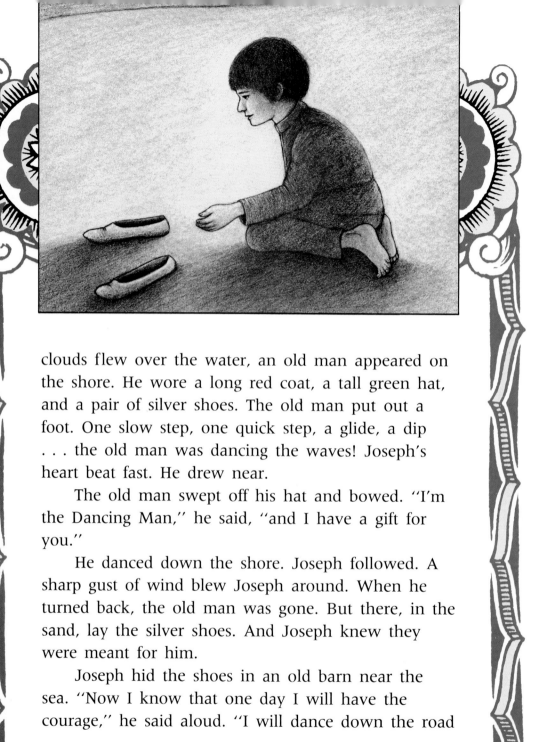

clouds flew over the water, an old man appeared on the shore. He wore a long red coat, a tall green hat, and a pair of silver shoes. The old man put out a foot. One slow step, one quick step, a glide, a dip . . . the old man was dancing the waves! Joseph's heart beat fast. He drew near.

The old man swept off his hat and bowed. "I'm the Dancing Man," he said, "and I have a gift for you."

He danced down the shore. Joseph followed. A sharp gust of wind blew Joseph around. When he turned back, the old man was gone. But there, in the sand, lay the silver shoes. And Joseph knew they were meant for him.

Joseph hid the shoes in an old barn near the sea. "Now I know that one day I will have the courage," he said aloud. "I will dance down the road

even as far as the southernmost sea. When the shoes
fit, I must be ready."

Every day Joseph watched the world around
him. Every day he felt in his bones all the ways the
world danced. The years flew by. And one day, the
shoes fit. Joseph came into the village. Slowly he
began to dance. A child followed. Then another.
Slowly the people turned to one another and smiled.
Slowly they joined hands. And Joseph danced with
the people in his silver shoes.

Joseph knew he was ready. He said good-bye to
the people. It was time to leave. He put out a foot.
One slow step. One quick step. One slow step. . . .
Suddenly he turned, he leaped, he pranced, he
danced down the road in his silver shoes.

He danced for his supper at an inn and slept
under the stars, his shoes on the earth beside him.

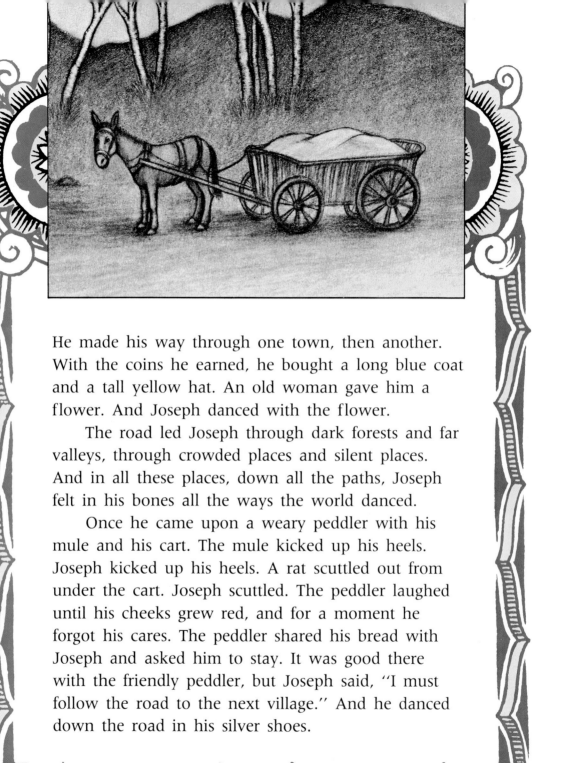

He made his way through one town, then another.
With the coins he earned, he bought a long blue coat
and a tall yellow hat. An old woman gave him a
flower. And Joseph danced with the flower.

The road led Joseph through dark forests and far
valleys, through crowded places and silent places.
And in all these places, down all the paths, Joseph
felt in his bones all the ways the world danced.

Once he came upon a weary peddler with his
mule and his cart. The mule kicked up his heels.
Joseph kicked up his heels. A rat scuttled out from
under the cart. Joseph scuttled. The peddler laughed
until his cheeks grew red, and for a moment he
forgot his cares. The peddler shared his bread with
Joseph and asked him to stay. It was good there
with the friendly peddler, but Joseph said, "I must
follow the road to the next village." And he danced
down the road in his silver shoes.

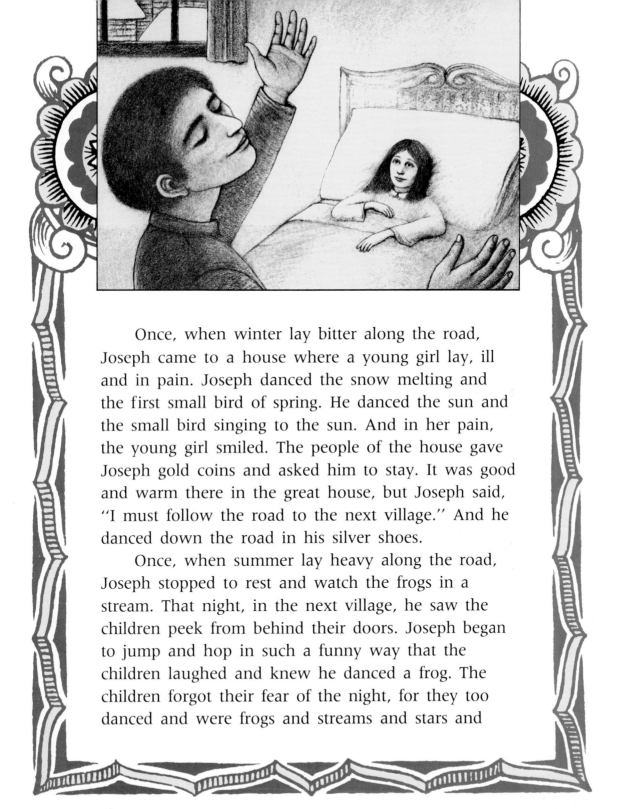

Once, when winter lay bitter along the road, Joseph came to a house where a young girl lay, ill and in pain. Joseph danced the snow melting and the first small bird of spring. He danced the sun and the small bird singing to the sun. And in her pain, the young girl smiled. The people of the house gave Joseph gold coins and asked him to stay. It was good and warm there in the great house, but Joseph said, "I must follow the road to the next village." And he danced down the road in his silver shoes.

Once, when summer lay heavy along the road, Joseph stopped to rest and watch the frogs in a stream. That night, in the next village, he saw the children peek from behind their doors. Joseph began to jump and hop in such a funny way that the children laughed and knew he danced a frog. The children forgot their fear of the night, for they too danced and were frogs and streams and stars and

moons. The children asked Joseph to stay. And, oh,
it was good and sweet there with the children. But
Joseph said, "I must follow the road all through the
land, even as far as the southernmost sea." And he
danced down the road in his silver shoes.

And once on a tired day . . . after many summers and winters, springs and autumns . . . Joseph
saw smoke curling from a sturdy farmhouse. Beside
the house he saw bountiful fields. He saw an old
farmer harvesting the fields. Joseph stood still in the
road. Suddenly the road seemed too long, the journey too lonely. The farmer is blessed with a good
life, thought Joseph. He lives in a snug house. He
works the land. He reaps a fine harvest.

Before he knew it, Joseph put out a foot. He
began to dance. He danced the sowing of the seeds
and the green crops growing. He danced the fruits
ripening. He danced the fine harvest. The farmer

leaned on his pitchfork and watched. Then his old
face shone with understanding. Joseph took his hand,
and together Joseph and the farmer danced in the
fields.

Suddenly Joseph laughed for joy. "Why, I too
am blessed," he said. "I too reap a fine harvest, a
harvest of dances. And I share my fine harvest with
everyone I meet."

Just then a soft wind came down the road. A
leaf twirled slowly in the wind. Slowly Joseph
twirled. The leaf twirled faster. Joseph twirled faster.
Before the farmer could ask him to stay, Joseph
called, "Good-bye, I must follow the road to the next
village." And Joseph twirled faster, faster, down the
road in his silver shoes.

On his way through the years, down all the
paths, fires still danced in hearths, trees danced with
the wind. And Joseph still felt in his bones how well

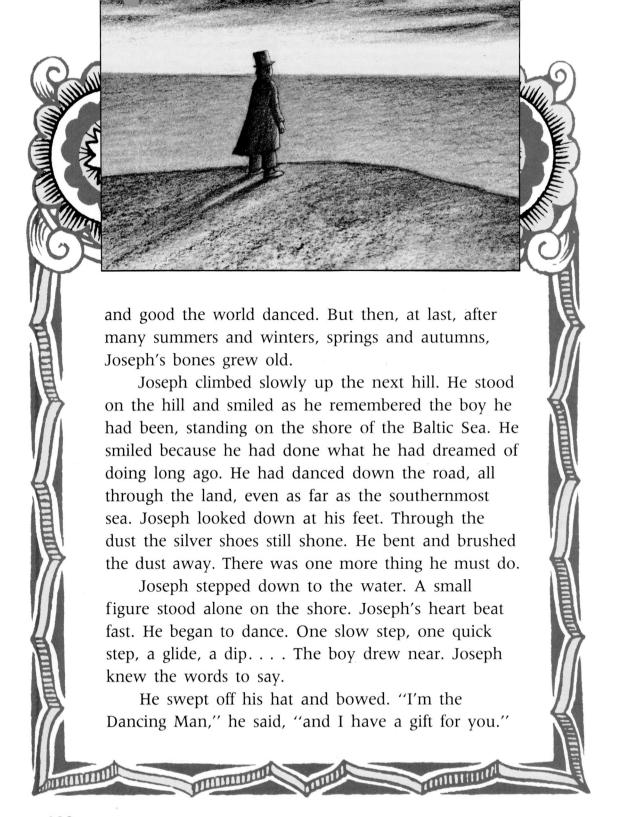

and good the world danced. But then, at last, after
many summers and winters, springs and autumns,
Joseph's bones grew old.

Joseph climbed slowly up the next hill. He stood
on the hill and smiled as he remembered the boy he
had been, standing on the shore of the Baltic Sea. He
smiled because he had done what he had dreamed of
doing long ago. He had danced down the road, all
through the land, even as far as the southernmost
sea. Joseph looked down at his feet. Through the
dust the silver shoes still shone. He bent and brushed
the dust away. There was one more thing he must do.

Joseph stepped down to the water. A small
figure stood alone on the shore. Joseph's heart beat
fast. He began to dance. One slow step, one quick
step, a glide, a dip. . . . The boy drew near. Joseph
knew the words to say.

He swept off his hat and bowed. "I'm the
Dancing Man," he said, "and I have a gift for you."

Thinking and Writing About the Selection

1. Why did Joseph have to wait before he could set out on his travels, dancing in the silver shoes?
2. How did Joseph know that he was ready to leave his village and begin dancing for others?
3. Why wouldn't Joseph stay with the family of the girl who was ill?
4. Do you have something that you would like to pass on to someone? Do you have a talent or skill that you would like to teach to someone? Explain what you would like to pass on or teach.

Applying the Key Skill
Plot, Setting, Mood

Read each phrase or sentence about "The Dancing Man" below. Then tell if each has to do with the Plot, Setting, or Mood.

1. In a poor village by the Baltic Sea
2. An old man appeared on the shore and left a pair of silver shoes on the sand.
3. The years flew by.
4. Joseph put on the silver shoes and danced.
5. He danced down the road, all through the land, even as far as the southernmost sea.
6. Suddenly the road seemed too long, the journey too lonely.

PLOT, SETTING, MOOD

Suppose you wanted to tell a friend about "The Dancing Man." You might begin by saying that "The Dancing Man" is a story about a boy named Joseph. Joseph is the main character in the story. Characters are very important. Without characters, there wouldn't be any stories. Just naming the characters, however, doesn't tell very much about a story.

If you wanted to give your friend a better idea of "The Dancing Man," you would probably tell what happened in the story. What happens in a story, or the series of events that takes place, is called the **plot**. Here is how you might explain the plot of "The Dancing Man":

> Joseph, a boy who loves to dance, is given a pair of silver shoes by the Dancing Man. When he is old enough for them to fit, Joseph puts the shoes on and begins to dance. For years, Joseph dances from village to village, bringing happiness and joy to the people who watch him. Joseph becomes the Dancing Man. Finally, when Joseph grows too old to dance, he gives the shoes to a young boy who also loves to dance.

How would you explain the plot of "Beezus and Her Little Sister"?

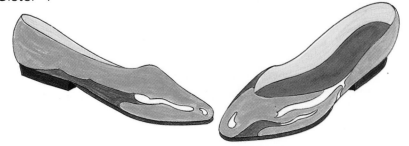

334

What important events would you include?

What else could you tell your friend about "The Dancing Man"? You might want to explain where and when the story took place. The time and place of the action in a story are called the **setting**. At the beginning of "The Dancing Man," you are told that Joseph lived in a village by the Baltic Sea. You can find out that the Baltic Sea is a large body of water in northern Europe by looking in an atlas or in an encyclopedia. You now know that the story took place in Europe. But when did the story take place? The author gives you a clue when she uses the word *once*. When an author begins a story with *once*, we can usually be sure that the story took place a long time ago. You now know that "The Dancing Man" took place in Europe in the past.

What is the setting of "Felita"?
When and where did it take place?

Finally, when telling about a story, you might want to talk about the mood. The **mood** of a story is the general feeling you get when you read the story. For example, a ghost story may give you a scary feeling, or a mystery story a mysterious feeling. The mood of "The Dancing Man" is generally happy. At the end, however, there is a feeling of sadness when the Dancing Man, now too old to dance, gives the silver shoes to a younger person.

How would you describe the mood of "Beezus and Her Little Sister"? How would you describe the mood of "Felita"?

ACTIVITY A Read the fable below.

The Seven Sticks

Long ago and far away, there was an old farmer who had seven children. When he thought that he was about to die, he gathered them about him. He told a servant to bring in a bundle of seven sticks tied together. Handing the bundle to his oldest child, the father said to him, "Now break the bundle."

The son tried with all his might, but he could not break the bundle. One by one, the other children tried. Not one of them was strong enough.

The father smiled, "Now my children, untie the bundle. Each of you take a stick and try to break it." This time they had no difficulty doing as their father bid them. In a few moments all the sticks were broken.

"In unity there is strength," said the father.

Write the answers to these questions on your paper.

1. Which sentence best describes the plot?
   a. A father uses a bundle of sticks to teach his children an important lesson.
   b. Brothers and sisters decide to work together to help their father.
   c. A father tricks his children into obeying him.

2. What is the setting?

3. Which word best describes the mood?
   a. sad   b. serious   c. humorous

ACTIVITY B Read the fable below. Then copy and complete the chart. Write a sentence to describe the plot. Write a phrase to describe the setting. Write a word to describe the mood at the beginning, and another word to describe the mood at the end.

The Crow and the Pitcher

Once upon a time, a thirsty crow came upon a pitcher, half full of water. With the greatest of joy, she stuck in her beak, for she was almost dead of thirst. But her beak was short and the water was very low in the pitcher. Try as she might, she could not reach a drop.

Just as she thought she would have to give up, she had a bright idea. She took a pebble in her beak and dropped it into the pitcher. Then she picked up another pebble and dropped it in, too. Another and another and another pebble went into the pitcher. Little by little, the water began to rise. At last, it was close enough for the crow to drink. She dipped her beak and drank till she was full.

"Where there's a will, there's a way," said she.

PLOT	
SETTING	
MOOD	

THANK YOU, JACKIE ROBINSON

Barbara Cohen

The year is 1948, and the Brooklyn Dodgers are scheduled to meet the Chicago Cubs at Ebbets field. It is only one game in the season, but for Sam Greene it is the most important game of the year.

Sam wanted to do something special for his friend Davy who was in the hospital. It didn't take Sam long to figure out that the best gift for a Dodgers' fan like Davy would be a baseball autographed by his favorite team. No matter what it takes, Sam is going to get that ball for Davy.

I had gone into the kitchen real early in the morning, before anyone else was up, and made myself a couple of egg-salad sandwiches. I had them and my money and the baseball in its little cardboard box. I walked the mile and a half to the bus station because there'd be no place to leave my bike if I rode there. I took the bus into New York City and I took a subway to Ebbets Field. Right in the middle of the subway was this big map of the subway system and Ebbets Field was marked right on it in large black letters. BMT, Brighton Local, downtown, get off at the station near Ebbets Field. I didn't even have to change trains.

You could see flags flying above the ball park when you climbed up out of the subway station. You had to walk three blocks and there you were. Inside it was as it always had been, as bright and green as ever, far from the sooty streets that surrounded it. In the excitement of being there, I almost forgot about Davy for a moment. I almost forgot why I had come. But then, when the Cubs' pitcher, Warren Hacker, began to warm up, I turned to Davy to ask him if he thought

Shotton was going to give Jackie's sore heel a rest that day, but Davy wasn't there, and I remembered.

I thought maybe I'd better start trying right away. My chances were probably better during batting practice than they would be later. I took my ball out of its box and stashed the box underneath my bleacher seat. Then I walked around to the first-base side and climbed all the way down to the box seats right behind the dugout. I leaned over the rail. Billy Cox was trotting back to the dugout from home plate, where Erskine had been throwing to him.

I swallowed my heart, which seemed to be beating in my throat, and called out, "Billy, hey Billy," waving my ball as hard and high as I could. But I was scared, and my voice wasn't very loud, and I don't think Billy Cox heard me. He disappeared into the dugout.

I decided this method would get me nowhere. I had to try something else before the game began and I'd really lost my chance. I looked around to see if there were any ushers nearby, but none was in sight.

I climbed up on the railing and then hoisted myself onto the roof of the dugout. I could have stood up and walked across the dugout roof to the edge, but I figured if I did that an usher surely would see me. I sneaked across the roof on my belly until I came to the edge and then I leaned over.

It was really very nice in the dugout. I had always kind of pictured it as being literally dug out of the dirt, like a trench in a war. But it had regular walls and a floor and benches and a water cooler. Only trouble was, there were just a couple of guys in there—Eddie Miksis and Billy Cox, whom I'd seen out on the field a few minutes before. I was disappointed. I had certainly hoped for Campy's signature, and Gil Hodges', and Pee Wee Reese's, and of course Jackie Robinson's. But I figured Davy would be thrilled with Miksis and Billy Cox, since their names on a ball would be more than he'd ever expected. Anyway, a few more guys might come meandering in before I was through.

No matter how hard I swallowed, though, my heart was still stuck in my throat. "Eddie," I called. "Eddie, Billy." Hardly any sound came out of my mouth at all.

Then all of a sudden I heard a voice calling real loud. Whoever it was didn't have any trouble getting the sound out of *his* mouth. "Hey you, kid, get down off that roof," the voice said. "What do you think you're doing?" I sat up and turned around. An angry usher was standing at the foot of the aisle, right by the railing, screaming at me. "Get yourself off that roof," he shouted. "Right now, or I'll throw you out of the ball park."

I scrambled down as fast as I could. Boy, was I a mess. My pants and my striped shirt were absolutely covered with dust and dirt from that roof. I guess my face and arms weren't any too clean either. I looked like a bum.

"I'm going to throw you out anyway," the usher said, "because you don't have a ticket."

"You can't throw me out," I shouted back at him. "I've got as much right to be here as you have." I had suddenly found my voice. I was scared of the ball players, but this usher didn't frighten me one bit. I pulled my ticket stub out of my pocket. "See?" I said, thrusting it into his face, "I certainly do have a ticket."

"I better not see you on that roof again," the usher said. "I'll have my eye out for you—and so will all the other ushers."

"Don't worry," I said.

Then I felt his hand on my shoulder. "As a matter of fact, kid," he said. "I think I'll escort you to your seat where you belong. Up in the bleachers where you can't make any trouble!"

Well, right then and there the whole plan would have gone up in smoke if old Jackie Robinson himself had not come trotting out onto the field from the dugout that very second. "Hey, Jackie," I called, "Hey, Jackie," in a voice as loud as a thunderbolt. I mean there were two airplanes flying overhead right that minute and Jackie Robinson heard me anyway.

He glanced over in the direction he could tell my voice was coming from, and I began to wave frantically, still calling "Jackie, hey, Jackie."

He lifted up his hand, gave one wide wave, and smiled. "Hey, kid," he called, and continued on his

344

way to the batting cage. In another instant he'd have been too busy with batting practice to pay attention to me.

"Sign my ball," I screamed. "Sign my ball."

He seemed to hesitate briefly. I took this as a good sign. "You have to," I went on frantically. "Please, please, you have to."

"Come on, kid," the usher said, "we're getting out of here." He was a big hulking usher who must have weighed about eight hundred pounds, and he began pulling on me. Even though I gripped the cement with my sneakers and held onto the rail with my hand, he managed to pull me loose. But he couldn't shut me up.

"Please, Jackie, please," I went right on screaming.

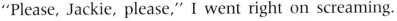

It worked. Or something worked. If not my screaming, then maybe the sight of that monster usher trying to pull me up the aisle and scrungy old me pulling against him for dear life.

"Let the kid go," Jackie Robinson said when he got to the railing. "All he wants is an autograph."

"He's a fresh kid," the usher said, but he let me go.

I thrust my ball into Jackie Robinson's face. "Gee, thanks, Mr. Robinson," I said. "Sign it, please."

"You got a pen?" he asked.

"A pen?" I could have kicked myself. "A pen?" I'd forgotten a pen! I turned to the usher. "You got a pen?"

"If I had," the usher said triumphantly, "I certainly wouldn't lend it to you!"

"Oh, come on," Jackie Robinson said. "What harm did the kid do, after all?"

"Well, as it happens, I don't have one," the usher replied smugly.

"Wait here," I said. "Wait right here, Mr. Robinson. I'll go find one."

Jackie Robinson laughed. "Sorry, kid, but I've got work to do. Another time, maybe."

"Please, Mr. Robinson," I said. "It's for my friend. My friend Davy."

"Well, let Davy come and get his own autographs," he said. "Why should you do his dirty work for him?"

"He can't come," I said. The words came rushing out of me, tumbling one on top of the other. I had to tell Jackie Robinson all about it, before he went away. "Davy can't come because he's sick. He had a heart attack."

"A heart attack?" Jackie Robinson asked. "A kid had a heart attack?"

"He's not a kid," I explained. "He's sixty years old. He's my best friend. He's a black man, like you. He's always loved the Dodgers, but lately he's loved them more than ever."

Now that I think about it, what I said could have annoyed Jackie Robinson very much. But at the time, it didn't. I guess he could tell how serious I was about what I was saying. "How did this Davy get to be your best friend?" he asked.

So I told him. I told him everything, or as near to everything as I could tell in five minutes. I told him how Davy worked for my mother, and how I had no father, so it was Davy who took me to my first ball game. I told him how they wouldn't let me into the hospital to see Davy, and how we had always talked about catching a ball that was hit into the stands and getting it autographed.

Jackie listened silently, nodding every once in a while. When I was done at last, he said, "Well, now, kid, I'll tell you what. You keep this ball you brought with you. Keep it to play with. And borrow a pen from someone. Come back to the dugout the minute, the very second, the game is over, and I'll get all the guys to autograph a ball for you."

"Make sure it's one you hit," I said.

What nerve. I should have fainted dead away just because Jackie Robinson had spoken to me. Here he was, making me an offer beyond my wildest dreams, and for me it wasn't enough. I had to have more. However, he didn't seem to care.

"O.K.," he said, "*if* I hit one." He had been in a little slump lately.

"You will," I said, "you will."

He did. He broke the ball game wide open in the sixth inning when he hit a double to left field, scoring Rackley and Duke Snider. He scored himself when the Cub pitcher, Warren Hacker, tried to pick him off

second base. But Hacker overthrew, and Jackie, with that incredible speed he had, ran all the way home. Besides, he worked two double plays with Preacher Roe and Gil Hodges. On consecutive pitches, Carl Furillo and Billy Cox both hit home runs, shattering the 1930 Brooklyn home-run record of 122 for a season. The Dodgers scored six runs, and they scored them all in the sixth inning. They beat the Cubs, 6-1. They were hot, really hot, that day and that year.

But I really didn't watch the game as closely as I had all the others I'd been to see. I couldn't. My mind was on too many other things—on Jackie Robinson, on what was going to happen after the game was over, on that monster usher who I feared would yet find some way of spoiling things for me, but above all on Davy and the fact that he was missing all of the excitement.

Then I had to worry about getting hold of a pen. You could buy little pencils at the ball park for keeping box scores, but no pens. I didn't see how I could borrow one from someone, since I'd never be able to find the person after the game to return it to him.

It didn't look to me like the guys in the bleachers where I was sitting had pens with them anyway. I decided to walk over to the seats along the first-base line to see if any of those fans looked more like pen owners. I had to go in that direction anyway to make sure I was at the dugout the second the ball game ended.

On my way over I ran into this guy selling sodas and I decided to buy one in order to wash down the two egg-salad sandwiches I had eaten during the third inning.

This guy had a pen in his pocket. As a matter of fact he had two of them. "Look," I said to him, as I paid him for my soda, "could I borrow one of those pens?"

"Sure," he said, handing it to me after he had put my money into his change machine. He stood there, waiting, like he expected me to hand it back to him after I was done with it.

"Look," I said again, "maybe I could sort of buy it from you."

"Buy it from me? You mean the pen?"

"Yeah."

"What do you want my pen for?"

"I need it because Jackie Robinson promised me that after the game he and all the other guys would autograph a ball for me."

"You don't say," the guy remarked. I could tell he didn't believe me.

"It's true," I said. "Anyway, are you going to sell me your pen?"

"Sure. For a dollar."

I didn't have a dollar. Not any more. I'd have to try something else. I started to walk away.

"Oh, don't be silly, kid," he called to me. "Here, take the pen. Keep it."

"Hey, mister, thanks," I said. "That's real nice of you." It seemed to me I ought to do something for him, so I added, "I think I'd like another soda." He sold me another soda, and between sipping first from one and then from the other and trying to watch the game, I made very slow progress down to the dugout. I got there just before the game ended in the top of the ninth. The Dodgers didn't have to come up to bat at all in that final inning, and I was only afraid that they'd all have disappeared into the clubhouse by the time I got there. I should have come down at the end

of the eighth. But Jackie Robinson had said the end of the game.

I stood at the railing near the dugout, waiting, and sure enough, Jackie Robinson appeared around the corner of the building only a minute or two after Preacher Roe pitched that final out. All around me people were getting up to leave the ball park, but a lot of them stopped when they saw Jackie Robinson come to the rail to talk to me. Roy Campanella, Pee Wee Reese, and Gil Hodges were with him.

"Hi, kid," Jackie Robinson said. He was carrying a ball. It was covered with signatures. "Pee Wee here had a pen."

"A good thing, too," Pee Wee said, "because most of the other guys left the field already."

"But these guys wanted to meet Davy's friend," Jackie Robinson said.

By that time, Preacher Roe had joined us at the railing. Jackie handed him the ball. "Hey, Preacher," he said, "got enough strength left in that arm to sign this ball for Davy's friend here?"

"Got a pen?" Preacher Roe asked.

I handed him my pen. I was glad I hadn't gone through all the trouble of getting it for nothing.

"Not much room left on this ball," Roe said. He squirmed his signature into a little empty space beneath Duke Snider's and then he handed me both the pen and the ball.

Everybody was waving programs and pens in the faces of the ball players who stood by the railing. But before they signed any of them, they all shook my hand. So did Jackie Robinson. I stood there, clutching

Davy's ball and watching while those guys signed the programs of the other fans. Finally, though, they'd had enough. They smiled and waved their hands and walked away, five big men in white uniforms, etched sharply against the bright green grass. Jackie Robinson was the last one into the dugout. Before he disappeared around the corner, he turned and waved to me.

I waved back. "Thank you, Jackie Robinson," I called. "Thanks for everything."

THE BROOKLYN DODGERS

THE DODGERS, 1949 NATIONAL LEAGUE CHAMPS . . .
On ground: batboy Stan Strull. Left to right, front row: Roy Campanella, Marv Rackley, Carl Erskine, Sam Narron, Jake Pitler, Clyde Sukeforth, Manager Burt Shotton, Milton Stock, Dick Whitman, Johnny Jorgensen and Duke Snider. Middle row: Doc Wendler, Eddie Miksis, Bruce Edwards, Gil Hodges, Erv Palica, Joe Hatten, Carl Furillo, Luis Olmo, Pee Wee Reese, Harold Parrott and John Griffin. Rear row: Billy Cox, Jackie Robinson, Gene Hermanski, Paul Minner, Jack Banta, Preacher Roe, Rex Barney, Ralph Branca, Don Newcombe and Mike McCormick.

Thinking and Writing About the Selection

1. What was the first method Sam tried to get a player's autograph? Did he succeed?
2. What kind of a boy is Sam?
3. Why do you think Jackie Robinson stayed to listen to Sam's story about Davy?

 4. Pretend that you are Sam. Write a note to Davy explaining how you got the autographed baseball.

Applying the Key Skill
Summarize

Read the paragraphs from "Thank You, Jackie Robinson" listed below. Then choose the best summary of the paragraph.

1. paragraph that begins, "So I told him. I told him everything. . . ."
   a. Sam told Jackie Robinson that Davy had taken him to his first ball game.
   b. Davy was in the hospital, and Sam wasn't allowed in to see him.
   c. Sam explained to Jackie Robinson why he wanted an autographed ball for Davy.
   d. Jackie Robinson listened while Sam told about Davy's special feeling for the Dodgers.

2. paragraph that begins, "He did. He broke the ball game wide open. . . ."
   a. During the sixth inning, Robinson hit a double.
   b. Jackie Robinson and the Dodgers played a great game and beat the Cubs 6−1.
   c. Warren Hacker's overthrow gave Jackie Robinson a chance to score.
   d. Jackie Robinson's hit led to three runs.

Field Goals and Foul Lines

In the story "Thank You, Jackie Robinson," Sam said that Robinson "hit a double." He also used the expressions "tried to pick him off second base" and "worked two double plays."

Expressions such as *double*, *pick off*, and *double play* are special to the game of baseball. Words or expressions used by people in a particular sport, occupation, or profession are called **jargon**. How much baseball jargon do you understand?

steal a base	to run toward the next base while the pitcher pitches and to get there before the baseman gets the ball from the catcher
home run (also four-bagger, round-tripper, circuit shot)	running a circle of all the bases from home plate back to home plate without stopping
bullpen	place where pitchers warm up
bases are loaded	there are players on all bases

Some jargon is common to several sports. Can you explain what a **benchwarmer** is? What is the **line-up**? What sport is a person playing to get a **hole-in-one**? To **sink a basket**? Can you give two or three examples of football jargon?

THE Gift

Helen Coutant

Illustrated by Vo-Dinh Mai

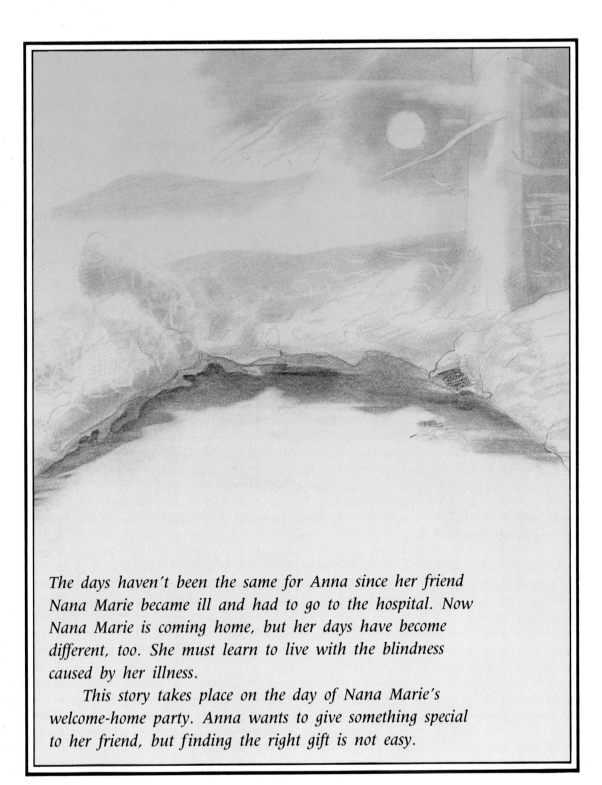

The days haven't been the same for Anna since her friend
Nana Marie became ill and had to go to the hospital. Now
Nana Marie is coming home, but her days have become
different, too. She must learn to live with the blindness
caused by her illness.

  This story takes place on the day of Nana Marie's
welcome-home party. Anna wants to give something special
to her friend, but finding the right gift is not easy.

There must be something she could do for Nana
Marie. Rita had said something about a present. But
what present could ever console a person who had
become blind?

Anna remembered a time she had imagined being
blind. Once in the middle of the night she had opened
her eyes thinking it was morning. The unexpected black-
ness pressed down on her. She turned her head this way
and that and saw nothing. Just when she was ready to
scream, her hand shot out and touched the light, nudging
it on. The brightness, which then appeared so suddenly,
dazzled her eyes. The patchwork quilt shone. The yellow
walls glistened as if they had been freshly painted, and

the air rushed out of her lungs in relief. Now she wondered how Nana Marie had felt waking up blind.

Anna broke into a trot. Ahead was a place she often came to, a small, deep spring in the woods. When she knelt to gaze into the bottomless pool, at first she saw nothing but darkness. Then as the sun came out, the water seemed to open up, reflecting the bark of silver beeches, shining like armor. The reflection of luminous silver reminded her of Nana Marie. She sat back on her heels, remembering.

Six months ago, at the end of summer, Anna and her parents moved to the house just up the hill from Rita's. A week later Anna started school. She didn't know anyone and found it hard to make friends with the other fourth graders. She was very lonely until one afternoon when she had looked up and saw Nana Marie's welcoming smile.

There was a small moving van outside Rita's house that day. From a safe distance, half concealed by bushes, Anna watched it being unloaded. Rita stood by, directing the operations. Anna could see the delight on Rita's face and wondered where this furniture was coming from.

As Anna watched, Rita's husband got out of his car, walked around it, and opened the door by the front seat. Then there was a long wait. Finally a white head emerged. An old woman rose and began to walk toward the house. Then, as if she felt Anna's eyes on her, the old woman looked up. Their eyes met, and Nana Marie smiled.

The next afternoon when Anna came home from school, she saw Nana Marie sitting in a rocking chair on the front porch. Slowly Anna approached, her school shoes raising little puffs of dust. The moment Nana Marie saw her she smiled, and the next thing Anna knew she was sitting cross-legged at Nana Marie's feet. Then they began to talk as if they had known each other for years. On and on till supper time they talked, "like old friends reunited," Nana Marie said.

Every day after that, when the school bus let Anna off at the bottom of the hill, she raced up to Rita's house to keep Nana Marie company. As long as the afternoons were warm they sat on the porch until twilight. When cold weather arrived, Anna climbed the steep stairs to

Nana Marie's room. Sitting by the window, they could see the world just as well as from the porch.

It was cozy in Nana Marie's room. There was a bed, a table, a large chest of drawers, and a trunk. As soon as Anna arrived, she would put her books on the trunk and boil water on the hot plate in one corner. Then the two of them would have tea and share the events of the day. As the weeks passed, Anna learned that every object in Nana Marie's room had a meaning and a story.

What at first had seemed to Anna only a small, cluttered room expanded to become a history of Nana

Marie's life, of her joys and sorrows and memories stretching over almost a century.

Gazing deep into the shining pool again, Anna decided that Nana Marie was like this spring. Each day of her old age she had quietly caught and held a different reflection. Stored in her depths were layers of reflections, shining images of the world. Many of these she had shared with Anna. But now that she was blind, would these images be gone, the way water became dark when there was no light? What would her days be like?

Anna's thoughts moved to the party that Rita would hold in the afternoon. She knew what the neighbors were likely to bring: fruit, scarves, flowers. She could do the same, yet none of these gifts would express what she felt for Nana Marie. Could any of them really make Nana Marie feel better?

Lost in thought, Anna continued to follow the path up the mountain. Slowly the world about her drew Anna in, just as if she had been with Nana Marie. The February sun was swallowed by a thick mist, which the mountain seemed to exhale with each gust of wind. Although the air was damp, it had an edge of warmth that had been absent in the morning. It felt almost like the beginnings of spring. As the hours passed, Anna picked up objects she thought Nana Marie would like: a striped· rock, a tiny fern, a clump of moss, an empty milkweed pod. None of them, on second thought, seemed a proper gift for Nana Marie. There had to be a way to bring the whole woods, the sky, and the fields to Nana Marie. What else would do? What else would be worthy of their friendship?

Suddenly Anna knew what her gift would be. It would be like no other gift, and a gift no one else could bring. All day long Anna had been seeing the world the way Nana Marie had shown her. Now she would bring everything she had seen to Nana Marie.

Eagerly she turned and began the long trudge back to Nana Marie's house. Her hands were empty in her pockets. But the gift she carried in her head was as big as the world.

Just as the sun went over the mountain, Anna emerged from the woods. Ahead of her was the road and Nana Marie's house. She looked at Nana Marie's room, the window directly over the front door. A light should be on by now. But the blinds were down as they had been all week, and the window was so dark it reflected, eerily, the reddish glow of twilight. Everyone must be downstairs at the party. Probably Rita hadn't even bothered to go upstairs and raise the blinds. Yet downstairs the windows were dark, too. What had happened? Where was Nana Marie?

Anna stopped to catch her breath. She hesitated, biting her lip, before she rapped softly on the glass part of the door. There was no answer. She knocked again, louder, then put her hand on the doorknob. It opened from the other side, and Rita stood there in her bathrobe. The kitchen table was covered with the remains of the party: tissue paper, stacked plates, and cups. So the neighbors had come and gone. Anna was too late for the party, but Nana Marie must be there!

"Well, here at last," Rita said. "I figured you went home and forgot. The party ended half an hour ago. I told Nana Marie it wasn't any use waiting up for you longer. I expect she's asleep by now. She was really disappointed you didn't come, though she got lots of nice things from everybody. Why don't you come back tomorrow when she's rested."

"Please, I can't," Anna said. "I have a present for Nana Marie. It won't take long."

"All right," said Rita. "But don't go waking her up."
Nodding, Anna headed for the stairs on tiptoe. The landing at the top of the stairs was dark, and the door to Nana Marie's room was closed. Anna's hand hesitated on the doorknob. Then she opened the door and shut it behind her.

Nana Marie's room was pitch black. There was no sound at all. Was the room empty? The window was straight ahead. Anna ran to it, groping for the cords. The blinds clattered up, crashing in the darkness. Then a faint light flowed into the room. Outside, in the winter twilight, a small frozen moon was wandering upward.

"Anna," Nana Marie was calling her name. She was not asleep after all. "Anna," Nana Marie said, and now there was surprise and joy in her voice. Nana Marie was sitting in her rocking chair. Her eyes were open and as blue as they had always been, like the sky on a summer morning.

"You came," Nana Marie said. "I thought maybe you were getting tired of having such a very old lady for a friend."

"I brought you a present," Anna said. "I'm late because it took me all day to get it."

"Gracious," said Nana Marie. "You shouldn't have done that! All the nice people who came this afternoon brought me presents as if I could see and were still of some use to someone!" She chuckled, gesturing toward the table and a new stack of boxes.

"Mine is different," Anna said. "I brought you a last day."

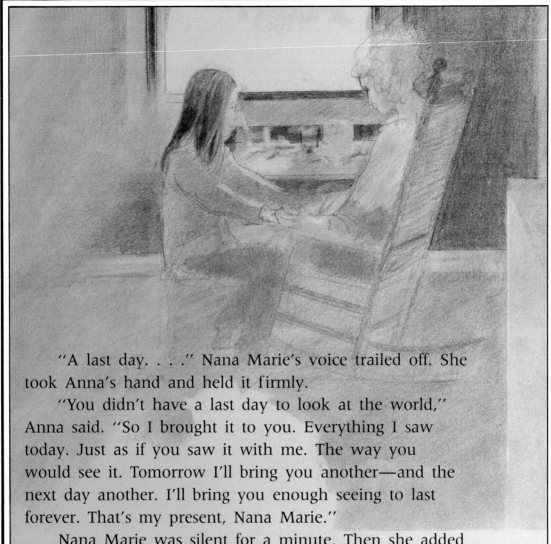

"A last day. . . ." Nana Marie's voice trailed off. She took Anna's hand and held it firmly.

"You didn't have a last day to look at the world," Anna said. "So I brought it to you. Everything I saw today. Just as if you saw it with me. The way you would see it. Tomorrow I'll bring you another—and the next day another. I'll bring you enough seeing to last forever. That's my present, Nana Marie."

Nana Marie was silent for a minute. Then she added softly, almost to herself, "Bless you, child, how did you ever think of that?" She leaned back in the rocking chair. One hand held on to Anna's. With the other she gestured toward a chair. "Pull it up right here, Anna," she said, "so we can look out over the valley and the moonlight together. The moon is out, isn't it, Anna? I can feel it." She closed her eyes.

Anna pulled Nana Marie's hand into her lap and held it with both of her own as she described the silver beeches reflected in the spring, the yellow mist breathing in and out, the pale sun—everything she had seen that day.

When Anna was finished, Nana Marie sat up and turned toward her. Nana Marie's blue eyes shone with contentment. "Thank you, Anna," she said. "That was beautiful." She paused briefly and when she continued it was almost as though she was speaking to herself. "*This is a day I'll always remember.*"

Anna sat holding on to Nana Marie's hand until the moon disappeared over the house. Even though Nana Marie was blind, she really hadn't changed. She could still marvel at the world, she could still feel the moon-light. Anna knew she was going to be all right.

Thinking and Writing About the Selection

1. How did Anna meet Nana Marie?
2. How did Anna discover the history of Nana Marie's life?
3. Was Anna's gift for Nana Marie "worthy of their friendship"? Explain your answer.
4. Do gifts always have to be something you can touch and see? Describe a gift you could give to someone that couldn't be touched or seen.

Applying the Key Skill
Predict Outcomes

Use complete sentences to answer the questions below.

1. What did Anna predict the neighbors would bring to Nana Marie's party?
2. Why did Anna know that she had found the right gift for Nana Marie?
3. What led Anna to believe that Nana Marie "was going to be all right"?

I ASKED THE LITTLE BOY WHO CANNOT SEE
Anonymous

I asked the little boy who cannot see,
"And what is color like?"
"Why, green," said he,
"Is like the rustle when the wind blows through
The forest; running water, that is blue;
And red is like a trumpet sound; and pink
Is like the smell of roses; and I think
That purple must be like a thunderstorm;
And yellow is like something soft and warm;
And white is a pleasant stillness when you lie
and dream."

SUMMARIZE

Have you ever had your mother or father ask, "What did you do today?" when you came home from school? When you told them, you probably mentioned only the most important things that happened. You probably left out what you felt was unimportant. When you describe something this way, you are **summarizing**.

Here are some rules for writing a summary.

1. Use as few words as possible.
2. Include the most important ideas or events.
3. Leave out details that are not important.

ACTIVITY A Read the paragraph below from "The Gift." Then read the three summaries. Decide which is the best. Write the summary on your paper.

> It was cozy in Nana Marie's room. There was a bed, a table, a large chest of drawers, and a trunk. As soon as Anna arrived, she would put her books on the trunk and boil water on the hot plate in one corner. Then the two of them would have tea and share the events of the day. As the weeks passed, Anna learned that every object in Nana Marie's room had a meaning and a story.

a. The furnishings of Nana Marie's room included a hot plate, where Anna boiled water for tea.

b. Anna and Nana Marie often sat in Nana Marie's cozy room drinking tea and talking.

c. As Anna and Nana Marie sat drinking tea and talking, Anna learned the stories behind the objects in Nana Marie's room.

ACTIVITY B Read the paragraph below from ''The Gift.'' Write a summary of the paragraph on your paper.

Suddenly Anna knew what her gift would be. It would be like no other gift and a gift no one else could bring. All day long Anna had been seeing the world the way Nana Marie had shown her. Now she would bring everything she had seen to Nana Marie.

THE THIRD GIFT

JAN CAREW

In this folk tale, you will read about an African tribe called the Jubas.
They receive three different gifts.
As you read, notice how the gifts change their lives.

In long-time-past days there was a black prophet named Amakosa. He was the leader of the Jubas, a clan of herdsmen and wanderers. Amakosa felt age nesting inside his tired limbs. He called all the Jubas together and said,

"Listen well to what I have to say. My face has beaten against many years. Now Mantop, Death's messenger, has sent for me. You must choose a leader to succeed me. When I have gone, all the young men must make their way up Nameless Mountain. The one that climbs the highest and brings back a gift of the wonders that he saw, him you must make your leader."

The Jubas were silent when Mantop led their prophet away. When sunset was casting long shadows, they saw the two walking towards the River of Night.

Then all the young men set out up Nameless Mountain. Up and up they climbed until all they could hear was the wind in the trees and the echoes of drums on the plains. Towards evening one man came

back weary and sleepy. The others followed, dragging their feet. But the one that climbed the highest came running deer-speed down the mountainside holding something in his hand high above his head. He didn't stop until he reached the village square. The Jubas crowded around him and shouted, "Show us the wonderful thing you brought, Brother-Man!"

The young man said, "Come closer and see." He opened his hand and said, "This is what I have brought. Eye never saw and hand never touched a gift like this."

The gift that the young man brought was a stone. When this stone caught the light, it had all the colors of mountain orchids and rainbows and more.

"But what is the message in this stone?" the people asked.

"This stone brings us the gift of Work," the young man said. "Since we wandered into this green country we have become lazy. Laziness is a more terrible threat than drought or hunger."

Looking at the stone, all of the Jubas had a vision of plowshares and ax blades, fields of maize and cassava, and harvest time filled with the singing of their drums.

Jawa, the man who had brought the gift of Work, ruled for a long time. The Juba nation grew, and the memory of hunger and laziness was pushed far away from them.

But the time came when Mantop, Death's messenger, knocked on Jawa's door. He, too, had to walk the trail to the River of Night.

So, once again at fore-day-morning, the young men set out up Nameless Mountain. Kabo, the man who climbed the highest this time, came down the mountainside soft-softly. He could not hurry because the gift he brought was a mountain flower. When he stood in the center of the village square holding this marvelous flower in his hand, it was clear for all to see that he had brought his people the gift of Beauty. They crowded around him to marvel at the curve of the petals and the colors and the way it shone in the light. The singing drums and the song-makers sang Kabo's praises far into the night.

Kabo ruled through many moons, and the Juba country became a place to wonder at. The door of every house had flowers painted on it in bright colors. The girls wore flowers in their hair. Flowers without

number were carved out of wood and stone. Every canoe was built with a flower sculpted on its prow.

But, the Jubas grew dissatisfied. They had Work and Beauty and yet they wanted more. Some began to say that they were thinking of moving to another country down the river and across the plains. When Mantop sent for Kabo, everyone knew that his successor would have to bring back a powerful gift from Nameless Mountain to hold the nation together.

Kabo went on his journey to the River of Night quietly, and for the third time the young men set out up Nameless Mountain. Amongst them was the dreaming, sad-faced son of Tiho the Hunter who was called Ika, the Quiet One.

Ika took a trail on the far side of Nameless Mountain where none of the others dared follow. When night fell and the fireflies brightened the fields and forests like fallen stars, everyone returned except Ika.

The weary ones who had returned said, "We saw him parting the clouds and climbing up and up, and none of us had the strength to follow him."

When Ika did not return by the next morning, the Jubas sent search parties to look for him and posted lookouts on the mountainside. Sun and Moon lengthened many shadows; still Ika did not return. There was plenty of talk about him and how he had gone his lonesome way to die on Nameless Mountain.

But one morning Ika came running down the mountainside, parting the long grass and leaping from rock to rock. He was clenching his fist and holding his hand high above his head. The people said, "Aye, aye,

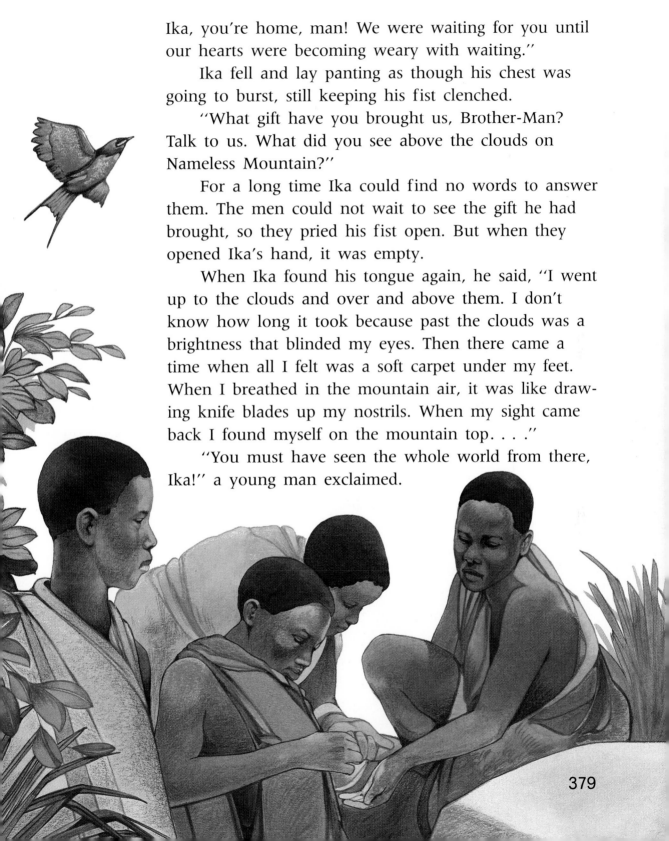

Ika, you're home, man! We were waiting for you until our hearts were becoming weary with waiting.''

Ika fell and lay panting as though his chest was going to burst, still keeping his fist clenched.

''What gift have you brought us, Brother-Man? Talk to us. What did you see above the clouds on Nameless Mountain?''

For a long time Ika could find no words to answer them. The men could not wait to see the gift he had brought, so they pried his fist open. But when they opened Ika's hand, it was empty.

When Ika found his tongue again, he said, ''I went up to the clouds and over and above them. I don't know how long it took because past the clouds was a brightness that blinded my eyes. Then there came a time when all I felt was a soft carpet under my feet. When I breathed in the mountain air, it was like drawing knife blades up my nostrils. When my sight came back I found myself on the mountain top. . . .''

''You must have seen the whole world from there, Ika!'' a young man exclaimed.

"Yes, and while I stood up there a soft white thing like rain started to fall . . . and yet it wasn't rain because it fell like leaves when there is no wind. I gathered this soft whiteness in my hand, but the farther down the mountainside I ran, the less of it I was holding, so I went back for more and ran down the mountain again. Four times I did this, and every time I was heading for home bird-speed, this magic thing melted in my hand. All I bring with me now is the memory of it, the feel of the sky and the bite of the wind—and the fire and ice burning my hand."

And the people listening believed, for this quiet young man, when he did speak, sounded like singing-birds-sweet. When he spoke, his words would grow inside your head like seeds.

Ika became prophet of the Jubas for he had brought the best gift of all, the gift of Imagination. So, with the gifts of Work and Beauty and Imagination, the Jubas became poets and creators, and they live at the foot of Nameless Mountain to this day.

Thinking and Writing About the Selection

1. What were the first two gifts?
2. Why did the Jubas need a powerful third gift to hold them together as a nation?
3. Was the third gift the best gift of all? Why or why not?
4. What other gift could have been brought to the Jubas? How would this gift have changed their lives?

Applying the Key Skill
Plot, Setting, Mood

Use complete sentences to answer the questions about "The Third Gift" below.

1. Where and when does the story take place? If you were making a picture of the setting, what would you draw?
2. If you were telling the story to a friend, what important events would you describe?
3. How would explain the mood of the story? What might you compare it to?

When You
Begin to Wonder

Meindert DeJong

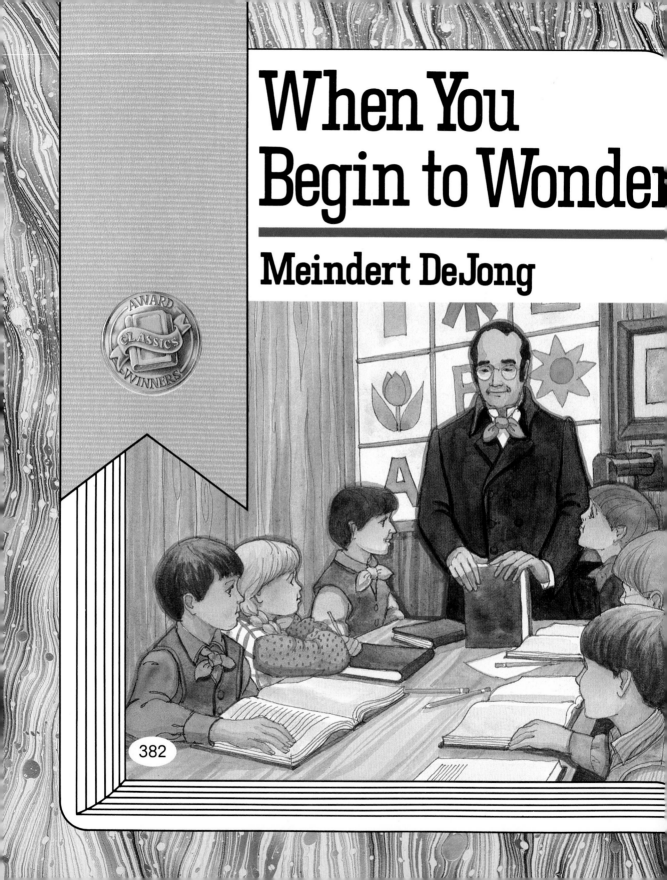

In the Dutch fishing village of Shora, there were only six school children. There were five boys: Jella, Eelka, Auka, and Pier and Dirk, who were twins; and then there was Lina, the only girl in the little Shora school.

One day, right in the middle of a lesson, Lina raised her hand and asked if she could read a story that she had written about storks. The teacher was so pleased that Lina had written something that he stopped the lesson and let her read to the class.

In Lina's story, she described storks as big white birds with long yellow bills and tall yellow legs. She said that storks do not sing but make a noise that sounds like clapping hands. She told how storks make big messy nests, even on rooftops. She explained that when storks do build a nest on the roof of a house, "they bring good luck to that house and to the whole village. . . . But I do not know much about storks," read Lina, "because storks never come to Shora."

fter Lina had finished reading her story, the room was quiet. The teacher stood there looking proud and pleased. Then he said, "That was a fine story, Lina, and you know quite a lot about storks!" He turned to Jella. "Jella," he said, "what do you know about storks?"

"About storks, Teacher?" Jella said slowly. "About storks—nothing."

"Oh," the teacher said. "Eelka," he said then, "what do you know about storks?"

Eelka thought awhile. "I'm like Lina, Teacher; I know little about storks. But if storks would come to Shora, then I think I would learn to know a lot about storks."

"Yes, that is true," the teacher said. "Now what do you think would happen if we all began to think a lot about storks? School's almost out for today, but if, from now until tomorrow morning when you come back to school, you thought and thought about storks, do you think things would begin to happen?"

They all sat still and thought that over. Eelka raised his hand. "I'm afraid I can't think much about storks when I don't know much about them. I'd be through in a minute."

Everybody laughed, but the teacher's eyes weren't pleased. "True, true," he said. "That's right, Eelka. We can't think much when we don't know much. But we can wonder! From now until tomorrow morning when you come to school again, will you do that? Will you wonder why and wonder why? Will you wonder why storks don't come to Shora to build their nests on the roofs, the way they do in all the villages around? For sometimes when we wonder, we can make things begin to happen.

"If you'll do that—then school is out right now!"

There they were out in the schoolyard—free! "What'll we do?" Jella said eagerly to the other boys.

Lina took charge. Since she had started it with her story about storks, she felt responsible. It was a wonderful day, the sky was bright and blue, and the dike was sunny. "Let's all go and sit on the dike and wonder why, just like the teacher said."

Nobody objected. They all dutifully set out for the dike.
384 They sat. Nobody seemed to know just how to begin to

wonder without the teacher there to start them off.

Jella looked along the quiet row. Everybody was just sitting, hugging his knees. Everybody looked quiet and awkward and uncomfortable. Suddenly Jella had had enough. He looked along the row of boys at Lina. "The teacher didn't say we had to sit in a row on the dike to wonder, now did he?"

"No," Lina said.

"Well, then," Jella said. All the boys jumped up eagerly.

Lina took off one of her wooden shoes and sat staring moodily into it. She often sat staring into her shoe. It somehow made her feel better and seemed to help her to think better, but she didn't know why.

Still thinking and dreaming about storks, Lina got up and wandered away from the dike, one shoe in her hand. She went slowly down the street, staring intently at the roofs of all the houses as if she'd never seen them before. The village street lay quiet and empty. Lina had it to herself all the way through the village to the little school. The school had the sharpest roof of all, Lina decided. All the roofs were sharp, but the school's was the sharpest.

A thin faraway shout and a shrill laugh came through to her. She turned. In the far, flat distance she could see the boys. She turned her back to them. It didn't matter that the boys were having fun. She knew why the storks didn't come to build their nests in Shora. The roofs were all too sharp! Not only did she know the reason why, she also knew what to do about it! They had to put a wagon wheel on top of one of the roofs—a wagon wheel just like her aunt in Nes had on her roof. Tomorrow morning she would

385

spring it on them in the schoolroom. They'd be surprised!

Lina started to hurry back to the village, almost as if she had to hurry to tell someone. There wasn't anyone there, she knew. Lina slowed herself by staring at a house. Once more Lina dawdled down the street, once more she stood a dreamy while before each house. Her shoe came off again. She was staring up at the roof of Grandmother Sibble III's house when the old lady came out. It startled Lina.

"I know I'm a nosy old creature," Grandmother Sibble III said, "but there you stand again, staring. I've been watching you wandering from the dike to the school and back again like a little lost sheep."

Lina laughed a polite little laugh. "Oh, I'm not exactly wandering. I'm wondering."

"Oh," said the old lady. "Well, I guess wondering is always better than wandering. It makes more sense."

They looked at each other. Lina thought how she had never talked much to Grandmother Sibble III except to say a polite "hello" as she walked by. Now she did not know just what to say to her.

The old lady was still looking at her curiously. "Is that why you have your shoe in your hand?" she said gently. "Because you were wondering so hard?"

In surprise Lina glanced down at her hand holding the wooden shoe. She reddened a bit and hastily slipped it on her foot. What must Grandmother Sibble think—not that she was her grandmother, she was just the grandmother of the whole village, the oldest old lady. It certainly must have looked silly, her hobbling down the street on one shoe,

carrying the other. No wonder Grandmother Sibble III had come out of the house!

"I . . ." Lina said, trying to explain. She giggled a little. "Oh, isn't it silly?" She fished in her mind for some sensible explanation. None would come. Lina decided to tell her. "I guess it does look silly and odd, but it somehow helps me think better to look into my shoe. Then when I get to thinking really hard, I forget to put it back on again," she said defensively.

"Why, yes," the old lady said immediately. "Isn't it funny how odd little things like that help? Now I can think much better by sort of rocking myself and sucking on a piece of candy, and I've done it ever since I was a little girl like you." She carefully settled herself on the top step of her brick stoop. She looked as if she was settling herself for a good long chat. "Now of course, I've just got to know what it was you were thinking about so hard it made you forget your shoe. If you don't tell me, I won't sleep all night from trying to guess."

They laughed together. Grandmother Sibble patted the stoop next to her. "Why don't you come and sit down with me and tell me about it?"

Lina eagerly sat down—close, exactly where the old lady had patted. She even understood silly things like looking into a wooden shoe. She understood it the way a friend—if you had a friend—would understand. A friend who also had silly tricks and secretly told you about them. Aloud Lina said, "I was thinking about storks, Grandmother Sibble. Why storks don't come and build their nests in Shora."

388   Grandmother Sibble looked thoughtful. "Well, that is a

thing to ponder all right. No wonder you had your shoe off. We here in Shora always were without storks."

"But I figured out why," Lina told the old lady proudly. "Our roofs are too sharp!"

"Well, yes. . . . Yes, I guess so," the old lady said carefully, sensing Lina's sharp excitement. "But that could be fixed by putting a wagon wheel on the roof, couldn't it?"

"Yes, I'd thought of that," Lina said promptly. "My aunt in Nes has a wagon wheel on her roof, and storks nest on it every year."

"Ah, yes," the old lady said, "but doesn't your aunt's house have trees around it, too?"

"Yes, it has," Lina said, looking in surprise at the little old lady. Why, Grandmother Sibble must have been thinking about storks, too. It seemed amazing, the old, old lady thinking about storks. "I guess I never thought about trees. Well, just because there are no trees in Shora—so I didn't think about trees." Lina's voice faded away. Here was a whole new thing to think about.

"Would a stork think about trees?" the old lady wanted to know. "It seems to me a stork would think about trees. It seems to me that in order to figure out what a stork would want, we should try to think the way a stork would think."

Lina sat upright. What a wonderful thing to say! Lina fumbled for her shoe while she listened eagerly.

"You see, if I were a stork, even if I had my nest on a roof, I think I would still like to hide myself in a tree now and then and settle down in the shade and rest my long legs. Not be on the bare peak of a roof for everybody to see me all the time."

389

"You see, years ago," Grandmother Sibble was explaining, "when I was the only girl in Shora, the way you are the only girl now, there were trees in Shora and there were storks! The only trees in Shora grew on my grandmother's place. She was Grandmother Sibble I.

"My grandmother's little house stood exactly where your school stands now but, oh, so different from your little school. My grandmother's house was roofed with reeds and storks like reeds. And my grandmother's house was hidden in trees. Storks like trees. Weeping willow trees grew around the edge of a deep moat that went all around my grandmother's house. Over the moat there was a little footbridge leading right to my grandmother's door. In one of the willows there was always a stork nest, and there was another nest on the low reed roof of my grandmother's house."

"Oh, I never knew," Lina said breathlessly.

Grandmother Sibble did not seem to hear. Her eyes were looking far, far back. She shook her head. "A storm came," she said. "The wind and waves roared up the dike for longer than a week. For a whole week the water pounded and the salt spray flew. When it was all done, there were only three willows left at my grandmother's house. Then even those three left-over trees sickened and died. I guess their leaves had just taken in too much salt.

"Later, after Grandmother Sibble I died, they came and tore down her house and chopped out the old rotted stumps of the willows and filled the moat with dirt. Then there was nothing for years until they built your little school

on the same spot. But the storks never came back."

Lina sat wide-eyed, hugging her knees, staring straight ahead, drinking it in, dreaming it over—the things the old lady had said—dreaming the picture. It sounded like a faraway tale, and yet it had been! Grandmother Sibble III had seen it!

Grandmother Sibble III roused herself. "So you see you mustn't think our sharp roofs are the whole story, must you?" she said softly. "We must think about other things, too. Like our lack of trees, our storms, our salt spray. We must think about everything. To think it right, we must try to think the way a stork would think!"

"Then have you been thinking about storks, too?" Lina asked in astonishment.

"Ever since I was a little girl. And ever since then I've wanted them back. They're lucky and friendly and, well, just right. It's never seemed right again—the village without storks. But nobody ever did anything about it."

"Teacher says," Lina told the old lady softly, "that maybe if we wonder and wonder, then things will begin to happen."

"Is that what he said? Ah, but that is so right," the old lady said.

The real wonder was that, just as the teacher had said, things *had* begun to happen. Begin to wonder why, the teacher had said, and maybe things will begin to happen. And they had! For there sat Grandmother Sibble III on the stoop of her little house, and suddenly she had become important. She wasn't just an old person any more, miles of years away, she was a friend. A friend, like another girl, who also wondered about storks.

*　　*　　*

In the morning it was school again. There they were in the schoolroom again, the five boys and Lina and the teacher. They sat quietly as the teacher stood looking at each one of them in turn. Then he said, "Who wondered why? Where did it lead you?"

Lina's hand shot up. To her amazement every hand shot up with hers, even Jella's and Eelka's. The teacher looked so happy and pleased about it, it made Lina furious. "Why, Teacher, they never did!"

392

The teacher looked at her a short moment. He seemed surprised. He turned away from her to Jella. Jella sat there in the front seat. The teacher was saying, "Well, Jella, and what did you think was the reason why storks do not come to Shora?"

"Oh, I didn't think," Jella told the teacher honestly. "I asked my mother."

The teacher smiled. "Well, next to thinking, asking is the way to become wise. What did your mother say?"

"She said storks don't come to Shora because they never did. She said storks go back every year to the same nesting spots. So if they never came to Shora, they never will. So there's just nothing to be done about it, she said."

Lina quivered with eagerness. Then she was waving her hand, almost getting up out of her seat. She had to tell them! Lina heard herself saying out loud, "Oh, but storks did once upon a time come to Shora!"

They all turned to her, even the teacher. The next moment Lina was excitedly telling the story that Grand-mother Sibble III had told her about Grandmother Sibble I and the storks and the willow trees all around. About storks right here in the exact spot where the school now stood!

When Lina was finished, Eelka raised his hand, and now he was saying in his slow way, "What Lina said about trees. You know, Teacher, that is exactly what I thought when I wondered why. Storks don't come to Shora because we have no trees!"

"All right, now," the teacher said. "Does everyone agree with Eelka that the number one reason why storks do not come to Shora is because we have no trees?" He turned to the blackboard and wrote in big letters:

THE REASONS WHY STORKS
DO NOT COME TO SHORA

Under the words he put a big number one and waited.

"I still think the number one reason is what my mother said," Jella spoke up.

"Ah, but Lina has just told us that storks used to come to Shora. In fact, Jella, Grandmother Sibble III has seen storks nesting above the spot where you are sitting now. Where our school now stands. Imagine it!" said the teacher.

"I guess maybe my mother was wrong," Jella said slowly. He seemed to hate to have to admit it. He looked up at the ceiling in a troubled way.

Then Auka raised his hand and quietly said, "Then the number one reason is still NO TREES."

"That's what Grandmother Sibble thinks, too," Lina told the class honestly. "She says storks like shelter and trees and hiding and a shady place to rest their long legs. She said she would if she were a stork! Grandmother Sibble told me the way to find out what a stork would want is to try to think like a stork."

The teacher stood looking at Lina. "Is that what Grandmother Sibble III told you? I think that is wonderful," he said. He turned back to the class. "Well, are we agreed then that the number one reason for no storks in Shora is no trees?" He turned toward the board with his chalk as if to write it down.

Lina frantically waved her hand to stop him. "Not trees—roofs!" she almost shouted when the teacher didn't turn around. "Teacher," she said desperately to the teacher's back, "even though Grandmother Sibble and everybody think it is trees, it has to be roofs. Storks don't just build nests in trees, they build their nests on roofs, too. But our roofs in Shora are too sharp! Oh, it just has to be roofs," she pleaded. "Because we can put wheels on the roofs for storks to build their nests on, but we can't do anything about trees."

Pier and Dirk said almost together, "Oh, man, imagine a nest on every roof in Shora!"

"Even on the roof of our school!" Auka shouted.

"That's just it. That's just it!" Lina all but shouted at them. "There's not a single wheel on any roof in Shora, because, just like Grandmother Sibble, everybody else must have figured it was no trees. So nobody ever put up a wheel. Nobody even tried! How can we know if we don't try?"

Lina sat back waiting breathlessly, hopefully looking at the teacher. Oh, she *had* to be right!

The teacher stood before the blackboard turning the piece of chalk in his hand in no hurry to write anything down. He looked at the boys who were still looking in surprise at Lina. He looked at Lina. Then he wrote on the blackboard Lina's reason in big white letters:

NO WHEELS ON OUR SHARP ROOFS

He turned back to the class. "Could it be?" he asked. "If we put wheels on our sharp roofs, could there be storks on every roof in Shora?"

"All that is a dream," Jella said scornfully.

"Ah, yes, that's all it is," the teacher said. "As yet! But that's where things have to start—with a dream. Of course, if you just go on dreaming, then it stays a dream and becomes stale and dead. But first to dream and then to do—isn't that the way to make a dream come true? Now sit for a moment, picture it for a moment: our Shora with trees and storks. Now Shora is bare, but try to see Shora with trees and storks and life. The blue sky above and the blue sea stretching behind the dike and storks flying over Shora. Do you see it?"

"Trees won't grow in Shora," Jella argued stubbornly. "It's the salt spray and the wind and storms."

"Well," asked the teacher, "couldn't we raise trees that could withstand the storms and salt spray—stouter and stronger than willows? There must be trees that grow along the sea. Or maybe we would have to protect the willows with a windbreak of poplar trees. The point is, if trees once grew here, couldn't we make them do it again?"

"Oh, but that would take too long," Dirk said. "That would take years."

"Making dreams become real often takes long," the teacher said. "I don't mean that it should be done at once. Our first problem is how to make just one pair of storks come to nest in Shora. That is what we are trying to do right now by first thinking out the reasons why the storks don't nest in Shora. But after that. . . . If trees once grew where our school now stands, wouldn't they grow there again? Think of it. Trees all around our school!"

"And a moat, too," Jella promptly added. "We could even dig it ourselves."

397

"Yes, Jella, now you are getting into the spirit of it. For that matter, we could even plant our own little trees. But first, before we can even start to think of all that, what must we do?"

"Find a wheel to put on a roof," Lina promptly cried.

"Ah, hah," the teacher said. "Now we are getting to something that we can do. Now do you see? We wondered why and we reasoned it out. Now we must do. Now we must find a wagon wheel, and then we must put it up on a roof. Behind doing that lies the long dream—storks on every roof in Shora. Trees! Maybe even a moat around the school. Can you picture our Shora like that! It's still a dream. We haven't even a wheel as yet; we don't even know what roof we'll put it on."

"Oh, yes, we do! Oh, yes, we do!" the whole class shouted. "It's got to go right on the roof of our school."

"Why, yes," the teacher said. "Why, yes, class! Then who's going to look for a wagon wheel? Look for a wagon wheel where one is and where one isn't; where one could be and where one couldn't possibly be?"

They were all too breathless to say a word. Jella blurted it out for all of them. "We all will. From the moment school is out until we find one."

The teacher nodded and nodded. "That's how we'll begin to make a dream come true. We'll begin at noon. It's Saturday, and we have our free afternoon before us. We'll have a whole afternoon to try to find a wagon wheel. We'll really work at it, because that is how to start to make a dream come true. . . ."

398   *   *   *

Would you like to find out if storks do come to Shora? "When You Begin to Wonder" is only part of a book called **The Wheel on the School.** *If you read the book, you will discover what can happen when you begin to wonder.*

399

Gifts

People give gifts for many reasons. Gifts can say, "Thank you," "I'm happy for you," or "I understand." Not all gifts are presents that can be wrapped in paper, tied with a ribbon, or even held in our hands. In *Gifts*, you read about people who gave gifts of understanding and friendship. You read about people who shared their talents or gifts with others. You also received some gifts—gifts of stories that made you laugh or smile, stories that made you think or wonder, and stories that may have been close to your own experiences and feelings.

Thinking and Writing About *Gifts*

1. What gift did the blue moose give to Mr. Breton?
2. What do you think Felita learned about the gift of friendship?
3. How did Joseph in "The Dancing Man" share his gift with others?
4. What helped Sam in "Thank You, Jackie Robinson" and Anna in "The Gift" know just what gifts to give to their friends?
5. In "The Third Gift," the third and last gift the Jubas received was the gift of imagination. What gifts could they create with the gift of imagination?

6. Imagine that you are a member of a group that is going to visit a school in another country. You have been asked to bring a gift from the students in your school. Describe the gift you would bring and write a message to the students who will receive the gift.

Introducing Level 10

CHANGES

Every year we see changes: winter turns to spring, spring to summer, and summer to fall. In this unit, you will read about places that scientists have studied: deserts, forests, and wetlands. You will learn about some of the changes that happen in these places, and you will meet some of the living things that grow in them. What changes in nature have you seen?

To every thing there is a season, and a time to every purpose under the heaven.

The Bible

The 17 Gerbils of Class 4A

William H. Hooks

The students in Class **4A** always enjoyed their science lessons. Mr. Rivera, their teacher, liked to plan interesting projects. When Roger Johnson brought two gerbils to class, they became part of a science lesson on desert animals. Chris kept a notebook of facts about gerbils. His classmates learned how to take care of them. When Roger and his family moved to California, he donated his gerbils to Class **4A**. Roger knew that there would be more gerbils by the end of the year. He left a will telling who should get them.

Roger's gift changed the classroom into a nursery as the two gerbils quickly became seventeen. When finding room for them to live became a problem, Mr. Rivera announced that it was time for the gerbils to go. That's when the science project turned into a math project. Read to find out how the gerbils helped Class **4A** learn more about science and arithmetic.

January 22

I, Roger Johnson, being of sound mind and body, do will all my present and future gerbils to my three friends Tommy, Cynthia, and Chris. The three before-mentioned friends are to share the gerbils in the following way:

1) Tommy is to own $\frac{1}{2}$ of them
2) Cynthia is to own $\frac{1}{3}$ of them
3) Chris is to own $\frac{1}{9}$ of them

Since it is hard to know how many gerbils you will have by the end of the school year, I think this will be the easy way to divide them up.

Witness to this paper: Signed:

Miguel Ortiz   Roger Johnson
whom I trust a lot.

"Wow, that Roger sounds like a real lawyer! He thinks of everything!" exclaimed Tommy while we were eating lunch.

I said, "That solves one part of our problem. Now we know how to divide the gerbils. I hope it will be as easy to convince our parents to let us bring them home."

"Roger, what have you done to us?" moaned Cynthia.

All I could think of was how much I'd like to box up all these little pets and mail them to Roger in California. The Johnson family had found a nice house in San Jose (san' hō zā'), California, but Roger never sent for Maxi and Mini. He found out that there's a law in California that says NO GERBILS. California has a lot of desert, and they're afraid the gerbils will get loose and run wild. That's how I got the first thing anybody ever willed me.

Tommy stopped chewing long enough to say, "Okay, let's figure out how many gerbils each of us gets."

Cynthia whipped out her pencil (always prepared, that girl) and wrote down a big 17. Then this strange look came over her face.

"What's wrong, Cynthia?" I asked her.

"We're in big trouble again," she announced.

"What trouble?" piped Tommy. "I get half of them. That's simple enough."

"Tommy," asked Cynthia in her I'm-being-very-patient voice, "how can you take home half of seventeen gerbils?"

"In a box," Tommy said, getting kind of huffy.

"Think a minute," said Cynthia, still being very patient. "Seventeen. Seventeen! How can you take half of seventeen?"

"Oh," says Tommy. "That comes to eight and a half gerbils."

"Cynthia," I asked kind of quietly, "how are we going to get your third of seventeen?"

Well, Cynthia's quick. She answered right back, "The same way we get your ninth of seventeen, Chris!"

Cynthia very carefully put all the figures down on a piece of paper. First, she put a big 17 at the top of the page. Then she divided things up the way Roger had left it in his will.

$$17$$

$$\frac{17}{1} \times \frac{1}{2} = \frac{17}{2} = 8\frac{1}{2}$$

$$\frac{17}{1} \times \frac{1}{3} = \frac{17}{3} = 5\frac{2}{3}$$

$$\frac{17}{1} \times \frac{1}{9} = \frac{17}{9} = 1\frac{8}{9}$$

"Well, Tommy, you get half the gerbils. That comes to exactly eight and one-half little animals, just as you figured," Cynthia announced.

"My third comes to five and two-thirds gerbils, and Chris, you get one and eight-ninths gerbils for your share." Cynthia held up the paper with her neat little rows of figures.

Tommy groaned. I just sat still, trying to think of something clever to say.

Cynthia piped up, "Listen, fellows. We have a real dilemma!"

"We have enough trouble with the gerbils without bringing up something else," moaned Tommy.

I didn't know what a *dilemma* was, so I just kept quiet. I smiled at Cynthia and looked interested. I knew I could depend on Tommy to put his foot in.

"Tommy, a *dilemma* is when you have trouble and you don't know how to get out of it," Cynthia explained.

"Yes, Tommy, we have had a real gerbil dilemma since Mr. Rivera made the announcement early this morning," I added. I told myself to hang on to that word. It could come in handy.

Before we got back to the classroom, we could tell there was a lot of excitement. My first thought was: *Gerbils! The gerbils have escaped again!*

Well, I was partly right. It was one gerbil out of his cage. Maxi. I could see someone holding Maxi. Roger! It was Roger. He was back to visit his grandmother and his school and gerbil friends.

Tommy and Cynthia and I pushed our way over to Roger. Everybody did a lot of friendly punching and horsing around. It got kind of crazy with everybody talking and yelling at the same time.

Mr. Rivera came into the room. He seemed pleased to have Roger back for a visit. He asked Roger to tell the class about his school in California.

Cynthia and Tommy and I thought we'd never get a chance to tell Roger about our dilemma with the gerbils. Finally we did.

Roger just smiled and said, "Don't worry, my good friends. I got you into this. Just watch me get you out. Right after school I'll solve the gerbil problem for you. Relax. No sweat, no problem. By the way, team, what names did you pick for Mini's last litter?" Roger asked.

"Do, Re, Mi, Fa, So, La, Ti, and Maxi Junior!" Tommy and Cynthia and I sang together.

Roger really laughed at that. He wouldn't tell us how he was going to solve our problem, though. I could hardly wait to find out what Roger was going to do.

Finally, it was three o'clock and time for Roger's magic act.

"Okay, Mr. Superfixer," said Cynthia. "Let's see you divide up these gerbils."

"Wait right here in front of the cages," Roger said, acting very mysterious. "I'll be right back."

In a few minutes, he was back with another gerbil he had borrowed from the room across the hall. Just what we needed! Roger put a blue ribbon on this new gerbil. Then he put the borrowed gerbil in one of the cages.

"Now," said Roger, "Tommy, how many gerbils do we have?"

"That makes eighteen now," answered Tommy. "Why?" Tommy asked, getting a little suspicious.

Roger went on. "Tommy, choose half of the gerbils in the two cages. Go ahead, pick your half

of the eighteen gerbils. Don't choose the one with the blue ribbon."

Tommy looked doubtful, but he went ahead and picked half of the eighteen. That came to nine whole gerbils.

Then Roger said to Cynthia, "Okay, Cynthia. Take a third of the eighteen gerbils. Skip the one with the blue ribbon."

"A third of eighteen is six," said Cynthia. "I know I can convince my mother to let me keep them." She sounded kind of uncertain for Cynthia. She quickly picked out six of the gerbils.

"Now, Chris," said Roger, "you take a ninth of the eighteen gerbils."

"A ninth of eighteen is two," I said out loud so they could all check me. I took my two gerbils.

You know what? There was still a gerbil left. The one with the blue ribbon was left over!

We couldn't believe it. We added it up again.

Tommy had nine.

Cynthia had six.

I had two.

Nine and six and two make seventeen!

Roger picked up the gerbil he had borrowed from across the hall and returned him. Then Roger quickly said, "I've got to run, gang. How about you three coming over to Gram's house tonight?"

We agreed, though we felt a little dazed. It had been some day!

Our dilemma was solved. At least part of it was. We had the gerbils divided up. None of us had counted on bringing gerbils home until school was out, though. We considered the gerbils ours, all right. In fact, we owned them legally. But neither Cynthia nor Tommy nor I had really settled it with our parents. We thought there was plenty of time to do that before summer vacation. Now all we had to do was convince our parents it was okay to take them home right away. That part seemed like it would be easy after what we had been through.

Everything was fine—except Cynthia kept turning the old problem around in her head. She'd sigh every now and then and mutter, "How did Roger do it?"

Finally she asked Mr. Rivera for help. Mr. Rivera did just what I expected—he turned our science project into a math project. He did give us one little hint. "Why don't you see if a half, a third, and a ninth add up to a whole?"

Then he left us to figure it out for ourselves.

Cynthia said, "Let's put it all in eighteenths." So we did.

$$\frac{1}{2} = \frac{1}{2} \times \frac{9}{9} = \frac{9}{18}$$

$$\frac{1}{3} = \frac{1}{3} \times \frac{6}{6} = \frac{6}{18}$$

$$\frac{1}{9} = \frac{1}{9} \times \frac{2}{2} = \frac{2}{18}$$

$$\frac{17}{18}$$

"That Roger!" yelled Cynthia. "I'll bet he knew all the time that it wouldn't add up to a whole."

"That's right," agreed Tommy. "That's why he went and got another gerbil. That gerbil made it possible to divide them up!"

"You are brilliant, Tommy," said Cynthia.

"That's why he had a gerbil left over when we all got our share," I chimed in.

"You, too, are brilliant," cried Cynthia.

We were all getting excited, and our voices were getting very loud. Mr. Rivera rejoined us. I think he was listening all the time.

"I think you're all pretty brilliant!" Mr. Rivera said.

Thirty-four gerbil legs began to drum against the floors of their cages.

I think they were applauding us.

Chris's Science Notebook

First Gerbils in the United States

Gerbils first came to the United States in 1954. They were not considered pets at that time. Eight pairs of males and females, plus six extra males, were imported for scientific experiments. The thousands of gerbils that we have today all came from these twenty-two. In 1964, gerbils were first sold in pet stores.

Gerbils and the Weather

Since gerbils come from the desert, you might think they would need a hot climate to do well. Not so. They can stand severe temperature changes. That's because the deserts they come from are very hot during the day and very cold at night. You don't have to worry about gerbils getting too cold on weekends when the heat is very low in the school building.

413

Claws and Ears

Strong claws and large ears help gerbils. With their claws they dig underground homes with connecting tunnels. They store their food underground and keep their babies there. Gerbils have big ears and very keen hearing. This helps them escape from enemies in the desert. I think it also may be why they get nervous when there is a lot of loud noise around them.

A Gerbil's Life Cycle

Gerbils are about an inch long when they are born. They start growing a soft brown coat of fur by the time they are a week old. Gerbils are also born with their eyes sealed. They open in about three weeks. Within three months a gerbil is grown. Gerbils live from three to five years.

Conclusion

It's easy to get hooked on gerbils.

Thinking and Writing About the Selection

1. Why didn't Roger send for his gerbils once he got to California?
2. What caused the gerbil dilemma?
3. Chris discovered many facts about gerbils and wrote them in his notebook. What are some other facts you would like to know about gerbils? How could you find out?
4. Would you like to have a gerbil for a pet? Why or why not?

Applying the Key Skill
Context Clues

Read the sentences about "The 17 Gerbils of Class 4A" below. Use context clues to choose the meaning of each underlined word. Then write each word and its meaning.

1. When Roger moved to California, he left a gift. He donated his gerbils to class 4A.
   - a. sold
   - b. delivered
   - c. gave
   - d. sent
2. "I'll solve the gerbil problem," Roger said, smiling. But Tommy looked doubtful.
   - a. unhappy
   - b. unsure
   - c. afraid
   - d. certain
3. Gerbils first came to America in 1954. Twenty-two gerbils were imported.
   - a. sent to other countries
   - b. brought in from a foreign country
   - c. very important
   - d. carried by hand

CONTEXT CLUES

In "The 17 Gerbils of Class 4A," Cynthia used a word that Tommy and Chris did not know. She said, "We have a real *dilemma*!" The boys found out what *dilemma* meant when Cynthia explained to Tommy, " a dilemma is when you have trouble and you don't know how to get out of it."

What do *you* do when you read or hear a word you don't know? You might ask someone to explain the meaning to you. You might also look up the word in the dictionary. But there is another way you can discover word meanings. You can find out the meaning of a word by using context clues. **Context clues** can be other words in the sentence that you do know. Other sentences can also provide you with context clues.

Read the sentences below from Chris's Science Notebook on Gerbils. Pay attention to the word *severe*.

> They (gerbils) can stand <u>severe</u> temperature changes. That's because the deserts they come from are very hot during the day and very cold at night.

If you don't know the meaning of the word *severe*, you can figure it out from the context clues. In the first sentence, *severe* is used to describe temperature changes. The second sentence explains that deserts are very hot during the day and very cold at night. These context clues should help you know that *severe* means "great or extreme."

Using context clues can help you be a word detective. As you read, try to figure out the meanings of unknown words by using the help that other words and sentences provide.

ACTIVITY A Number your paper from 1 to 3. Use context clues to help you choose the correct meaning of each underlined word. Write the word and its meaning on your paper.

1. You can express many meanings without using words by miming.

    a. shouting   b. acting out silently   c. writing

2. The acrobats made sure the rope was taut. If it were loose, they could easily fall.

    a. high   b. straight   c. tight

3. Mr. Wilson reads a newspaper or watches a newscast every day. He likes to keep up with current events.

    a. belonging to the present   b. past   c. unusual

ACTIVITY B Write a meaning for each underlined word on your paper. Check your definition in a dictionary. Then write a sentence of your own using the underlined word.

1. We usually extinguish the lights when we tell ghost stories. It's scarier in the dark.

2. The players were jubilant when the final score was announced. It had been a perfect season!

417

THE LIVING DESERT
Barbara Brenner

Alan Pippin loves lizards. When his sister Jan invites him to spend the summer with her in Arizona, it is a dream come true. Alan can hardly wait to see the lizards that live in the Sonoran Desert of southern Arizona. He has a field guide that describes all his favorite lizards. It is Jan, however, who teaches Alan how to find what he is looking for. She is a botanist (bot' ən ist), or scientist who studies plants. She spends a lot of time studying the plants in the desert. She knows about the living things in the desert and what it takes to find them.

In less than an hour we were deep in the desert. It was unreal—like a foreign country or another planet. Nothing was familiar. Where my eye was used to seeing tree-lined streets and shady woods, there were flat sunbaked roads and sand. There were almost no trees. The few we saw didn't look anything like our Connecticut maples and oaks and birches.

We talked about deserts. Jan told me what defines them—water. A desert, she said, is a place where the rainfall is no more than ten inches a year.

Water is the key to the desert. It even shapes it. Cuts out the canyons and rubs the stones smooth. Water even shapes the plants and animals.

"Take desert plants," said Jan. "Out here the most important thing is to conserve water. Desert plants, like other plants, carry water in their stems and leaves. If they had big leaves, they'd lose a lot of water through evaporation. So they've developed small leaves. Or no leaves, like the cactus. They have long roots that reach down and get water from deep underground, or spread out and soak up whatever rainwater falls onto the surface of the desert." Jan told me that some desert plants have roots that run for thirty or forty feet just below ground.

We'd been driving around most of the morning, looking for a spot where we could watch wildlife. We'd been circling, doubling back, trying little dirt roads, when suddenly we came on it. A stretch of pure desert, in full color, rimmed by mountains, and looking really pretty under a June sun.

The spot we had picked was divided into two parts. On one side was a gentle slope called a *bajada* (bä hä' də). It was covered with low-growing plants and tall *saguaro* (sə gwär' ō) cacti.

At the base of the bajada was a sandy flatland. Here the ground was hot and dry. Everything was beige and tan and brown. Jan called off the names of the plants for me. *Creosote* (krē' ə sōt'). *Mesquite* (mes kēt'). *Cholla* (choi' yə). They were all pale desert colors.

There was a dry streambed which separated the bajada from the flatland—an *arroyo* (ə roi' ō). It was about two feet deep and was cut into the earth in a clear path from the mountains.

There were trees along the banks of the arroyo— unfamiliar desert trees. *Paloverde* (pal' ō vėr' dē). *Acacia* (ə kā' shə). *Ironwood*. Jan knew them all. She said they were there to catch the water that sometimes ran down from the mountains and through the arroyo.

I began to have a feeling that something was missing. I finally realized what it was. "There's nothing here," I remember blurting out to Jan.

Jan didn't get my point at all. For her, there was plenty there—all kinds of low-growing plants and grasses, cacti, and bushes. She could have spent a year and still not investigated all the plants in that desert.

"I mean there are no *living* things," I said.

She was annoyed. "What do you think all those plants are?"

"I mean where is everything? Where are all the animals? There aren't even any birds."

Jan tried to ease my disappointment. "It's getting to the hottest part of the day. This is when the birds go higher in the sky to catch the cooler currents of air. And you know the lizards go underground to cool off." I agreed that that was where they must be.

"You'll have to learn to be patient in the desert or you won't see anything," said Jan. "Why don't we have some lunch and then come back?"

While we ate and drank in the shade of the car, Jan explained to me that the desert requires a different kind of looking. "You have to learn to look *under* and *inside* and *overhead*," she said. "Your eye has to tune in to tiny movements and to small differences in the shape of the ground. Then you'll begin to see things."

After lunch we tried again. The first things we began to see were birds' nests. Soon we began to see birds. The cactus wrens hung out in the cholla, and the gila (hē′ lə) woodpeckers popped in and out of holes in the saguaro. A hawk flew high over our heads, scouting mice and ground squirrels and lizards.

The hawk and I were having about the same luck with the lizards. By two o'clock I was sure there wasn't a single lizard in the whole Sonoran Desert. *The living desert, my foot*, I thought.

Then I saw it out of the corner of my eye. A small movement near where Jan was standing. It had been scrambling up our side of the arroyo when Jan had moved and frightened it. It shot past us and made for a bush. But not so fast that I didn't see its long tail and pointed snout, its tiny body and the stripes.

I clutched my field guide happily and read aloud about the western whiptail. My first lizard.

> The western whiptail (*Cnemidophorus tigris*) (nē′ mə dä′ fər əs tī′ grəs) is one of about twelve species of whiptails found in the United States. Whiptails are all smooth, slim lizards, and they all have long ''noses'' and long tails.

I was to see a lot of western whiptails before the summer was out. In fact, the "nemmies," as we got to call them, seemed to be almost everywhere we went.

We found "nemmies" among rocks, under bushes, and in sandy washes. Many times the sound of our

footsteps would bring one out of hiding. Sometimes one would let me get close before it dashed away under a bush. At other times our presence would send it dashing down any hole that was nearby. After a while, though, it got so I could catch the streak of a "nemmy" out of the corner of my eye and get a good look before it took off.

After about a week at Jan's, I discovered that there were whiptails in her courtyard. They weren't wanderers from the desert; they lived there.

Lizards don't range very far from a home base. If a lizard travels more than a few hundred feet in its whole lifetime, it's a lot. So if you're a lizard, it's important to be born in a good spot. The whiptails in Jan's courtyard were lucky. The courtyard was sheltered from the hottest rays of the sun. There were lots of plants and plenty of food in the form of ants, beetles, spiders, and moths. There were no animals that could prey on them. There was one other thing that made it an ideal home— plenty of water.

You could always find a whiptail around one of the outside faucets, catching the drips. They seemed to know where the faucets were and would visit them, like people going to a water fountain. Each time the flowers were watered, we'd see a half dozen little whiptails lapping water from the leaves with their tongues.

I started to make notes on where I saw certain ones. One in particular, a large checkered whiptail, seemed to hang around by the faucet outside my bedroom. I began to think of "Checkers," as I called it, as a pet. I thought perhaps handling it might make it more tame, so every time I saw Checkers, I'd try to catch it.

I didn't notice that the handling made it any more willing to stay around or any more relaxed. But it didn't seem any more scared than it had been, so I still had hopes.

One day as I was handling the whiptail, the phone rang. I dropped the whiptail into a jar. I meant to come right back, but somehow I forgot. About a half hour later I remembered the lizard. I rushed out to the courtyard. Checkers was lying in the bottom of the jar, which stood in direct sunlight. The temperature inside that jar must have been 140 degrees. I didn't know how long it had been in the sun but I knew my lizard was in trouble. Like all reptiles, it had to move around from heat to cool to keep its body temperature within safe limits. I'd locked it in a container where it was cooking!

It took the lizard about an hour to recover. It took *me* a week to get over what I'd done. It certainly showed me what it means for an animal to have to depend on outside sources to maintain its body temperature. Suddenly I felt lucky to be a mammal with an inner thermostat to keep me at 98.6 degrees.

Thinking and Writing About the Selection

1. What is a desert?
2. Why do you have to be patient in order to see animals in the desert?
3. What did Alan mean when he said the lizard was "cooking" in the container?
4. If you had a whiptail for a pet, what kind of home would you make for it?

Applying the Key Skill
Cause and Effect

Read the following incomplete sentences about cause-and-effect relationships in "The Living Desert." Choose the best ending. Then write the complete sentence.

1. There are few trees in the desert because ___.
    a. it is too hot
    b. the soil is too sandy
    c. there is little rainfall
2. The cactus loses little water through evaporation since ___.
    a. it has no leaves
    b. it has long, deep roots
    c. it stores its water in its stem
3. Desert animals stay hidden in the afternoon in order to ___.
    a. escape from their enemies
    b. keep cool
    c. look for food

Has anybody seen
A lizard in a tin?
A tiny little tin
That you'd keep a lizard in?

Has anybody heard
A lizard in a tin?
A little lizard sounding
As if he's growing thin?

Has ANYBODY seen it
Or heard a scratching sound
Of a desperate little lizard
Scrabbling round and round?

LOST-A LIZARD
by Irene Gough

CHARTS AND TABLES

In "The Living Desert" you were given a lot of information about the desert. The writer used sentences and paragraphs to tell you about the Sonoran Desert, its plants, and its animals.

When writers have a lot of information to tell, they often use a chart or table. A **chart** presents information in a way that is easy to read. A chart also makes it easy to compare information.

Look at the chart below. Notice that it is divided into three columns. Each column has a heading.

A chart is read from left to right. For example, if you look at the first row beneath the column headings, you will see that the Mojave Desert is located in California and its size is 15,000 square miles.

Some Important Deserts of the United States

Name	Location	Size in square miles
Mojave Desert	California	15,000
Painted Desert	Arizona	7,500
Great Salt Lake Desert	Utah, Nevada	5,500
Colorado Desert	California	2,000
Black Rock Desert	Nevada	1,000

430

ACTIVITY A Number your paper from 1 to 4. Use the chart to answer the questions. Write the answers on your paper.

1. What is the largest desert listed on the chart?
2. What two deserts are found in California?
3. Where is the Black Rock Desert located?
4. Which desert is larger, the Colorado Desert or the Painted Desert? About how much larger?

ACTIVITY B Number your paper from 1 to 4. Use the chart below to answer the questions. Write the answers on your paper.

The Five Largest Deserts in the World

Name	Continent	Size (square miles)
Sahara	Africa	3,500,000
Great Australian Desert	Australia	1,250,000
Gobi	Asia	600,000
Arabian Desert	Asia	500,000
Turkestan	Asia	450,000

1. What is the largest desert in the world? In what continent is it found?
2. How many of the five largest deserts in the world are found in Asia?
3. What desert named on the chart is found in Australia?
4. Which desert is larger, the Gobi or the Arabian Desert? How much larger is it?

The Desert Is Theirs
Byrd Baylor
illustrated by Peter Parnall

Many people couldn't imagine wanting to live in a hot, dry desert. But one group of people, the Papago (päp' ə gō') Indians, couldn't imagine living any-place else. This selection, part of a poem, tells about the special feeling the Papagos have for all the living things that share the desert.

This is no place
for anyone
who wants
soft hills
and meadows
and everything
green
green
green . . .

This is for hawks
that like only
the loneliest canyons
and lizards
that run
in the hottest sand
and
coyotes
that choose
the rockiest trails.

It's for them.

And for
birds
that nest
in cactus
and sing out over
a thousand thorns
because
they're where
they want to be.

It's for them.

And for
hard skinny plants
that do without water
for months
at a time.

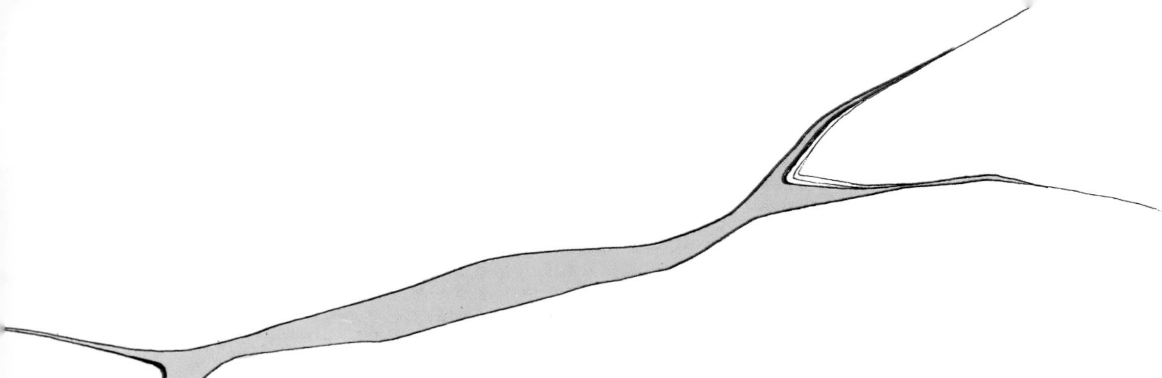

And it's for
strong brown Desert People
who call the earth
their mother.

They *have* to see
mountains
and *have* to see
deserts
every day . . .
or they don't feel right.

They wouldn't leave
even for rivers
or flowers
or bending grass.
They'd miss
the sand too much.
They'd miss
the sun.

So
it's for them.

Talk to Papago Indians.
They're
Desert People.

They know
desert secrets
that no one else
knows.

Ask
how they live
in a place
so harsh and dry.

They'll say
they *like*
the land they live on
so they treat it well—
the way you'd treat
an old friend.
They sing it songs.
They never hurt it.

And the land knows.

Papagos try
not to anger
their animal brothers.
They don't
step on
a snake's track
in the sand.
They don't disturb
a fox's bones.
They don't shove
a horned toad
out of the path.
They know
the land belongs
to spider and ant
the same as it does
to people.

They never say,
"This is my land
to do with as I please."
They say,
"We share . . .
we only share."

And they *do* share.

435

Women weave grass
into their baskets
and birds weave it
into their nests.

Men dig
in the earth
for soil
to make houses—
little square adobe houses
the color of the hills.
And lizards
dig burrows
in the same
safe earth.

Here animals and people know
what plants to eat
when they are sick.
They know what roots
and weeds
can make them well again.

No one has to tell
Coyote or Deer
and no one has to tell
the Papagos.

They share in other ways, too.
They share
the feeling
of being
brothers
in the desert,
of being
desert creatures
together.

A year that is hard
for people
is hard for
scorpions, too.
It's hard for everything.

Rain is a blessing
counted
drop
by
drop.
Each plant
finds its own way
to hold
that sudden water.
They don't waste it
on floppy green leaves.
They have thorns
and stickers
and points
instead.

Yucca
sends roots
searching
far far underground—
farther than you'd ever dream
a root
would go.

And Saguaro is fat
after rain—
fat with the water
it's saving
inside its great stem.
Give it one summer storm.
It can last a year
if it has to.
Sometimes it has to.

The desert's children
learn to be patient.

Hidden in his burrow,
Kangaroo Rat
spends each long day
waiting
for the heat to fade,
waiting
for darkness
to cool the desert
where he runs.
Just so he runs sometime . . .

A weed
may wait
three years
to bloom.
Just so it blooms sometime . . .

A toad
may wait
for months
to leave
his sandy hiding place
and sing toad songs
after a rain.
Just so he sings sometime . . .

Desert People
are patient, too.
You don't see them rushing.
You don't hear them shouting.

They say you plant happier corn
if you take your time
and that squash tastes best
if you've sung it
slow songs
while it's growing.
They do.

Anyway,
the desert has
its own kind of time
(that doesn't need clocks).
That's
the kind of time
snakes go by
and rains go by
and rocks go by
and Desert People
go by, too.

That's why
every desert thing
knows
when the time comes
to celebrate.

Suddenly . . .
All together.
It happens.

Cactus blooms
yellow and pink and purple.
The Papagos begin
their ceremonies
to pull down
rain.
Every plant joins in.
Even the dry earth
makes a sound of joy
when the rain touches.
Hawks call across the canyons.
Children laugh for nothing.
Coyotes dance in the moonlight.

Where else
would
Desert People
want to be?

Thinking and Writing About the Selection

1. What do the Papagos share with the plants and animals of the desert?
2. Why is rain a cause for celebration to the people, plants, and animals of the desert?
3. What does the author mean when she says "The desert's children learn to be patient"?

 4. The Papagos share with the plants and animals of the desert. How can you share with the plants and animals that live around you?

Applying the Key Skill
Author's Purpose

Authors usually have more than one purpose for writing. Which of the following purposes do you think the author had in mind when she wrote "The Desert Is Theirs"? Write your choices.

a. to explain how desert plants and animals survive
b. to describe the beauties of the desert
c. to persuade people to move to the desert
d. to tell about the ways the Papagos treat the plants and animals in their desert home
e. to show how people can harm nature
f. to tell a serious story
g. to describe a way of life that many people don't know about
h. to persuade people to help the Papagos

Byrd Baylor

"I want to know the things that hawks and horned toads know. I want to understand dust devils and falling stars. I want to follow coyote trails wherever they go. I like to talk to people who remember sunsets they saw five years ago. . . ."

Is there a special place in your life where you feel especially at home? For Byrd Baylor, the Southwest is not only home. It is also the inspiration for most of her books. She was born in San Antonio and spent most of her childhood in Texas, Arizona, and Mexico. She remembers always being outside as a child. This is not surprising because her father worked in the mining industry. She later attended the University of Arizona.

Byrd Baylor began her writing career as a reporter for an Arizona newspaper. Her interests, however, soon ran toward the past as well as the present. "I go to Indian ceremonials and search for ancient ruins and Indian treasures," she explains. Out of this interest have come such books as *Before You Came This Way*, about Indian rock drawings, and *When Clay Sings*, which grew out of her discovery of some ancient Indian pottery.

Byrd Baylor's love of the desert comes through in all her work. *Desert Voices* recognizes the animals of the desert, just as *The Desert Is Theirs* honors the people who live there.

More to Read

Everybody Needs a Rock; Hawk, I'm Your Brother

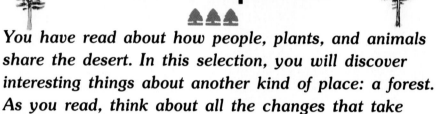

HOW THE FOREST GREW

William Jaspersohn

🌲🌲🌲

You have read about how people, plants, and animals
share the desert. In this selection, you will discover
interesting things about another kind of place: a forest.
As you read, think about all the changes that take
place as a forest grows.

BOB HERSEY

443

Have you ever wondered where forests come from, and how they grow? Most forests grow the same way. To find out how a forest grows, we must go back in time.

Two hundred years ago the land that is now a forest was open and green. Then the farmer and his family who owned the land, and who had cleared it, moved away. Changes began. The wind blew seeds across the fields. Birds dropped seeds from the air. The sun warmed the seeds. The rain watered them, and they grew.

In a few years the land was filled with weeds— with dandelions and goldenrod and milkweed. And ragweed and black-eyed Susans. Each spring new plants took root. The land began to look different. Burdock and briars grew among the weeds, making the land moist and brushy.

Blackberries grew. Birds came to eat them— song sparrows and catbirds. Meadow mice and cottontail rabbits made their nests in the tall grass. Woodchucks and moles dug their tunnels in the ground. Snakes came to feed on the small animals. Hawks and owls hunted over the land for their food. Time passed.

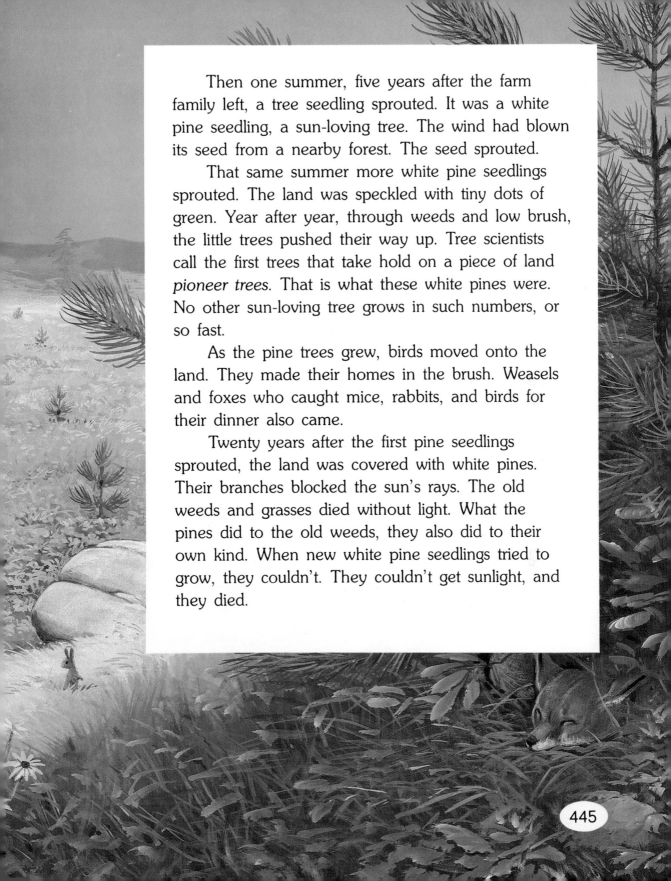

Then one summer, five years after the farm family left, a tree seedling sprouted. It was a white pine seedling, a sun-loving tree. The wind had blown its seed from a nearby forest. The seed sprouted.

That same summer more white pine seedlings sprouted. The land was speckled with tiny dots of green. Year after year, through weeds and low brush, the little trees pushed their way up. Tree scientists call the first trees that take hold on a piece of land *pioneer trees*. That is what these white pines were. No other sun-loving tree grows in such numbers, or so fast.

As the pine trees grew, birds moved onto the land. They made their homes in the brush. Weasels and foxes who caught mice, rabbits, and birds for their dinner also came.

Twenty years after the first pine seedlings sprouted, the land was covered with white pines. Their branches blocked the sun's rays. The old weeds and grasses died without light. What the pines did to the old weeds, they also did to their own kind. When new white pine seedlings tried to grow, they couldn't. They couldn't get sunlight, and they died.

Only those seedlings that liked the shade grew beneath the white pines. Ash trees, red oak, red maple—these were the trees that the white pines helped the most.

In less than fifteen years the new trees were crowding the white pines for space. A struggle had begun, and only the strongest trees would survive. Scientists call this change from one kind of tree or animal to a new kind *succession*. They say that one kind of tree or animal succeeds, or follows, another.

As the new trees on the land began to succeed the old pines, the animal life on the land changed, too. The meadow mice moved because their food supply was gone, and there was no more grass for them to build their nests. White-footed mice took their place. They made their nests in hollow stumps and logs. They ate seeds from the trees and shrubs.

For the first time deer came to live on the land. Now there were places for them to hide and tender shoots for them to eat.

Cardinals perched in the trees. So did redstarts and ovenbirds. Squirrels and chipmunks brought nuts onto the land. Some of these sprouted with the other seedlings.

Forty years had passed since the farmer and his family had left. Then one summer afternoon, fifty years after the farm family had gone, a storm broke over the land. Lightning struck the tallest pines, killing some of them and damaging others. Strong winds uprooted more pines, and lightning fires burned branches.

This is how forests grow. The death of some of the pine trees made room for new and different trees that had been sprouting on the forest floor. As time passed, insects and disease hurt the other pines. Every time one of them died, a red oak, white ash, or red maple tree took its place.

447

The forest grew. By the year 1860, more than eighty years after the farm family had left, the weeds were all gone. The pioneer white pines were nearly all gone. Red oaks, red maples, and ash trees were everywhere. The forest had reached its *middle stage*.

Now on the forest floor came the last of the new seedlings. These were the beeches and the sugar maples, trees that like the deep shade. The other seedlings—the red oak, red maple, and ash seedlings—needed more light. Some of them needed more water and different kinds of soil to grow in. So they died, and the beech and the sugar maple seedlings took their place.

Every autumn the trees lost their leaves. They fell to the ground with dead twigs and branches. All of these things decayed and made a rich layer of stuff called humus (hū′ məs). Then, slowly, bacteria and worms turned the humus into soil from which the trees got food and water. Sometimes an animal or an insect died, and its body became part of the humus, too.

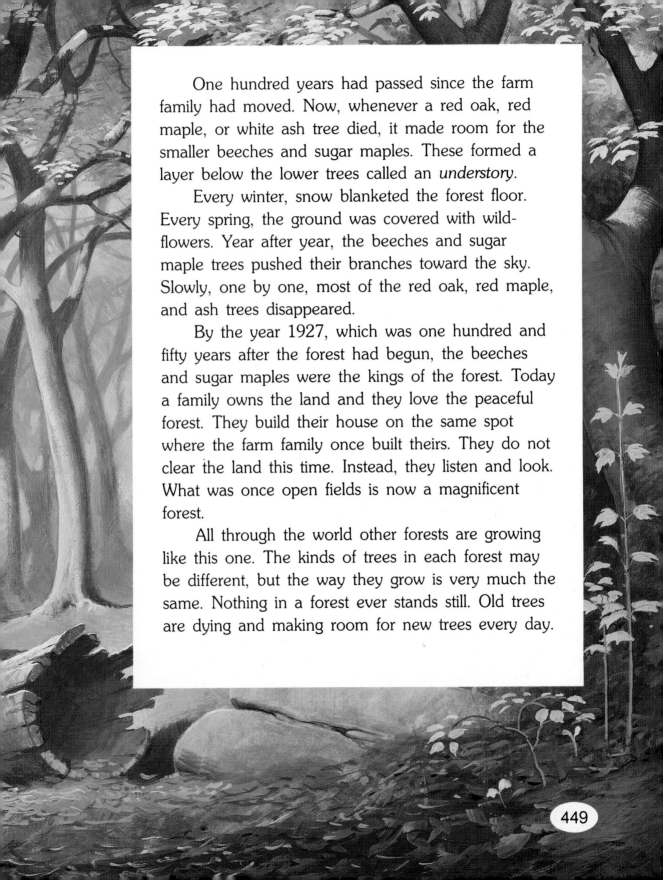

One hundred years had passed since the farm family had moved. Now, whenever a red oak, red maple, or white ash tree died, it made room for the smaller beeches and sugar maples. These formed a layer below the lower trees called an *understory*.

Every winter, snow blanketed the forest floor. Every spring, the ground was covered with wildflowers. Year after year, the beeches and sugar maple trees pushed their branches toward the sky. Slowly, one by one, most of the red oak, red maple, and ash trees disappeared.

By the year 1927, which was one hundred and fifty years after the forest had begun, the beeches and sugar maples were the kings of the forest. Today a family owns the land and they love the peaceful forest. They build their house on the same spot where the farm family once built theirs. They do not clear the land this time. Instead, they listen and look. What was once open fields is now a magnificent forest.

All through the world other forests are growing like this one. The kinds of trees in each forest may be different, but the way they grow is very much the same. Nothing in a forest ever stands still. Old trees are dying and making room for new trees every day.

Thinking and Writing About the Selection

1. How did the first tree seedling come to sprout on the land?
2. Why did other kinds of trees succeed the white pines?
3. Why is humus important to a forest?
4. The family that bought the land decided not to clear it. Does this mean that the forest will stay the same? Why or why not?

Applying the Key Skill
Sequence of Events

Read each pair of events from "How the Forest Grew" below. Decide which event happened first. Then write all the events in the correct sequence.

1. Birds and winds carried seeds to the land.
   The land was covered with weeds and grasses.
2. Grasses and weeds died.
   Tall pines blocked the sun's rays.
3. The small and weakest pines died.
   Red oak, red maple, and ash trees grew up and fought for space.
4. Most of the trees of the forest's middle age died out.
   Beeches and sugar maples formed an understory.

Dandy Lions and Tiger Lilies

One of the first flowers on the land where the forest grew was the dandelion. Where did the dandelion get its name? Was it the yellow blossom that looks like a lion's mane? Or was it the jagged leaves that look like a lion's teeth?

The answer is "lion's teeth," or "lion's tooth." The word dandelion comes from the French words *dent de lion* which mean "lion's tooth." How do you think the tiger lily got its name?

Many flower names have stories behind them. Some flowers, like the dandelion and the tiger lily, were named because of what they look like. The tulip also got its name that way. The word *tulip* comes from a Turkish word for turban. Does the tulip remind you of a turban?

Some flowers got their names because of what they do. If you touch a touch-me-not, its seed pods will burst open. Do snapdragons really snap? What happens to four-o'clocks at four o'clock? Try to find out by using an encyclopedia.

While you're looking, try to figure out how a daisy is like an eye, and how a jack-in-the-pulpit is like a church.

Other flower names you can look up are:

aster   **iris**   **gladiolus**   **Queen Anne's Lace**

MAIN IDEA

You know that the most important idea in a paragraph is called the **main idea**. Writers often state the main idea in a single sentence.

Not all main ideas are stated in one sentence, however. Writers sometimes use two sentences to state the main idea. You must combine information from both sentences to state the main idea.

Read the following paragraph from "How the Forest Grew."

> Twenty years after the first pine seedlings sprouted, the land was covered with white pines. Their branches blocked the sun's rays. The old weeds and grasses died without light. What the pines did to the old weeds, they also did to their own kind. When new white pine seedlings tried to grow, they couldn't, they couldn't get sunlight, and they died.

Part of the main idea of this paragraph is found in the sentence: *The old weeds and grasses died without light.* The other part is found in the sentence: *When new white pine seedlings tried to grow, they couldn't, they couldn't get sunlight, and they died.* Information from both sentences can be combined to state the main idea: Old weeds and grasses, as well as new white pine seedlings, died without the light they needed to grow.

ACTIVITY A Read the paragraph below. Then write the sentence that best states its main idea.

Forest products were important to early settlers. The forest provided wood for fires, and fruits and nuts to eat. Many pioneer homes were made of wood. Forest products are still important to people today. We use forest products for food and fuel, too. Like the pioneers, people today need wood for building materials.

a. People today use many forest products.
b. Forest products were important to early settlers, and they are still important to people today.
c. Forests provide building materials, food, and fuel.

ACTIVITY B Read the paragraph below. Combine the information from two sentences to state the main idea. Write the main idea on your paper.

You know that a tree is a plant. You probably think of a tree as the part that we see above the ground. The part of a tree that grows above the ground is called the crown. The crown is made up of the trunk, the branches, and the leaves. There is a very important part of a tree that grows beneath the ground, however. It is the root. The roots of a tree may take up as much room underground as the crown does above the ground.

THIS IS OUR PARK

The United States government has set aside some of our country's land as parks in order to protect it. In this selection, you will meet Mia Monroe, who works in one of these protected places. Mia talked about her job in an interview.

Lisa Yount

Just seventeen miles (about 27 kilometers) north of the city of San Francisco, California, is a special, hidden place. It is called Muir (mūr) Woods. Muir Woods is a small, narrow valley, or canyon. A creek runs through the canyon's bottom. A thick forest of redwood trees grows along the canyon's sides. Redwoods are some of the tallest trees on earth. Some of the redwoods in Muir Woods are 260 feet (about 79 meters) high. That's about as high as a 26-story building!

Almost two million visitors come to Muir Woods each year. In this beautiful forest they can see what part of North America was like a very long time ago. Some of the trees in Muir Woods are more than a thousand years old. Long ago, trees much like them covered large parts of North America.

People can visit Muir Woods today because of a man named William Kent. Kent bought the canyon in 1905. Five years later, he gave the land to the United States government. He asked that the woods be preserved and named in honor of a man called John Muir. Muir, like Kent, loved nature deeply. He had helped to persuade the government to protect some of the country's wild lands by making them into national parks. Today Muir Woods is a national monument (mon' yə mənt). A monument is a place preserved for its interesting natural features or historical importance. The National Park Service takes care of it.

Mia Monroe is a park ranger who works in Muir Woods. She has seen many changes come to the woods in the year and a half she has been there. Her job is to make sure that the changes are good ones.

"The purpose of the Park Service is to preserve and protect the parks and help people enjoy them. That's my job, too," Mia says. "Everything I do in the woods is related to that."

Mia preserves and protects Muir Woods in many ways. "A large part of my day is spent just patrolling the trails," she says. "By being out there all the time, I know what's going on. I notice when the first wild-flowers are out. I notice where the deer are hiding. I notice which pools the baby fish are swimming in."

Mia sees many changes in Muir Woods as the seasons change. Around November, for example, the rainy season begins. "With the first rains, everything greens up," Mia says. "The forest looks completely different after just a week or so." Mixed with the green are big red and yellow maple leaves that dot the trails.

The rains bring changes to the animals of Muir Woods, too. "As the rains continue, Redwood Creek gets full of water," Mia explains. "The young trout and salmon that were born in the creek in the spring begin to make their way down to the ocean. They're called fingerlings at this age because they're about as big as your finger.

"A little later, in December or January, adult salmon swim in from the ocean. They're three or four feet long. They come back up the creek to spawn, or lay their eggs. Then they die."

The only large animals in Muir Woods are black-tailed mule deer. They are very busy in the fall, too. "The bucks, the male deer, are testing out their antlers. They rub them against the trees and fences. They begin to fight each other and set up territories. Soon after that, the mating season starts."

The deer go into the open grasslands around the forest during the winter. Then, in the spring, the female deer, or does, come back with their babies, the fawns. "If you peek under the trees, you'll see fawns hiding among the plants," Mia says. "Later on you can see the fawns testing their legs."

The deer are not afraid of people. They often come so close to the trails that visitors can almost touch them. Mia reminds people that the deer are still

wild animals, though. In fact, she often does something
that shocks people.

"I wait until everyone has taken pictures and
gotten a good look at the deer. Then I kick and scream
at the deer to frighten them away. We don't want them
to get too friendly with people. Both the deer and the
people can get hurt that way."

Visitors, like the seasons, can bring changes
to Muir Woods. Part of Mia's job is to see that the
changes are not harmful.

"One of our most important rules is 'Please stay
on the trails,'" she explains. "Redwoods are very tall,
but they have a very shallow root system. They depend
on their roots to bring them nutrients and water. When
lots of people walk over the ground, their feet press
the soil down. It gets almost like concrete. Then the
nutrients and the water can't get to the tree roots.
The tree is almost choked to death."

People are sometimes unhappy or angry when
Mia tells them to stay on the trails. They may be
disappointed when she tells them they can't have

picnics in Muir Woods, either. She tries to explain why these rules are important. She also reminds them that there are large areas of park land around Muir Woods where they can picnic, walk, and camp.

One of Mia's favorite jobs is taking classes of students through the woods. Sometimes she begins by having them do "redwood exercises."

"Reach up to the sun—way up! Now hug yourselves like you do when it's cold and windy. That's just what redwood trees do."

Mia often shows the class special things she has collected. She might show them a fossil cone from a redwood tree that lived thousands of years ago. She might show them a banana slug and explain that its job in the forest community is to make the soil richer.

Mia tells students how she finds things in the woods. "I really tell all my secrets," she laughs. "I explain how I know where to go to find the snakes, the banana slugs, the salamanders. It's because I know the habits of the animals. I tell how to listen for things and then look to see where the sound is coming from. I show how to find clues to where animals have been and what they were doing there."

The skills Mia teaches are useful in many places besides Muir Woods. "If I go to work in another forest, I could use all these same skills there," she tells her classes. "You can use what I teach you in other national parks or in a city park or in your own back-yard. You can use these skills all your lives."

Another part of Mia's job is directing work crews who help take care of Muir Woods. Some of the crews

are teenagers doing summer jobs. They may move fallen trees off the trails or out of the creek.

Other crews are volunteers, just as Mia was when she was younger. Sometimes a school class or a Scout troop "adopts" a part of the forest. Mia shows them how to look for "plant travelers" that do not belong in the forest. These plants grow faster than the natural plants and choke them out, just as weeds do in a garden. The class comes in every few months and pulls up the harmful plants in its part of the forest.

Sometimes volunteers decide that they want to work in a park as a regular job. "There are all kinds of jobs in the Park Service," Mia says. "Other rangers do the kinds of jobs I do. Secretaries and other people work in offices. Scientists study living things in the parks. Maintenance workers keep the parks clean. Whatever kind of work you do, you can do it for the Park Service." If a volunteer wants to know more about a certain kind of job, Mia introduces him or her to the people who do that job in Muir Woods.

If young people do decide to work for the Park Service, Mia hopes they will love their jobs as much as she loves hers. "I love working with people, and I love the land," she says. "The whole goal of my life is to set up the best possible relationship between the land and the people.

"Muir Woods is here because people felt it was important," Mia tells people. "I'm here because I feel it's important. It will go on being here because you feel it's important."

"This isn't my park," Mia says. "This is *our* park."

Thinking and Writing About the Selection

1. What is the job of the National Park Service?
2. Why is it important for Mia Monroe to spend time patrolling the trails?
3. Do you think it is important to set aside land as national parks and monuments? Why or why not?

 4. "Please stay on the trails" is one of the most important rules at Muir Woods. What do you think another rule might be? Why would it be important?

Applying the Key Skill
Cause and Effect

Copy the chart below. Then fill in the missing information about cause-and-effect relationships from "This Is Our Park."

CAUSE	EFFECT
	People can visit Muir Woods today.
Mia doesn't want the deer to get too friendly with people.	
	People must stay on the trails in Muir Woods.
"Plant travelers" can choke out the natural plants in Muir Woods.	

My Forest House

Ruth Simpson
Age 10

I know a place with a roof of green
And the floor is much the same.

This place I call my forest house.
It's great for playing games.

I love this place more than anything else
With the bluebirds and robins that sing.

This beautiful` place, this wonderful place,
Is my forest house in the spring.

I know a place with a gold-green roof
For the sun is peeking through.

The crickets chirp, the robins sing
As I sit and play in the dew.

I love this place more than anything else
Where the woodpecker is the drummer.

This beautiful place, this wonderful place,
Is my forest house in the summer.

I know a place with a roof of gold
And a cool soft floor of green.

This place I call my forest house.
It's the best house ever seen.

I love this place more than anything else
Though I don't live here at all.

This beautiful place, this wonderful place,
Is my forest house in the fall.

I know a place with no roof at all
And the floor is cold and white.

This place I call my forest house.
It's always shimmering bright.

I love this place more than anything else
And couldn't say this any simpler.

This beautiful place, this wonderful place,
Is my forest house in the winter.

465

AUTHOR'S PURPOSE

If you think about it, you will realize that you say and do things for many different reasons. The reason for doing or saying something is sometimes called the **purpose**. For example, suppose you want a new bike. When you talk with your parents about it, your purpose is **to persuade**, or convince, them to buy you one. When you explain the rules of a game to someone who doesn't know the game, your purpose is **to inform**. When you tell a joke to a friend, your purpose is **to entertain**.

Authors, too, have different purposes when they write. Their purpose may be to persuade, inform, or entertain you.

People who write ads try to get you to buy a product or use a service. Their purpose is to persuade.

You often read books and articles that teach you new things. The author presents you with many facts. The author's purpose is to inform.

Many times you read a story for enjoyment. The author's purpose in writing the story is to entertain. Stories do not have to be funny to be entertaining. Folk tales, mysteries, and legends can entertain readers.

ACTIVITY A Read the passages below. Then on your paper, tell the author's purpose by writing to persuade, to inform, or to entertain.

1. Yellowstone National Park is our oldest national park. It was established in 1872. It includes more than two million acres of land in Wyoming, Idaho, and Montana.

2. When you visit the park, please remember the rules and obey them. Stay on the trails. Walking off the trails may destroy many beautiful and rare plants.

3. TED: Where is Katmai National Park?
   ED: I don't know.
   TED: Neither do I, but Sue does. Alaska.

ACTIVITY B The following selections are ones that you have read in this unit. Tell whether the author wrote the selection to inform and, to entertain, or both. Write **to inform** and/or **to entertain** next to each number on your paper.

1. Lost—A Lizard

2. The 17 Gerbils of Class 4A

3. How the Forest Grew

4. This is Our Park

5. The Living Desert

6. My Forest House

The MONTH-BROTHERS

retold by **Samuel Marshak**
illustrated by Diane Stanley

The sequence of the seasons never changes. Spring is always followed by summer, fall by winter. Spring cannot come in the middle of winter, or can it?

In this folk tale of long ago, you will read about a girl who lived with her stepmother and her stepsister. She spent most of her time doing chores. Many of them had to be done outdoors, so she knew well the cold of winter and the heat of summer, the rains of fall and the winds of spring. Once she also got to know the twelve month-brothers who lived in the forest near her house.

It was winter, the middle of January. Toward dusk
the stepmother opened the door a bit and watched the
blizzard outside. Then she said to her stepdaughter,
"Go on out into the woods and pick some snowdrops.
Tomorrow is your sister's birthday."

The girl looked at her stepmother. Was she joking,
or was she really sending her into the forest? How could
you ever find snowdrops now? You couldn't find them
until March no matter how hard you looked.

Her stepsister said to her, "Be off with you, and
don't come home without the flowers. Here, take this
basket."

Weeping, the girl wrapped herself in a tattered shawl
and went outside. The snow blown by the wind stung
her eyes and kept trying to tear her shawl away from
her. She marched ahead, just barely able to move
through the deep drifts.

Everything grew dark. She entered the forest, and there it was completely black; she couldn't see her hands in front of her face.

Suddenly, far off, a light gleamed from between the trees—like a star caught in the branches. The girl went in the direction of the light. She quickened her stride and soon she emerged into a clearing. There she came to a startled halt.

The clearing was bright, bright like sunlight. In the middle of it a big bonfire was burning, and its flames leaped upward nearly to the sky. Around the bonfire men were seated, some close to the fire and some farther back. They were sitting there and conversing quietly. They were all beautifully dressed—some in silver, some in gold, some in green velvet.

The girl began to count them, and there were twelve. Three were old, three were of middle age, three were young. And the three remaining were mere boys.

All of a sudden one old man—the tallest, with a beard and with bushy eyebrows—turned about and looked at the girl. The old man asked loudly, "Where are you from? What do you want here?"

The girl showed him her empty basket and said, "I have to fill this basket with snowdrops."

The old man laughed. "Snowdrops in January? You must be joking!"

"It wasn't my idea," the girl replied. "It was my stepmother who sent me here to pick snowdrops and who told me not to come home with an empty basket."

Then and there all twelve looked at her and began to talk with each other. The girl stood there and listened, but she did not understand their words, which were like the sound of the wind in the leaves. They talked and talked and then fell silent.

The tall old man turned to the girl and asked, "What will happen to you if you don't find snowdrops? After all, they don't appear until March."

"I will stay in the forest," said the girl. "I will wait for the month of March. It's better to freeze in the woods than to return home without snowdrops." She started sobbing.

Then all of a sudden, the youngest of the twelve got up and went over to the old man. "Brother January, let me take your place for just an hour!"

The old man stroked his long beard and said, "I would let you take my place, but you can't have March coming before February."

"Oh, all right," said another old man. "Go ahead and let him take your place. I'm not going to object! We all know the girl very well; we have run into her at the ice hole with buckets and in the woods with bundles of firewood. We have to help her now."

"Well, so be it," said January.

He knocked with his icy crook and things grew quiet in the forest. The trees stopped crackling from the frosts, and snow fell in large, soft clumps.

"Well, now it's your turn," said January, and he gave the crook to his brother February.

February in his turn knocked with the crook. Just then a stormy, wet wind howled through the branches. Snow clumps whirled in the air, and white gales stormed over the earth.

Then February gave his icy crook to his younger brother and said, "Now it's your turn, brother March."

The younger brother took the crook and struck the earth. The girl watched and saw it was no longer an icy crook. It was a big branch covered with buds.

The girl spread her arms in astonishment. Beneath her feet lay the soft earth of early spring. All about her she heard the sounds of dripping, flowing, gurgling. The buds on the branches were bursting, and the first little green leaves were already peering out from under the dark carpet of leaves.

"What are you standing there for?" March asked her. "You'd better hurry! My brothers made a gift to us of just one hour."

The girl ran into the forest to look for snowdrops. They were all over! She picked a basketful and filled her apron, too. Soon she returned to the clearing where the bonfire had been burning, where the twelve brothers had been sitting.

But now there was no bonfire, and there were no brothers. The clearing was bright—but not as before. The light came not from a bonfire but from a full moon that had risen over the forest.

The girl felt sorry that there was no one to thank. She ran home, and the full moon floated behind her. She ran right up to her own door, and the moment she got indoors once again, the winter blizzard howled outside and the moon hid behind clouds.

"Well, well!" exclaimed the stepmother and her daughter. "So you've come home? But where are the snowdrops?"

The girl poured the snowdrops from her apron onto the table and put the basket alongside it. The stepmother and her daughter exclaimed, "Where did you find them?"

The girl told them exactly what had happened to her. They didn't know whether to believe her or not. It was hard to believe her, but right there on the table lay a whole pile of snowdrops.

The stepmother and her daughter looked at one another and asked her, "Did the months give you anything else?"

"I didn't ask them for anything else."

"What a little fool you are!" said the sister. "You had the good luck to meet all the twelve months, and you didn't ask them for anything except snowdrops! Now if I had been in your place, I would have known what to ask for. I would have asked one of them for sweet apples and pears. I would have asked another for ripe strawberries and another still for mushrooms and still another for cucumbers!"

"You're very clever, daughter dear!" said the stepmother. "Strawberries and pears could bring any price at all in wintertime. We could have sold them and made much money! Get dressed as warmly as you can, daughter, and go to that clearing. They won't outsmart *you*, even though there are twelve of them and one of you."

"Certainly not!" the daughter replied. She wrapped her shawl about her head and ran off into the forest.

She hurried along, following her sister's tracks. The forest kept getting thicker and thicker, darker and darker.

She saw a light at a distance, just like a star caught in the branches. She went in the direction of the light. She walked and she walked, and finally she emerged into a clearing. In the middle of the clearing a big bonfire was burning, and around the bonfire sat twelve brothers, the twelve months. They sat there and conversed quietly.

The stepmother's daughter went right up to the bonfire. She did not bow, and she did not utter a word of friendly greeting. She picked the warmest place of all and started to warm herself.

The month-brothers kept their silence. The forest fell silent. Suddenly January knocked with his crook on the ground. "Who may you be?" he asked. "Where did you come from?"

"From home," the stepmother's daughter replied. "Just now you gave my sister a whole basket of snow-drops. I followed her trail here."

"We know your sister," said January. "But you we have never seen before. Why did you come to us?"

"For some gifts. I want the month of June to pour some strawberries into my basket, and I want them to be large ones, too. I want July to give me fresh cucumbers and the very best mushrooms. I want August to give me some apples and sweet pears. From September I want ripe walnuts. From October . . ."

"Just wait a minute," said January. "Summer cannot come before spring, nor spring before winter. It's a long time till June. Right now I am master in the forest. And I intend to rule here for thirty-one days."

"I didn't come to talk to you anyway," said the stepmother's daughter. "There's nothing to be had from you but snow and frost. I need the summer months."

January frowned. "Just you try to find summer in the winter!" he said.

He waved his great sleeve, and a snowstorm rose from the ground up to the heavens. The snowstorm wrapped itself around the stepmother's daughter. She fell into a drift and the snow covered her over.

The stepmother kept waiting and waiting for her daughter. She kept looking out the window and running to the door. But the daughter did not come. So the stepmother dressed herself up warmly and went into the forest. She walked and walked and searched and searched until she herself froze. And that's how both of them remained in the forest to wait for summer.

The stepdaughter lived a long life. She grew up and got married and raised a family.

People say that she had about her house a garden more wonderful than anything you have seen. In it the flowers bloomed, the berries and apples and pears ripened before anyplace else. When elsewhere it was hot, there it was cool. When elsewhere there was a snowstorm, there things were quiet.

People used to say, "That woman has all the months of the year as her guests."

Who knows? Maybe that is how it was.

Thinking and Writing About the Selection

1. How did the girl get the snowdrops her stepmother asked her to bring home?
2. Why was March the youngest of the Month-Brothers?
3. Why do you think the Month-Brothers refused to give the stepmother's daughter what she wanted?
4. What is your favorite season? Why do you like it more than the others?

Applying the Key Skill
Sequence of Events

Complete the following sentences about the events in "The Month-Brothers."

1. The stepmother told her stepdaughter to go into the woods and find snowdrops because the next day was ___.
2. The girl thought her stepmother was joking because it was ___ and you usually couldn't find snowdrops until ___.
3. When Brother January knocked with the icy crook, ___.
4. When Brother February knocked with the crook, ___.
5. When the younger brother struck the earth, ___.
6. As soon as the girl was safely inside the house, ___.

CAUSE AND EFFECT

You know that an **effect** is a result, or what happens. You also know that a **cause** is the reason something happens. Figuring out cause-and-effect relationships is one way to understand what you read.

Writers often use signal words such as *because*, *in order to*, *since*, or *so* to relate a cause and effect. When signal words are not used, you can still find causes and effects. You can ask yourself, "Are the two events related?" If the answer is yes, you can go on to the next step. Ask yourself, "How are they related? What happened? Why did it happen?"

Read the sentences below. Look for a cause-and-effect relationship.

Chlorophyll (klôr′ ə fil) is a green substance found in many plants. The leaves of these plants are green.

EFFECT: Leaves are green.
CAUSE: Leaves contain chlorophyll.

ACTIVITY   Read the paragraphs about leaves. Then copy the chart. Fill in the missing information about the cause-and-effect relationships.

Leaves, like other living things, are made up of cells. Chloroplasts (klôr′ ə plasts) are small "packages" inside leaf cells. These packages contain substances of different colors. Chlorophyll is green. Other substances are yellow and orange. In the summer, the green color covers up the yellow and orange colors. That is why leaves are green all summer.

Leaves get water through tubes in their stems. In the fall, a layer of cork grows over these tubes. No water can get into the leaf. Without water, the green chlorophyll fades and disappears. Then the orange and yellow colors can be seen. That is why many leaves turn yellow or orange in the fall.

CAUSE	EFFECT
	Leaves are green in summer.
A layer of cork grows over the tubes in a leaf's stem.	
	Leaves are yellow or orange in the fall.

Wetlands

Lewis Buck

You have read about
deserts and forests.
This article introduces
another kind of place—
wetlands. As you read,
notice the changes
that take place in
the watery worlds the
author describes.

When most of us look around the places where we live, we see mainly dry land. If you look at a globe of the earth, however, you will see less dry land than land covered by water—the oceans, seas, and lakes. In fact, more than two-thirds of the earth is water.

If there were no mountains and valleys under the oceans and on the land, we would all have to be very good swimmers. The sea would be about a mile and a half deep everywhere.

Water does cover the land in some places. These places are not deep enough to be called by watery names like pond, lake, sea, or ocean. They are deep enough, however, so that they are not called fields and forests. We call these places marshes, swamps, and bogs. The name we give them all together is *wetlands*.

Places where water stands upon the land and grasses grow are *marshes*. Not all the plants that live in marshes are

483

grasses, but to most people they look like grasses.

Wetlands where trees are growing with their roots beneath the water are called *swamps*. Sometimes people, or beavers, may dam a woodland stream. Water will flood the surrounding forest. For a while such places may look like a swamp. But the trees will not live another year. Only certain trees can live with their roots always under water and make a swamp.

Perhaps the strangest wetland of all is the *bog*. From its edge you can see that the bog is covered with low bushes. The ground looks solid and a little lumpy. When you walk on the ground, though, you find that it bounces. The real floor of the bog may be fifteen feet below you. You are standing on a layer of plants that are floating on water.

MARSH

SWAMP

BOG

Floating Plants

Water

485

The Changing Earth

All wetlands are places that are slowly changing from water to dry land. It may take many years, but every pond or lake is changing to a forest.

Let us see how these changes come about. We'll use a pond for an example. For a pond you have to have a hole in the ground. When it rains, water runs into the hole. Is that all that runs in? How about dirt? Dirt is pushed into the hole by the rain water. After many years the rain washes in enough dirt to fill the hole.

Something else is happening at the same time. Things other than dirt are getting into the hole. Plants and animals are moving in.

The first plants may live completely under water. They may be so small that you need a microscope to see them. Or they may have roots in the dirt and long stems and leaves. They do not need to stick their leaves out into the air. We call

POND

MARSH   SWAMP

486

FOREST

these *submergent plants.* They grow, make new plants, and die. The dead ones sink to the bottom of the pond and help build up the soil.

Then come plants that are rooted to the bottom, with their stems, leaves, and flowers standing up above the water. They could not live if the water did not cover their roots at least part of the time, but their tops need the air. We call these *emergent plants.* They are the beginning of the marsh.

As more and more plants die and become part of the soil, there is less and less room for water. The soil becomes firmer. Bushes and trees can grow. The pond has become a swamp.

As time goes on, more dead plants are added to the soil. More dirt washes in. The ground becomes higher and drier. Trees that do not need wet soil all the time will take the places of the swamp trees. The swamp has become a forest.

487

Wetland Communities

In order to live, plants and animals need food, shelter, and room to grow. The plants and animals that live together in one place and provide food for each other make up a *community*. There are many different kinds of wetland communities.

Along slow rivers, where the water spreads out over low ground, we find freshwater marshes and some swamps. Arrowhead, bulrush, and cattail grow in the river marshes. You can see the homes of muskrats and hear the calls of blackbirds.

The swamps do not all look alike. Drier swamps will look much like an ordinary forest. Where water covers the ground all the time you will find trees like the bald cypress. Its roots grow up in knobs that look like "knees" poking out of the water. In the swamps you might also catch a glimpse of wood ducks. They build nests in holes in trees high over the water.

Where rivers empty into the ocean, fresh and salt water mix together. We call this mixture *brackish water*.

In brackish water very tall grasses called reeds, build marshes with their roots. The roots grow in a thick tangle. They catch and hold dirt and mud washed down by the river.

Reeds have been used in the past to thatch roofs, to make musical pipes, and even to build small boats. Because they help to clean water that has been polluted, they are very useful right where they grow.

What's There to Eat?

Animals that live in salt and brackish marshes stay out of sight most of the time. If you want to find them you have to be patient.

You may see a marsh hawk or a short-eared owl flying low over the marsh searching for mice and small birds. Or you may see herons that visit the marsh to eat. They are long-legged birds that wade in

489

shallow water. They catch fish and crabs with their long bills.

You will be lucky if you catch a glimpse of sparrows that nest and feed in the marsh. They do not fly far even when you scare them up. Sparrows creep about in the grass so that you might mistake them for mice. Easier to see are the ducks that nest and feed in the salt marshes.

You will probably have no trouble finding mosquitoes and tiny biting flies. At least, they will have no trouble finding you. They are only two out of many kinds of insects that have been found in salt marshes. Most of them will not bother you. Many of them eat plants. Some eat other insects.

Like every other animal in a community, insects are part of a *food chain*. Plants make their own food with the help of sunlight, soil, water, and air. Some animals eat the plants. Still other animals eat them.

Even mosquitoes are an important part of a food chain. Young insects, called larvae, feed on decaying plants. Small fish, such as the killifish, eat all the larvae they can get. In turn, the killifish are eaten by larger fish from the sea, such as the bluefish. Bluefish are a favorite seafood of many people.

Who Needs It?

Many people have looked at a marsh and asked, "Who needs it?" It seems empty and flat and useless. It isn't shady and cool like a forest. It isn't dry like a meadow. You can't have a picnic and play baseball in it.

Some marshes have been used as dumps. They have been filled with trash. Others have been filled with rocks and dirt. They have been covered with cement to make parking lots or to build houses or factories.

When this is done, the marshes are gone. When the marshes go, the seafood fishers will go because there will be nothing to catch.

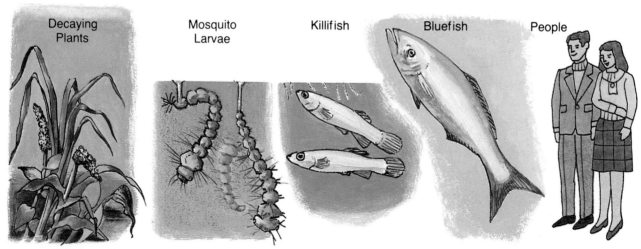

Decaying Plants   Mosquito Larvae   Killifish   Bluefish   People

FOOD CHAIN

Along the coast, the marsh food chain is part of the food chain of the sea. Young fish of many kinds seek food and shelter in the marshes. Other fish that may not enter the marshes also get food from them.

A salt or a brackish marsh produces more food in a year than a farm the same size would. You don't even have to farm it. In fact, a marsh is better off if you leave it alone. The plants and animals of the marsh live—and die—and decay. They become foodstuff this way.

Each time the tide goes out it carries some of the decaying foodstuff with it to waiting shellfish, like mussels, clams, oysters, shrimp, crabs, and lobsters.

For anyone who can see the fishing boats beyond the marshes, the answer to "Who needs marshes?" is: "People need marshes."

People need all kinds of wetlands. They need bogs to explore and enjoy. They need marshes to shelter and feed ducks and geese and muskrats. They need swamps to slow down floods and to keep big storm waves from washing away the land.

People need wetlands. But wetlands could get along nicely without people.

Thinking and Writing About the Selection

1. What are three kinds of wetlands? What are all wetlands slowly changing into?
2. How do reeds help keep the water in a marsh clean?
3. Why would destroying the mosquitoes in a marsh be harmful?
4. Do you think "wetlands could get along nicely without people"? Why or why not?

Applying the Key Skill
Main Idea

Read the paragraphs listed from "Wetlands" below. Then choose the best main idea statement for each paragraph.

1. third paragraph
   a. Water covers the land in some places.
   b. Some bodies of water are called pond, lake, sea, or ocean.
   c. Wetlands include marshes, swamps and bogs.
2. sixth paragraph
   a. The bog is probably the strangest wetland.
   b. A bog is really a layer of plants that are floating on water.
   c. The real floor of a bog may be fifteen feet below the surface you walk on.
3. fourth paragraph under "The Changing Earth"
   a. Some submergent plants are so small that you need a microscope to see them.
   b. The leaves of submergent plants do not stick out into the air.
   c. Submergent plants live completely under water.

COMPARISON PARAGRAPHS

Prewrite

"The Living Desert" and "Wetlands" describe two important kinds of places in our world. These two kinds of places, while different, are also alike. The desert and wetlands are alike because water is important to both. They are also alike because people can be dangerous to their survival.

You are going to write two comparison paragraphs. In your paragraphs you will compare and give examples of how the desert and wetlands are alike.

Read these questions and then reread the selections. Make notes of possible answers. As you reread, try to compare what you already know about these places to the information the authors give. Discuss possible answers with other students.

1. How is water the key to the origin of the desert and the wetlands?

2. How does water maintain plant life?
   Think: Why do paloverde, acacia, and ironwood grow on the banks of the arroyo?
   Think: Why do reeds grow in marshes by the sea?

3. How could people be a danger to wetlands and the desert?
   Think: How could building homes and communities be a danger to the desert and wetlands?
   Think: How could pollution be a danger?

Write

1. Reread your notes. The first paragraph should use the answers to Questions 1 and 2. One way to write a main idea sentence for your paragraph is to turn Question 1 into a statement.

> Water is the key to the origin of the desert and wetlands.

2. Your second paragraph will present your answers to Question 3. Again, try turning the question into a statement for the main idea sentence.

3. Try to use Vocabulary Treasures in your paragraphs.

4. Now write the first draft of your paragraphs.

VOCABULARY TREASURES

conserve	dilemma
require	necessary

Revise

Read your paragraphs. Have a friend read them, too. Think about this checklist as you revise.

1. Do the detail sentences in each paragraph relate to the main idea sentence?

2. Did you use verbs in your sentences other than *is*, *are*, *was*, and *were*? Use Vocabulary Treasures or the Glossary for help.

3. Did you proofread your paragraphs for correct spelling and end punctuation in sentences?

4. Did you try to join some sentences with *but* or *however* to show comparison?

5. Now rewrite your paragraphs to share.

ELISABETH and the MARSH MYSTERY

Felice Holman

*Strange sounds are coming from the marsh.
Elisabeth wants to know who or what is making
them. Elisabeth's father thinks that it might be
their neighbor, Stewart Peebles. Stewart has a
bugle that he likes to play. Elisabeth knows that
ever since Stewart got braces, he hasn't been
playing his bugle. Mrs. Peebles and another
neighbor, Mrs. Munch, have reported seeing a
strange bird—a long-legged one that half flew
and half ran into the marsh.*

*Elisabeth and her father try to identify the
bird described by their neighbors. First they look
for clues in a bird book. Then they decide to ask
for help from Mr. Thew, who works at a wildlife
museum. Mr. Thew believes that the bird could be
an escaped "exotic," a bird from another country
that may have escaped from a zoo. Mr. Thew
agrees to join Elisabeth and her father one evening
to search in the marsh for the mysterious bird.*

Elisabeth and Papa set out to meet Mr. Thew in
the marsh. They had walked only two steps, from
the kitchen door to the middle of the porch, when
Papa tripped over something. Then the something
sat up and said, "Hello," in a husky voice.

"Stewart!" exclaimed Elisabeth. "What are you
doing?"

"Waiting for you to come and hunt for it. I knew
you would."

"Oh, you are clever, Stewart!" Stewart grinned
with pleasure, the bright silver braces on his teeth
gleaming and flashing. Elisabeth was glad Stewart
had joined them.

As they neared the marsh, the reeds got thicker and the ground wetter. Then the bugle call suddenly sounded.

"That's him!" cried Elisabeth.

"We really need a blind for this kind of work," said Stewart. Then he explained to Elisabeth, "That means we need someplace to hide so that the bird doesn't see *us* but we can see *him*. Maybe we should all climb a tree."

Papa looked about for a good place. "In this case, I agree with you, Stewart. This ground is awfully wet to sit on, or even stand on, for long." With that, Elisabeth climbed up to the low limb of a willow tree, where she was nearly hidden by its weeping branches. Stewart and Papa settled on branches near Elisabeth.

Just then the bugle sounded again, and there was a sudden splash.

A night heron unbent his legs, unfolded his neck, and, giving a loud *guark*, flew off over the marsh.

The splash was Stewart. He had fallen out of the tree into the shallow water. "I guess I dozed off," he said sleepily. "Gosh, that sound was close!"

Papa climbed down from the tree and pulled Stewart out of the muddy water. Elisabeth was climbing down from her branch just as Mr. Thew arrived.

"Hello, everybody," he said. "Quite a stalking party! Now tell me all over again about this matter."

Everybody talked at once. Mr. Thew tapped his forehead and looked thoughtful. "Well, let's creep

along here quietly and see what we can see," he decided.

Just then the bugle sounded quite close. Mr. Thew looked surprised. "My word!" he said. "Let's get down low."

They lay very still in the deep grasses, looking toward a clearing in the meadow. Suddenly, right in front of them, the bugle call sounded loud and clear. And then they saw the most extraordinary thing! Right there at the edge of the marsh an enormous gray bird began dancing. *Dancing!*

He leaped high in the clearing, then turned and bowed to an imaginary partner. He leaped again, turned, bowed; leaped, turned, bowed. Then he gave one of his loud bugle calls and leaped again; a few small dancing steps, a turn, a bow, a leap, and a bugle call.

Elisabeth, Stewart, Papa, and Mr. Thew watched, their eyes wide with amazement. Quite suddenly the bird stopped dancing, stepped into the water, and started to look for fish and frogs. He walked slowly out of sight.

"I don't believe it!" said Papa.

"In all my life," said Elisabeth, "I never saw a bird dancing."

"For a good reason," said Mr. Thew. "This bird, as far as I know, is scarcely ever, *if* ever, seen in this part of the country. He belongs way out West."

"But what *is* it?" asked Elisabeth.

"A sandhill crane," said Mr. Thew. "*A sandhill crane!* I don't believe it myself."

"This crane doesn't live around here," said Papa. "That's why, even when I saw his picture in the bird

book, I didn't give him a second thought. Besides, you'll remember that neither Mrs. Peebles nor Mrs. Munch mentioned its most special marking."

"His bright-red forehead!" said Elisabeth. "No one said a word about it. All they said was how big he was. But how did he get here?"

"My guess," said Mr. Thew, "is that he got lost." He picked up a stick and drew an outline on

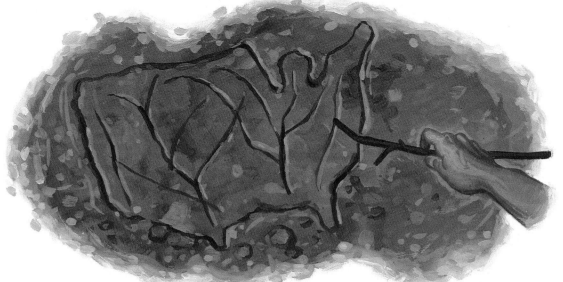

the ground. "Look, this is a rough drawing of the United States. Now, there are four important flyways where birds migrate. See, like this—one on each coast and two up the middle. The flyways cross each other in some places. This crane is probably a young first-year bird who may have gotten a little mixed up at the crossroads and, perhaps, joined up with a flight of geese who were coming this way."

"Now he's all alone," cried Elisabeth. "All his family and the other cranes are somewhere else. What can he do? Can he ever find them?"

Mr. Thew looked thoughtful. "You see, sandhill cranes all migrate along these middle flyways. That's a long way from here. Mmmmm. Now, let's think."

While they sat there the moon came up, and the sounds of the marsh sounded stranger than ever in the night. Elisabeth and Stewart started to get sleepy, but Papa and Mr. Thew went on talking quietly. Suddenly Mr. Thew said, "Aha! That's it!" and jumped up and went off toward the road.

"Where's he going?" Elisabeth asked, coming awake suddenly.

"He's got a few useful things in the museum truck that he left parked out on the lane. I'll let him show you what he has in mind himself."

Mr. Thew was back in a few minutes with some tools on his back and what looked like a hammock under his arm. Then, by the light of the moon and the flashlights held by Elisabeth and Stewart, Papa and Mr. Thew began to put together a very strange contraption.

Right on the edge of the marsh meadow, where they had last seen the sandhill crane, they dug a deep hole. The hole gathered a bit of water at the bottom because of the damp ground. Then they laid the hammock-looking thing across the hole and attached it by ropes to two nearby trees.

When Elisabeth heard that it was called a snare, she was worried. "You won't hurt him," she begged.

"Not a bit," said Mr. Thew. "You see, when the bird steps on it, the net will sink into the hole with the crane right on it. Meanwhile, these ropes will

close the top of the net like a bag. Then we'll handle him very carefully."

"Well, that's all right, then, I guess," said Elisabeth. "But when we have him, what will we do with him?"

"I'll tell you *that* when we get him," said Mr. Thew.

"Now, all we have to do is wait," Papa said. Just then a voice from across the meadow called, "Stewart! Time for bed!"

"Time for you, too," Papa said to Elisabeth. "We won't catch this bird until he gets up in the morning, so you won't miss a thing."

"I'll come by for you in the museum truck first thing in the morning," Mr. Thew said. "Good night."

"Good night," they called to Mr. Thew as they walked back through the meadow in the moonlight.

It was very early and still dark when Papa awakened Elisabeth. "Get dressed warmly," he said.

Just as Papa and Elisabeth stepped out onto the lawn, Mr. Thew drove up in the museum truck. There was an enormous wooden crate on the back of it. "Hop in!" he said.

"Let's stop for Stewart," said Elisabeth. "He won't want to miss it."

They didn't even have to ring the bell at the Peebles'. Stewart was waiting.

Mr. Thew drove on down the lane and parked the truck as close to the marsh as he could get. Then they walked across the meadow.

The long grasses brushed them wetly as they neared the edge of the marsh, where the snare was set. Mr. Thew, who was leading the way, suddenly held up his hand.

They all stood still in silence for a moment, and then Mr. Thew walked to the snare. He waved his arm, signaling them to come closer.

There he was! The sandhill crane—quiet now and probably puzzled—wrapped like a gift in netting.

"The *exotic!*" gasped Elisabeth. "But the thing is, now that we have him, what *are* we going to do with him?"

"Aha!" said Papa. "I think perhaps Mr. Thew will tell you about that now."

"Well, here's the story," said Mr. Thew as he started untying the ropes from the trees. "We all know sandhill cranes just don't belong around here. Right?"

"Right!" Elisabeth and Stewart said at once.

"Now, since birds migrate on a pretty good timetable, like the trains, you can tell where they'll be a certain time of year. It just happens we know that a very large flock of sandhill cranes is due at this time at a big reservation in Indiana. I spoke to one of the bird experts at the zoo. What we think is that we might be able to put him on an airplane that will set him down right near the reservation so that he can join the rest of the cranes."

Mr. Thew cut a long pole from a sapling, and he and Papa arranged it so that they could carry the sandhill crane in its net to the truck. There they set him gently in the crate, loosened the net, and put the top on the crate.

Stewart was dropped off at his house. He couldn't go with them to the airport because there

was something else he had to do. Papa, Elisabeth, Mr. Thew, and the sandhill crane rode into the city and out to the airport.

It took a long time to work things out with the airline people. Finally everything was arranged, and the great plane took off in a *whoosh*—almost, Elisabeth thought, like a heron in the marsh.

When they got back home it was late. Elisabeth dropped tiredly, but happily, into the big chair in Papa's study. It seemed a long, long time since she had sat in this chair looking at the bird book with Papa. But it was just yesterday, at this same time of day.

Papa sat down, too, and put his head back and sighed. Then, suddenly, he sat up very straight.

"Oh, no! Not again!" he exclaimed.

"What is it, Papa?" Elisabeth asked.

"Listen!" Papa shouted. "Just listen to that! It's *another* exotic."

Elisabeth closed her eyes tight and listened for a moment. Sure enough, an unmistakable sound was carried on the evening breeze, across the marsh and the meadow, and into the house.

Then Elisabeth laughed. "Oh, Papa, *that's Stewart!* That's what he had to do today—have the braces taken off his teeth. *Now* he can play the bugle. Isn't that wonderful!"

Papa wrinkled up his forehead in what started to be a frown. Then he looked at Elisabeth and laughed instead. "Wonderful!" he said.

Thinking and Writing About the Selection

1. What extraordinary thing did the sandhill crane do?
2. Why wasn't the crane frightened by all the people who had come to find it?
3. Do you think the sandhill crane could have found its way to Indiana without help? Explain your answer.

 4. Write a short description of the sandhill crane. Make sure you don't forget any important details.

Applying the Key Skill
Context Clues

Read the sentences about "Elisabeth and the Marsh Mystery" below. Use context clues to choose the meaning of each underlined word. Then write each word and its meaning.

1. Roger, Elisabeth, and Elisabeth's father met to search for the strange bird. "This is quite a stalking party," said Mr. Thew.
   a. hunting   b. large
   c. dangerous   d. sneaky

2. Mr. Thew untied the ropes from the trees. Then he cut a long pole from a sapling.
   a. stick   b. young tree
   c. bush   d. small branch

3. Papa was positive that he heard another crane. The sound was unmistakable.
   a. barely heard   b. not clear
   c. easily seen   d. plain

AWARD CLASSICS WINNERS

SOUNDS OF SPRING

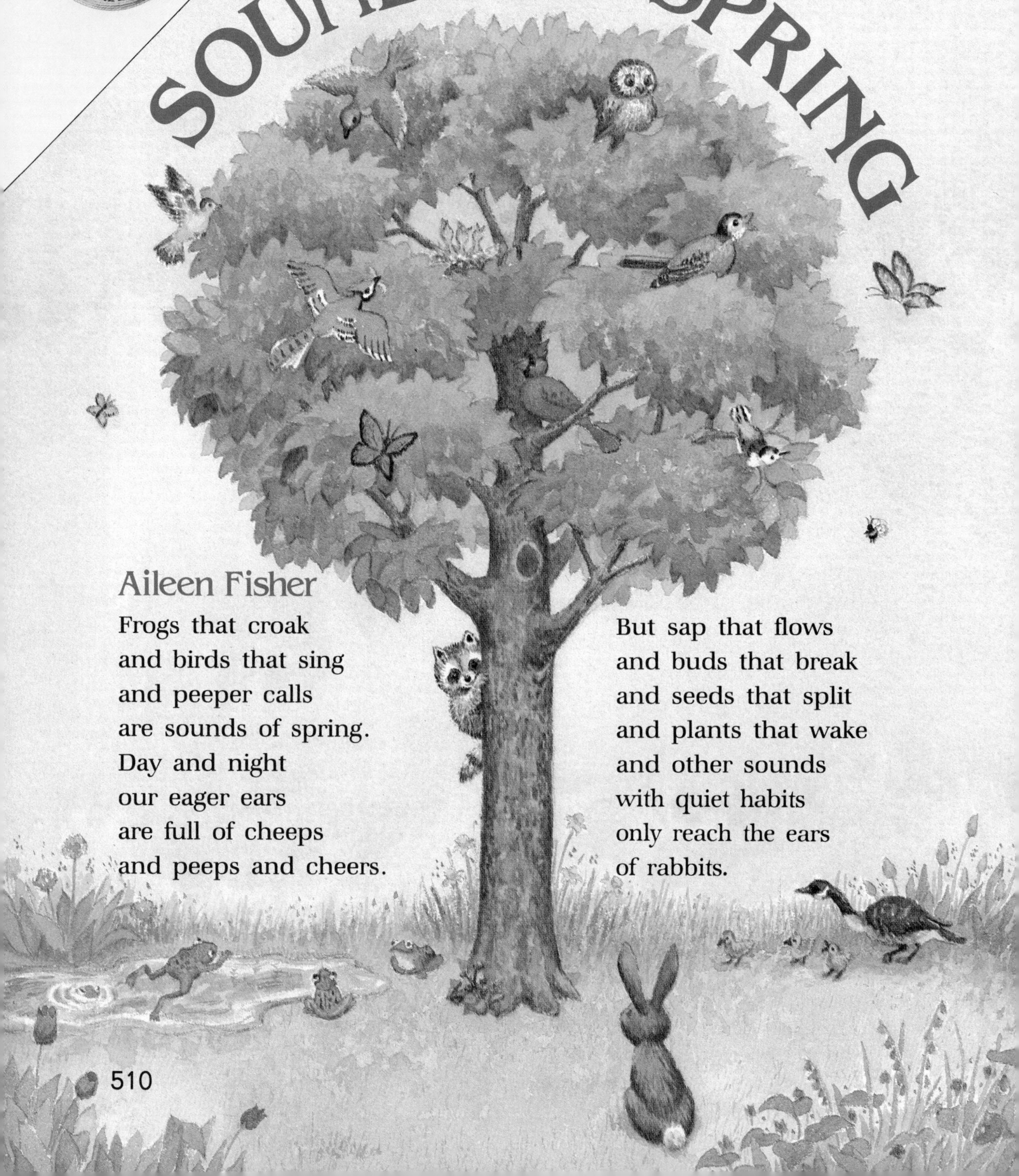

Aileen Fisher

Frogs that croak
and birds that sing
and peeper calls
are sounds of spring.
Day and night
our eager ears
are full of cheeps
and peeps and cheers.

But sap that flows
and buds that break
and seeds that split
and plants that wake
and other sounds
with quiet habits
only reach the ears
of rabbits.

Fizz, Buzz, and Sizzle

What do the words *splash*, *croak*, *cheep*, and *peep* have in common? Read the words aloud and listen to their sounds. The words all describe sounds, and the sound of each word itself has something to do with its meaning. *Splash*, *croak*, *cheep*, and *peep* are examples of special kinds of words we call onomatopoetic (on′ ə mat′ ə pō et′ ik) words. **Onomatopoetic** words are words whose sounds echo or suggest their meanings. The use of onomatopoetic words is called *onomatopoeia* (on′ ə mat′ ə pē′ ə). *Onomatopoeia* comes from two Greek words meaning "to make a word or name." Onomatopoetic words were made up to name sounds.

Onomatopoetic words are often found in poetry. They are also found in other kinds of writing and used in everyday speech. Onomatopoeia helps make our language, especially as it is spoken, more expressive. Compare these two sentences by reading them aloud: *The cat made a contented sound. The cat purred.* Which is more poetic? Now reread the poem "Sounds of Spring" to see how the author used onomatopoeia.

If you say a word aloud, you can usually decide whether it is onomatopoetic. Which words below are onomatopoetic?

hoot	plop	call	meow	fizz
hit	write	hiss	clink	keep
sizzle	buzz	roar	answer	soar

Can you think of other examples of onomatopoetic words? Can you make some up?

The Trumpeter Swans

E.B. WHITE

Spring has come to the Canadian wilderness. Animals wake up to the good smell of the thawing earth. The sound of birds fills the air. One sound rises above the rest, "ko-hoh, ko-hoh," the trumpeting of swans. Two trumpeter swans descend to the shore of a pond. After a long journey, they have found the place to build their nest.

Sam Beaver, who is camping with his father, hears the cries of the swans. He will soon discover their nesting place.

he swan stepped cautiously out onto the island. The spot seemed made to order—just right for a nesting place. While the male swan floated close by, watching, she snooped about until she found a pleasant spot on the ground. She sat down, to see how it felt to be sitting there. She decided it was the right size for her body. It was nicely located, a couple of feet from the water's edge. Very convenient. She turned to her husband.

"What do you think?" she said.

"An ideal location!" he replied. "A perfect place! And I will tell you *why* it's a perfect place," he continued, majestically. "If an enemy—a fox or a coon or a coyote or a skunk—wanted to reach this spot with murder in his heart, he'd have to enter the water and get wet. And before he could enter the water, he'd have to walk the whole length of that point of land. And by that time we'd see him or hear him, and I would give him a hard time."

The male stretched out his great wings, eight feet from tip to tip, and gave the water a mighty clout to show

513

his strength. This made him feel better right away. When a Trumpeter Swan hits an enemy with his wing, it is like being hit by a baseball bat. A male swan, by the way, is called a "cob." No one knows why, but that's what he's called. A good many animals have special names: a male goose is called a gander, a male cow is called a bull, a male sheep is called a ram, a male chicken is called a rooster, and so on. Anyway, the thing to remember is that a male swan is called a cob.

The cob's wife pretended not to notice that her husband was showing off, but she saw it, all right, and she was proud of his strength and his courage. As husbands go, he was a good one.

The cob watched his beautiful wife sitting there on the tiny island. To his great joy, he saw her begin to turn slowly round and around, keeping always in the same spot, treading the mud and grass. She was making the first motions of nesting. First she squatted down in the place she had chosen. Then she twisted round and around, tamping the earth with her broad webbed feet, hollowing it out to make it like a saucer. Then she reached out and pulled twigs and grasses toward her and dropped them at her sides and under her tail, shaping the nest to her body.

The cob floated close to his mate. He studied every move she made.

"Now another medium-sized stick, my love," he said. And she poked her splendid long white graceful neck as far as it would go, picked up a stick, and placed it at her side.

"Now another bit of coarse grass," said the cob, with great dignity.

The female reached for grasses, for moss, for twigs—anything that was handy. Slowly, carefully, she built up the nest until she was sitting on a big grassy mound. She worked at the task for a couple of hours, then knocked off for the day and slid into the pond again, to take a drink and have lunch.

"A fine start!" said the cob, as he gazed back at the nest. "A perfect beginning! I don't know how you manage it so cleverly."

"It comes naturally," replied his wife. "There's a lot of work to it, but on the whole it is pleasant work."

"Yes," said the cob. "And when you're done, you have something to show for your trouble—you have a swan's nest, six feet across. What other bird can say that?"

"Well," said his wife, "maybe an eagle can say it."

"Yes, but in that case it wouldn't be a swan's nest, it would be an eagle's nest, and it would be high up in some old dead tree somewhere, instead of right down near the water, with all the conveniences that go with water."

They both laughed at this. Then they began trumpeting and splashing and scooping up water and throwing it on their backs, darting about as though they had suddenly gone crazy with delight.

"Ko-hoh! Ko-hoh! Ko-hoh!" they cried.

Every wild creature within a mile and a half of the pond heard the trumpeting of the swans. The fox heard,

the raccoon heard, the skunk heard. One pair of ears heard that did not belong to a wild creature. But the swans did not know that.

One day, almost a week later, the swan slipped quietly into her nest and laid an egg. Each day she tried to deposit one egg in the nest. Sometimes she succeeded, and sometimes she didn't. There were now three eggs, and she was ready to lay a fourth.

As she sat there, with her husband, the cob, floating gracefully nearby, she had a strange feeling that she was being watched. It made her uneasy. Birds don't like to be stared at. They particularly dislike being stared at when they are on a nest. So the swan twisted and turned and peered everywhere. She gazed intently at the point of land that jutted out into the pond near the nest. With her sharp eyes, she searched the nearby shore for signs of an intruder. What she finally saw gave her the surprise of her life. There, seated on a log on the point of land, was a small boy. He was being very quiet, and he had no gun.

"Do you see what I see?" the swan whispered to her husband.

"No. What?"

"Over there. On that log. It's a boy! *Now* what are we going to do?"

"How did a boy get here?" whispered the cob. "We are deep in the wilds of Canada. There are no human beings for miles around."

"That's what I thought too," she replied. "But if that isn't a boy over there on that log, my name isn't Cygnus Buccinator."

The cob was furious. "I didn't fly all the way north into Canada to get involved with a *boy*," he said. "We came here to this idyllic spot, this remote little hideaway, so we could enjoy some well-deserved privacy."

"Well," said his wife, "I'm sorry to see the boy, too, but I must say he's behaving himself. He sees us, but he's not throwing stones. He's not throwing sticks. He's not messing around. He's simply observing."

"I do not *wish* to be observed," complained the cob. "I did not travel all this immense distance into the heart of Canada to be observed. Furthermore, I don't want *you* to be observed—except by me. You're laying an egg— that is, I *hope* you are—and you are entitled to privacy. It has been my experience that all boys throw stones and sticks—it is their nature. I'm going over and strike that boy with my powerful wing, and he'll think he has been hit with a billy club. I'll knock him cold!"

"Now, just wait a minute!" said the swan. "There's no use starting a fight. This boy is not bothering me at the moment. He's not bothering you either."

"But how did he *get* here?" said the cob, who was no longer talking in a whisper but was beginning to shout. "How did he get here? Boys can't fly, and there are no roads in this part of Canada. We're fifty miles from the nearest highway."

"Maybe he's lost," said the swan. "Maybe he's starving to death. Maybe he wants to rob the nest and eat the eggs, but I doubt it. He doesn't look hungry. Anyway, I've started this nest, and I have three beautiful eggs, and the boy's behaving himself at the moment, and I intend to go right ahead and try for a fourth egg."

"Good luck, my love!" said the cob. "I shall be here at your side to defend you if anything happens. Lay the egg!"

For the next hour, the cob paddled slowly round and around the tiny island, keeping watch. His wife remained quietly on the nest. Sam sat on his log, hardly moving a muscle. He was spellbound at the sight of the swans. They were the biggest water birds he had ever seen. He had heard their trumpeting and had searched the woods and swamps until he had found the pond and located the nest. Sam knew enough about birds to know that these were Trumpeters. Sam always felt happy when he was in a wild place among wild creatures. Sitting on his log, watching the swans, he had the same good feeling some people get when they are sitting in church.

After he had watched for an hour, Sam got up. He walked slowly and quietly away, putting one foot straight ahead of the other, Indian-fashion, hardly making a sound. The swans watched him go. When the female left the nest, she turned and looked back. There, lying safely in the soft feathers at the bottom of the nest, was the fourth egg. The cob waddled out onto the island and looked in the nest.

"A masterpiece!" he said. "An egg of supreme beauty and perfect proportions. I would say that that egg is almost five inches in length."

His wife was pleased.

When the swan had laid five eggs, she felt satisfied. She gazed at them proudly. Then she settled herself on the nest to keep her eggs warm. Carefully, she reached down with her bill and poked each egg until it was in just the right spot to receive the heat from her body. The cob cruised around close by, to keep her company and protect her from enemies. He knew that a fox prowled somewhere in the woods; he had heard him barking on nights when the hunting was good.

Days passed, and still the swan sat quietly on the five eggs. Nights passed. She sat and sat, giving her warmth to the eggs. No one disturbed her. The boy was gone—perhaps he would never come back. Inside of each egg, something was taking shape. As the weeks went by, the days grew longer, the nights grew shorter. When a rainy day came, the swan just sat still and let it rain.

"My dear," said her husband, the cob, one afternoon, "do you never find your duties onerous or irksome? Do you never tire of sitting in one place and in one position, covering the eggs, with no diversions, no pleasures, no escapades, or capers? Do you never suffer from boredom?"

"No," replied his wife. "Not really."

"Isn't it uncomfortable to sit on eggs?"

"Yes, it is," replied his wife. "But I can put up with a certain amount of discomfort for the sake of bringing young swans into the world."

"Do you know how many more days you must sit?" he asked.

"Haven't any idea," she said. "But I notice that the ducks at the other end of the pond have hatched their young ones; I notice that the Red-winged Blackbirds have hatched theirs, and the other evening I saw a Striped Skunk hunting along the shore, and she had four little skunks with her. So I think I must be getting near the end of my time. With any luck, we will soon be able to see our children—our beautiful little cygnets."

"Don't you ever feel the pangs of hunger or suffer the tortures of thirst?" asked the cob.

"Yes, I do," said his mate. "As a matter of fact, I could use a drink right now."

The afternoon was warm; the sun was bright. The swan decided she could safely leave her eggs for a few minutes. She stood up. First she pushed some loose feathers around the eggs, hiding them from view and giving them a warm covering in her absence. Then she stepped off the nest and entered the water. She took several quick drinks. Then she glided over to a shallow place, thrust her head underwater, and pulled up tender greens from the bottom. She next took a bath by tossing water over herself. Then she waddled out onto a grassy bank and stood there, preening her feathers.

The swan felt good. She had no idea that an enemy was near. She failed to notice the Red Fox as he watched her from his hiding place behind a clump of bushes. The fox had been attracted to the pond by the sound of splashing water. He hoped he would find a goose. Now he sniffed the air and smelled the swan. Her back was turned so he began creeping slowly toward her. The cob, her husband, was still floating on the pond. He spied the fox first.

"Look out!" he trumpeted. "Look out for the fox who is creeping toward you even as I speak, his eyes bright, his bushy tail out straight, his mind lusting for blood, his belly almost touching the ground! You are in grave danger, and we must act immediately."

While the cob was making this elegant speech of warning, something happened that surprised everybody. Just as the fox was about to spring and sink his teeth in the swan's neck, a stick came hurtling through the air. It struck the fox full on the nose, and he turned and ran away. The two swans couldn't imagine what had happened. Then they noticed a movement in the bushes. Out stepped Sam Beaver, the boy who had visited them a month ago. Sam was grinning. In his hand he held another stick, in case the fox should return. But the fox was in no mood to return. He had a very sore nose, and he had lost his appetite for fresh swan.

"Hello," said Sam in a low voice.

"Ko-hoh, ko-hoh!" replied the cob.

"Ko-hoh!" said his wife. The pond rang with the trumpet sounds—sounds of triumph over the fox, sounds of victory and gladness.

Sam was thrilled at the noise of swans, which some people say is like the sound of a French horn. He walked slowly around the shore to the little point of land near the island and sat down on his log. The swans now realized, beyond any doubt, that the boy was their friend. He had

525

saved the swan's life. He had been in the right place at the right time and with the right ammunition. The swans felt grateful. The cob swam over toward Sam, climbed out of the pond, and stood close to the boy, looking at him in a friendly way and arching his neck gracefully. Once, he ran his neck far out, cautiously, and almost touched the boy. Sam never moved a muscle. His heart thumped from excitement and joy.

The female paddled back to her nest and returned to the job of warming the eggs. She felt lucky to be alive.

That night before Sam crawled into his bunk at camp, he got out his notebook and found a pencil. This is what he wrote:

> I don't know of anything in the entire world more wonderful to look at than a nest with eggs in it. An egg, because it contains life, is the most perfect thing there is. It is beautiful and mysterious. An egg is a far finer thing than a tennis ball or a cake of soap. A tennis ball will always be just a tennis ball. A cake of soap will always be just a cake of soap—until it gets so small nobody wants it and they throw it away. But an egg will someday be a living creature. A swan's egg will open and out will come a little swan. A nest is almost as wonderful and mysterious as an egg. How does a bird know how to make a nest? Nobody ever taught her. How does a bird know how to build a nest?

Sam closed his notebook, said good night to his father, blew out his lamp, and climbed into his bunk. He lay there wondering how a bird knows how to build a nest. Pretty soon his eyes closed, and he was asleep.

Changes

As you grow, you change in many ways. Plants and animals also change. Places can change, too. In *Changes*, you read about three different places: deserts, forests, and wetlands. You found out about changes that happen in these places. You also discovered how scientists observe and record these changes. Perhaps after reading this unit, your understanding of and appreciation for nature has changed.

Thinking and Writing About *Changes*

1. What did Alan of "The Living Desert" think of the desert when he first saw it? How did his viewpoint change after he spent time there?
2. Do you think the Papago Indians described in "The Desert Is Theirs" would welcome changes in the desert places where they live? Why or why not?
3. What kinds of changes does Mia Monroe try to prevent in Muir Woods?
4. If you could live in a place that had only one season instead of four, what season would you choose? Why would you choose that season instead of the others?
5. What changes could result if one part of a food chain were changed in some way?
 6. Choose an area in your neighborhood that you see every day. It can be a field or a park, a yard or even a large tree. Describe the area in a detailed way. Tell about what you see and hear, smell and feel. Then wait a week. Return to the area and write about the changes that have taken place.

Glossary

This glossary can help you to pronounce and find out the meanings of words in this book that you may not know.

The words are listed in alphabetical order. Guide words at the top of each page tell you the first and last words on the page.

Each word is divided into syllables. The way to pronounce each word is given next. You can understand the pronunciation respelling by using the key below. A shorter key appears at the bottom of every other page.

When a word has more than one syllable, a dark accent mark (´) shows which syllable is stressed. In some words, a light accent mark (´) shows which syllable has a less heavy stress.

The following abbreviations are used in this glossary:

n. noun   *v.* verb   *adj.* adjective   *adv.* adverb   *pl.* plural

Glossary entries are adapted from the Macmillan *School Dictionary.*

PRONUNCIATION KEY

Vowel Sounds

/a/ bat
/ā/ cake, rain, day
/ä/ father
/är/ car
/ãr/ dare, hair
/e/ hen, bread
/ē/ me, meat, baby, believe
/ėr/ term, first, worm, turn

/i/ bib
/ī/ kite, fly, pie, light
/ir/ clear, cheer, here
/o/ top, watch
/ō/ rope, soap, so, snow
/ô/ saw, song, auto
/oi/ coin, boy
/ôr/ fork, ore, oar

/ou/ out, cow
/u/ sun, son, touch
/ù/ book, pull, could
/ü/ moon
/ū/ cute, few, music
/ə/ about, taken, pencil, apron, helpful
/ər/ letter, dollar, doctor

Consonant Sounds

/b/ bear
/d/ dog
/f/ fish, phone
/g/ goat
/h/ house, who
/j/ jar, gem, fudge
/k/ car, key
/l/ lamb

/m/ map
/n/ nest, know
/p/ pig
/r/ rug, wrong
/s/ city, seal
/t/ tiger
/v/ van
/w/ wagon

/y/ yo-yo
/z/ zoo, eggs
/ch/ chain, match
/sh/ show
/th/ thin
/th/ those
/hw/ where
/ng/ song

A

ab·sence (ab′ səns) *n.* the state of being away or not being present.

ab·strac·tion (ab strak′ shən) *n.* a work of art that emphasizes the color, shape, pattern or design of objects.

a·bue·lit·a (ä′ bwä lē′ tä) *n.* an affectionate term for grandmother in Spanish.

ac·cept (ak sept′) *v.* to take or receive something that is given.

ac·com·pa·ny (ə kum′ pə nē) *v.* **ac·com·pa·nied, ac·com·pa·ny·ing. 1.** to perform music to go along with something, such as a movie, or an-

ad·dress (ə dres′) *v.* **1.** to direct one's writing or speech to. **2.** to speak formally to.

ad·mire (ad mīr′) *v.* **ad·mired, ad·mir·ing.** to feel a great respect for.

a·do·be (ə dō′ bē) *adj.* con-structed or made of adobe, a mud or clay brick that has been dried in the sun.

adobe

a·dopt (ə dopt′) *v.* to agree to or approve, especially by formal vote.

ad·ver·tis·ing a·gen·cy (ad′ vər tī′ zing ā′ jən sē) *n., pl.* **a·gen·cies.** a company that prepares advertisements, or public announcements, for other companies or people.

ad·vice (əd vīs′) *n.* an idea that is offered to a person about what he or she should do.

Ah·yo·ka (ä yō′ kə) the daughter of Sequoyah.

aisle (īl) *n.* the space between two rows or sections of something; for example, the aisles in a movie theater or auditorium.

am·ble (am′ bəl) *v.* **am·bled, am·bling.** to walk in a relaxed, easy way.

am·mu·ni·tion (am′ yə nish′ ən) *n.* **1.** anything used in attack or defense. **2.** bullets, shells, grenades, bombs, and other things that can be fired.

an·nounce·ment (ə nouns′ mənt) *n.* the act of announcing or making something known to the public.

an·noy (ə noi′) *v.* to bother or disturb.

a·non·y·mous (ə non′ ə məs) *adj.* written or done by someone whose name is not known.

anx·ious (angk′ shəs) *adj.* **1.** eager; looking forward to. **2.** worried or fearful.

ap·pear (ə pir′) *v.* **1.** to come into view. **2.** to seem.

ap·plause (ə ploz′) *n.* a clapping of the hands in order to show approval or enjoyment.

ap·pre·ci·ate (ə prē′ shē āt′) *v.* **ap·pre·ci·at·ed, ap·pre·ci·at·ing.** to be thankful, or grateful, for.

ap·pren·tice (ə pren′ tis) *v.* **ap·pren·ticed, ap·pren·tic·ing.** to work for a skilled worker, usually for a fixed period of time, in order to learn a trade or skill.

ap·proach (ə prōch') *v.* to come near or close to.

arch (ärch) *v.* to form something into an arch; curve.

ar·mor (är' mər) *n.* a covering for the body, usually made from metal. In former times it was worn for protection during battle.

armor

ar·range·ment (ə rānj' mənt) *n.* **1.** a group of things placed in a special way. **2.** the act of putting in order.

ar·roy·o (ə roi' ō) *n.* a dry streambed.

as·sign·ment (ə sīn' mənt) *n.* something that is assigned, such as a task or a job.

as·sist·ant (ə sis' tənt) *adj.* serving as a helper to another person.

as·ton·ish·ment (ə ston' ish mənt) *n.* surprise or amazement.

at·ten·tion (ə ten' shən) *n.* **1.** careful watching or listening. **2.** notice or consideration.

au·di·ence (ô' dē əns) *n.* a group of people gathered to hear or see something.

au·di·to·ri·um (ô' də tôr' ē əm) *n.* a large room in a school, theater, or other building where a group of people can gather.

awk·ward (ôk' wərd) *adj.* **1.** difficult or embarrassing; self-conscious; unsure. **2.** clumsy.

B

bac·te·ri·a (bak tir' ē ə) *n. pl.* very tiny one-celled animals that can only be seen through a powerful microscope.

ba·ja·da (bä hä' də) *n.* a gentle slope.

bale (bāl) *n.* a large bundle of things tied together tightly for shipping or storage.

ba·nan·a slug (bə nan' ə slug') *n.* a slow-moving, slimy animal like a snail without a shell, living mostly in forests, gardens, and damp places.

batch (bach) *n., pl.* **batch·es. 1.** an amount baked at one time. **2.** a group of things.

bel·lows (bel' ōz) *n. pl.* a device that makes a strong current of air when it is pumped open and closed. A bellows is often used to make a fire.

bellows

ben·e·fit (ben' ə fit) *n.* something that helps a person or thing; advantage.

bit·ter (bit' ər) *adj.* harsh or biting; for example, bitter cold.

---

a bat, ā cake, ä father, är car, âr dare; e hen, ē me, ėr term; i bib, ī kite, ir clear; o top, ō rope, ô saw, oi coin, ôr fork, ou out; u sun, u̇ book, ü moon, ū cute; ə about, taken

blind (blīnd) *n.* a hiding place for hunters or bird and animal watchers.

blurred (blėrd) *adj.* not clear; difficult to see.

blurt (blėrt) *v.* to say suddenly or without thinking.

blush (blush) *v.* to become red in the face because of shame, embarrassment, or confusion.

bog (bog) *n.* wet, spongy ground.

boll (bōl) *n.* the rounded seed pod of a cotton or flax plant.

bo·ta·nist (bot' ən ist) *n.* a person who is an expert on plant life.

boun·ti·ful (boun' ti fəl) *adj.* producing much food; fertile; abundant.

box score (boks' skôr') *n.* a printed score of a game (like baseball) giving the names and positions of the players and a record of their plays in the form of a table.

brack·ish (brak' ish) *adj.* salty; briny.

branch (branch) *n., pl.* **branch·es. 1.** a small river that goes out from a main river. **2.** anything that goes out or away from a main part.

brief (brēf) *adj.* lasting for a short time.

brisk·ly (brisk' lē) *adv.* in a quick or lively way.

buc·ca·neer (buk' ə nir') *n.* a pirate.

buck·skin (buk'skin') *n.* a yellowish-tan leather made from the skins of deer or sheep. Clothes made of buckskin were often worn by early settlers.

buckskin

bur·row (bėr' ō) *n.* a hole dug in the ground by an animal for living or hiding in.

bust·ling (bus' ling) *adj.* full of activity; busy.

C

cac·tus (kak' təs) *n., pl.* **cac·tus·es, cac·ti** (kak' tī). a plant that has a thick stem covered with sharp spines instead of leaves.

ca·fe (ka fā') *n.* a small restaurant; coffee house.

cactus

can·vas (kan' vəs) *n.* a strong, heavy cloth made of cotton, flax, or hemp.

can·yon (kan' yən) *n.* a deep valley with steep sides, usually with a stream running through it.

ca·per (kā' pər) *n.* **1.** a trick or prank. **2.** a playful leap or jump.

car·ni·val (kär' nə vəl) *n.* a fair or festival that has games, rides, and other amusements.

carve (kärv) *v.* **carved, carv·ing.** to make, shape, or decorate by cutting.

cas·sa·va (kə sä' və) *n.* a plant grown in warm regions for its edible roots.

cast (kast) *n.* the actors in a play or other show.—*v.* **cast, cast·ing. 1.** to assign a role in a play or movie to someone. **2.** to cause to fall upon. **3.** to throw.

cast·ing (kast′ ing) *n.* the act of giving out the parts of a play or movie to the actors.

cat·e·go·ry (kat′ ə gôr′ ē) *n., pl.* **cat·e·go·ries.** a group or class of things.

cau·tious·ly (kô′ shəs lē) *adv.* in a cautious way; carefully.

cease (sēs) *v.* **ceased, ceas·ing.** to stop; come to an end.

cel·e·brate (sel′ ə brāt′) *v.* **cel·e·brat·ed, cel·e·brat·ing.** to observe or honor a special day or event with ceremonies and other activities.

cel·e·bra·tion (sel′ ə brā′ shən) *n.* the ceremonies and special activities carried on to honor a special day or event.

cen·tu·ry (sen′ chər ē) *n., pl.* **cen·tu·ries.** a period of one hundred years.

cer·e·mo·ny (sãr′ ə mō′ nē) *n., pl.* **cer·e·mo·nies.** a formal act done on special or important occasions.

chal·lenge (chal′ ənj) *n.* **1.** something that calls for work, effort, and the use of one's talents. **2.** a call to take part in a contest or fight.

cham·pi·on·ship (cham′ pē ən ship′) *n.* the position or honor of being a champion, or winner of first place in a contest or game.

chat (chat) *v.* **chat·ted, chat·ting.** to talk in a light, familiar, or friendly way.

chau·dière de clam (shō dyãr′ də klam′) clam chowder pronounced with a French accent.

Cher·o·kee (chãr′ ə kē) *n., pl.* **Cher·o·kees, Cher·o·kee. 1.** a member of a tribe of North American Indians that used to live in the southeastern United States. Many Cherokee live in Oklahoma. **2.** the language of this tribe.

chief·ly (chēf′ lē) *adv.* **1.** mainly; mostly. **2.** above all; especially.

Chi·na·ber·ry tree (chī′ nə bãr′ ē trē′) *n.* a soapberry tree of the southern U.S., known for its quick-growing lacy foliage.

Chinaberry tree

chink (chingk) *n.* a plug of material, often mud, that was used to seal a crack or hole in a wall.

chore (chôr) *n.* a small job or task.

chute (shüt) *n.* a steep passage or slide through which things may pass.

claim (klām) *n.* **1.** something that is claimed, such as a piece of land. **2.** things that are asked for or demanded as one's own.

clan (klan) *n.* a group of families who believe they are descended from the same ancestor.

clear·ing (klir′ ing) *n.* a piece of land, especially within a thickly wooded area, that is free of trees or brush.

clench (klench) *v.* to close together tightly.

---

a bat, ā cake, ä father, ãr car, ãr dare; e hen, ē me, ėr term; i bib, ī kite, ir clear; o top, ō rope, ô saw, oi coin, ôr fork, ou out; u sun, ů book, ü moon, ū cute; ə about, taken

cling (kling) *v.* **clung, cling·ing. 1.** to hold tightly. **2.** to stick closely.

clout (klout) *n. Informal.* a heavy blow, as with the hand.

clump (klump) *n.* a thick mass or lump of something.—*v.* to walk heavily and noisily.

clutch (kluch) *v.* to grasp or hold tightly or firmly.

coarse (kôrs) *adj.* thick or rough.

cob·ble·stone (kob' əl stōn') *n.* a round stone. In the past, cobblestones were used to pave streets.

Co·lo·ni·al (kə lō' nē əl) *adj.* having something to do with the thirteen British colonies that became the United States of America.

Co·man·che (kə man' chē) *n., pl.* **Co·man·ches, Co·man·che.** a member of a tribe of North American Indians who lived in the southern part of the Great Plains.

com·et (kom' it) *n.* a bright heavenly body made up of ice, frozen gases, and dust particles. A comet has a starlike head and a long tail.

comet

com·fort·ing (kum' fər ting) *adj.* easing someone's pain or sadness.

com·mis·sar·y (kom' ə sãr' ē) *n., pl.* **com·mis·sar·ies.** a store that sells food and supplies, especially in an army, lumber, or mining camp.

com·mu·ni·cate (kə mū' ni kāt') *v.* **com·mu·ni·cat·ed, com·mu·ni·cat·ing. 1.** to exchange or pass along feelings, thoughts, or information. **2.** to make known or understood.

com·mu·ni·ty (kə mū' nə tē) *n., pl.* **com·mu·ni·ties. 1.** a group of animals and plants living together in the same area. **2.** a group of people living in the same area.

com·pan·ion (kəm pan' yən) *n.* a person who often goes along with another; friend.

com·part·ment (kəm pärt' mənt) *n.* a separate division or section, as a glove compartment in a car.

com·pose (kəm pōz') *v.* **com·posed, com·pos·ing. 1.** to make oneself quiet or calm. **2.** to put together; create.

com·po·si·tion (kom' pə zish' ən) *n.* **1.** something composed, especially a work of writing, art, or music. **2.** the parts that make up a whole.

con·ceal (kən sēl') *v.* to put or keep out of sight; hide.

con·clu·sion (kən klü' zhən) *n.* **1.** a final opinion reached by reasoning. **2.** the final part of something; end.

con·crete (kon' krēt) *n.* a mixture of cement, pebbles, sand, and water that becomes very hard when it dries.

Con·fed·er·a·cy (kən fed' ər ə sē) *n.* the eleven southern states that withdrew from the Union in 1860 and 1861.

Con·gress (kong′ gris) *n.* the branch of the government of the United States that makes the laws of our country.

con·sec·u·tive (kən sek′ yə tiv) *adj.* following one after another without a break.

con·serve (kən sėrv′) *v.* **con·served, con·serv·ing.** to keep or preserve; protect from loss or waste.

con·sid·er (kən sid′ ər) *v.* thought about carefully before deciding.

con·sist (kən sist′) *v.* to be made up or composed.

con·sole (kən sōl′) *v.* **con· soled, con· sol·ing.** to comfort or cheer.

con·stel·la·tion (kon′ stə lā′ shən) *n.* a group of stars forming a pattern in the sky that looks like an object, animal, or figure from a myth.

constellation

con·struct (kən strukt′) *v.* to put together; build.

con·tent·ment (kən tent′ mənt) *n.* the state of being happy and content; satisfaction.

con·trap·tion (kən trap′ shən) *n.* something unusual made or invented for a particular purpose.

con·ven·ience (kən vēn′ yəns) *n.* something that gives ease and comfort.

con·ven·ient (kən vēn′ yənt) *adj.* **1.** meeting one's needs; giving ease and comfort. **2.** within easy reach; near.

con·ver·sa·tion (kon′ vər sā′ shən) *n.* a friendly and informal talk.

con·verse (kən vers′) *v.* **con·versed, con·vers·ing.** to talk together in an informal and friendly way.

con·vince (kən vins′) *v.* **con·vinced, con·vinc·ing.** to cause a person to do or believe something; persuade.

cop·y·book (kop′ ē bùk′) *n.* a book containing examples of handwriting for students to copy.

cot·ton gin (kot′ ən jin) *n.* a machine for separating cotton from its seeds.

coun·cil (koun′ səl) *n.* a meeting of people called together to give advice, discuss a problem, or make a decision.

court·yard (kôrt′ yärd′) *n.* an open area that is surrounded by walls or buildings.

crank (krangk) *n.* a part of a machine that has a handle attached to a rod.—*v.* to turn a crank so that something will work.

crank

a bat, ā cake, ä father, är car, âr dare; e hen, ē me, ėr term; i bib, ī kite, ir clear; o top, ō rope, ô saw, oi coin, ôr fork, ou out; u sun, ù book, ü moon, ū cute; ə about, taken

craw·fish (krô′ fish′) *n., pl.* **craw·fish, craw·fish·es.** a small shellfish that looks like a lobster and lives in fresh water.

crawfish

crea·ture (krē′ chər) *n.* a living thing, usually an animal.

crew (krü) *n.* a group of people who work together on a job.

crit·i·cism (krit′ ə siz′ əm) *n.* the act of saying what is good or bad about something.

crook (krůk) *n.* a staff or pole with a hooklike curve at one end.

cross·roads (kros′ rōdz′) *n.* the place where two or more roads cross each other.

crossroads

cruise (krüz) *v.* **cruised, cruis·ing.** to move or ride from place to place.

cud (kud) *n.* food that comes back into the mouth from the first stomach of cows and some other animals so that they can chew it again.

cu·ri·os·i·ty (kūr′ ē os′ ə tē) *n., pl.* **cu·ri·os·i·ties.** a strong wish to learn about things that are new, strange, or interesting.

cu·ri·ous·ly (kūr′ ē əs lē) *adv.* with a strong wish to know or find out about something, especially something new or strange.

cyg·net (sig′ nit) *n.* a young swan.

D

dair·y (dãr′ ē) *n., pl.* **dair·ies.** a farm where cows are raised, milk and cream are pro-duced, and butter and cheese are made.

dairy

dam·age (dam′ ij) *n.* harm or in-jury that makes something less valuable or useful.

dam·ag·ing (dam′ ij ing) *adj.* causing harm or injury.

dart (därt) *v.* to move suddenly and swiftly.

dash (dash) *n., pl.* **dash·es.** a short race. —*v.* to move suddenly and with great speed; rush.

daw·dle (dôd′ əl) *v.* **daw·dled, daw·dling.** **1.** to walk aimlessly or without a purpose. **2.** to waste time; linger.

daz·zle (daz′ əl) *v.* **daz·zled, daz·zling.** to make almost blind with too much light.

de·cay (di kā′) *v.* to rot slowly.—*adj.* **de·cay·ing.** rotting slowly.

de·clare (di klãr′) *v.* **de·clared, de·clar·ing.** to announce; make known.

ded·i·ca·tion (ded′ ə kā′ shən) *n.* the act of dedicating or setting apart something for a special purpose or use.

de·fen·sive·ly (di fen′ siv lē) *adv.* in a way that would keep one from being attacked or harmed.

de·fine (di fīn′) *v.* **de·fined, de·fin· ing. 1.** to determine or fix the limits or extent of. **2.** to state the meaning of a word or phrase.

def·i·nite·ly (def′ ə nit lē) *adv.* without a doubt; positively; certainly.

de·light (di līt′) *n.* great pleasure; joy.

de·mand (di mand′) *v.* to ask for forcefully.

de·ny (di nī′) *v.* **de·nied, de·ny·ing.** to say that something is not true.

de·pos·it (di poz′ it) *v.* **1.** to set or lay down. **2.** to put money or valuable things in a bank or other safe place.

de·pot (dē′ pō) *n.* a railroad or bus station or terminal.

depth (depth) *n.* the distance from top to bottom or from front to back. **the depths.** the deepest or lowest part.

de·scend (di send′) *v.* to move from a higher place to a lower one; come or go downward.

de·scribe (di skrīb′) *v.* **de·scribed, de· scrib·ing.** to give a picture of something in words; tell or write about.

de·scrip·tion (di skrip′ shən) *n.* **1.** a statement that describes. **2.** the act of giving a picture using words.

de·sign (di zīn′) *v.* to make a drawing, plan, or outline of.—*n.* a plan, drawing, or outline made to serve as a guide or pattern.

de·sire (di zīr′) *v.* **de·sired, de·sir·ing.** to wish for; request; want.

des·per·ate·ly (des′ pər it lē, des′ prit lē) *adv.* with a willingness to take any risk; recklessly.

de·tail (di tāl′, dē′ tāl) *n.* a small or less important part of a whole; item.

de·ter·mined (di tėr′ mind) *adj.* having one's mind made up; firm.

de·vel·op (di vel′ əp) *v.* **1.** to cause to grow or expand. **2.** to change slowly. **3.** to work out in detail.

dew (dü, dū) *n.* moisture from the air that forms drops on cool surfaces. Dew forms on grass, plants, and trees during the night.

dig·ni·ty (dig′ nə tē) *n., pl.* **dig·ni·ties.** the state of being noble, worthy, or honorable.

dike

dike (dīk) *n.* a dam or high wall of earth built to hold back the waters of a sea or other body of water.

di·lem·ma (di lem′ ə) *n.* a situation that calls for a choice between two or more things that are equally unpleasant; a difficult choice.

dis·ap·point·ed (dis′ ə poin′ tid) *adj.* with a feeling of disappointment, or failure to live up to one's hopes.

dis·ap·prov·al (dis′ ə prü′ vəl) *n.* the act of disapproving or frowning upon.

---

a **bat**, ā **cake**, ä **father**, är **car**, âr **dare**; e **hen**, ē **me**, ėr **term**; i **bib**, ī **kite**, ir **clear**; o **top**, ō **rope**, ô **saw**, oi **coin**, ôr **fork**, ou **out**; u **sun**, u̇ **book**, ü **moon**, ū **cute**; ə **about, taken**

dis·card·ed (dis kär′ did) *adj.* given up or thrown away as useless, worthless, or unwanted.

dis·cuss (dis kus′) *v.* to talk over; speak about.

dis·ease (di zēz′) *n.* sickness or illness; harmful condition.

dis·miss (dis mis′) *v.* **1.** to send away or allow to leave. **2.** to fire someone from a job.

dis·turb (dis tėrb′) *v.* to upset or change the order or arrangement of things.

di·ver·sion (di vėr′ zhən) *n.* amusement; entertainment; pastime.

di·vert (di vėrt′) *v.* to draw someone's attention away from something.

do·nate (dō′ nāt) *v.* **do·nat·ed, do·nat·ing.** to give to; contribute.

doubt (dout) *n.* a feeling of uncertainty or disbelief.

doubt·ful (dout′ fəl) *adj.* full of doubt; not sure; uncertain.

drear·y (drir′ ē) *adj.* dull or gloomy; depressing.

drift (drift) *n.* something that has been piled up by the force of wind or water, such as a snow drift.

drift

drought (drout) *n.* a long period of dry weather with little or no rainfall.

due (dü) *adj.* owed, as in a debt.

dune (dün, dūn) *n.* a hill of sand that is heaped up by the wind.

dusk (dusk) *n.* the time of day just before nightfall.

du·ti·ful·ly (dü′ ti fəl lē, dū′ ti fəl lē) *adv.* with a sense of duty or obedience.

E

ea·ger·ly (ē′ gər lē) *adv.* **1.** with much interest or enthusiasm. **2.** with a strong feeling of desire.

ea·ger·ness (ē′ gər nis) *n.* the state of being very interested in or enthusiastic about something.

ease (ēz) *v.* **eased, eas·ing.** to make less; lighten.

ea·sel (ē′ zəl) *n.* a tall stand or rack used to hold artists' paintings or signs.

Eb·bets Field (e′ bəts fēld) the Brooklyn Dodgers' playing field in the 1940s.

Ed·i·son, Thom·as Al·va (ed′ i sən, al′ və) 1847–1931, U.S. inventor.

ed·i·tor-in-chief (ed′ ə tər in chēf′) *n.* the highest ranking editor of a newspaper or other publication.

ee·ri·ly (ir′ i lē) *adv.* in a strange and frightening way; weirdly.

e·lect (i lekt′) *v.* to choose by voting, as when a town elects a mayor.

el·e·gant (el′ ə gənt) *adj.* fine; showing good taste, dignity, or style.

em·bar·rass·ing (em bâr′ ə sing) *adj.* making one feel shy, uncomfortable, or ashamed.

em·bar·rass·ment (em bâr′ əs mənt) *n.* a feeling of shyness or shame.

e·merge (i mėrj′) *v.* **e·merged, e·merg·ing.** to come out; come into view.

e·mer·gent (i mėr′ jənt) *adj.* of or relating to plants whose roots are
usually covered by water, but whose
stems, leaves, and flowers are
above the water.

en·ter·tain·ment (en′ tər tān′ mənt) *n.*
the act of entertaining; something
that entertains, interests, or amuses.

en·tire (en tīr′) *adj.* whole; complete.

ep·i·sode (ep′ ə sōd′) *n.* a single happening or group of happenings in
real life or in a story.

e·quip·ment (i kwip′ mənt) *n.* anything
needed for a particular purpose or
use.

es·ca·pade (es′ kə pād′) *n.* an action
that is wild, dangerous, or full of
adventure.

es·cort (es kôrt′) *v.* to guide, lead, or
go along with someone.

es·say (es′ ā) *n.* a short written composition on a subject.

etch (ech) *v.* **1.** to outline or draw
boldly. **2.** to cut
a picture or
design onto
metal by letting
acid burn into
parts of it.

etch

e·vap·o·ra·tion (i vap′ ə rā′ shən) *n.* a
change from a liquid or solid state
into a vapor, or tiny particles of matter such as mist, steam, or smoke.

e·vent (i vent′) *n.* anything that happens, especially an important
happening.

ex·claim (eks klām′) *v.* to speak or cry
out suddenly.

ex·ot·ic (eg zot′ ik) *adj.* **1.** something
that comes from another part of the
world. **2.** something very unusual or
colorful.

ex·pand (eks pand′) *v.* to make or
grow larger.

ex·per·i·ment (eks pãr′ ə mənt) *n.* a
test that is performed to discover or
prove something.

ex·pert (eks′ pėrt) *n.* a person who
knows a great deal about a certain
thing.

ex·pla·na·tion (eks′ plə nā′ shən) *n.* **1.**
something that makes a thing clear
or understandable; a reason or
meaning. **2.** the act of making something understandable.

ex·press (eks pres′) *v.* to say or
show.

ex·pres·sion (eks presh′ ən) *n.* a particular look on the face that
expresses a thought or feeling.

ex·tra (eks′ trə) *n.* a person hired to
play a lesser, usually nonspeaking
part in a motion picture or other pro-
duction.

ex·traor·di·nar·y (eks trôr′ də nãr′ ē,
eks′ trə ôr′ də nãr′ ē) *adj.* very unusual; remarkable.

eye con·tact (ī′ kon′ takt) *n.* eye-to-
eye contact, or meeting, between
two persons; for example, between a
speaker and individual members of
his or her audience.

---

a bat, ā cake, ä father, är car, ãr dare; e hen, ē me, ėr term; i bib, ī kite,
ir clear; o top, ō rope, ô saw, oi coin, ôr fork, ou out; u sun, ù book,
ü moon, ū cute; ə about, taken

F

fade (fād) v. **fad·ed, fad·ing. 1.** to lose color or brightness. **2.** to die down; disappear gradually.

fa·mil·iar (fə mil′ yər) adj. **1.** knowing something well. **2.** often heard, seen, or experienced.

fam·ine (fam′ in) n. a very great and widespread lack of food.

fan·ta·sy (fan′ tə sē) n., pl. **fan·ta·sies.** a story or invention of great imagination and creativity.

fes·ti·val (fes′ tə vəl) n. a celebration or holiday, especially one that takes place every year.

fic·tion (fik′ shən) n. **1.** a written work that tells a story about characters or events that are not real. **2.** something made up or imagined.

field guide (fēld′ gīd′) n. a book used to identify things found in nature such as birds, rocks, plants, or animals.

fig (fig) n. the small, sweet, edible fruit of a fig tree.

file (fīl) n. a set of papers, cards, or records arranged in order, often in a drawer, cabinet, or box.

firm (fėrm) adj. solid; stable.

flee (flē) v. **fled, flee·ing.** to run away or try to escape from.

flour·ish (flėr′ ish) n., pl. **flour·ish·es.** a bold or fancy stroke in writing.

flur·ry (flėr′ ē) n., pl. **flur·ries.** a sudden outburst or stir; bustle; commotion.

fly·way (flī′ wā′) n. a particular path in the air along which certain birds fly regularly.

fo·cus (fō′ kəs) v. **fo·cused, fo·cus·ing. 1.** to adjust a lens in order to make a clear picture. **2.** to fix or direct one's attention on something.

folk tale (fōk′ tāl) n. a story that has been handed down among a group of people and usually tells a part of their history.

foot·bridge (fut′ brij′) n. a bridge that is only for people walking on foot.

for·bid·den (fər bid′ ən) adj. not allowed; prohibited.

for·eign (fôr′ ən) adj. of or from another country.

for·tune (fôr′ chən) n. **1.** great wealth; riches. **2.** something good or bad that will happen to a person.

fos·sil (fos′ əl) n. the remains or traces of a plant or animal that lived long ago. Fossils are usually found in rocks.

fossil

fran·ti·cal·ly (fran′ tik lē) adv. in a worried, fearful, or wildly excited way.

freight (frāt) n. goods that are transported; cargo.

fron·tier (frun tir′) n. the newly settled area of a country that lies along the border of land that is still unsettled or undeveloped.

fum·ble (fum′ bəl) v. **fum·bled, fum·bling.** to look for in a clumsy way.

fu·ri·ous (fūr′ ē əs) adj. very angry; full of rage.

G

gale (gāl) *n.* a very strong wind.

ga·losh·es (gə losh′ iz) *n. pl.* over-shoes made of rubber or plastic.

gaze (gāz) *v.* **gazed, gaz·ing.** to look at something a long time without looking away.

gear (gir) *n.* a wheel having a toothed edge designed to fit into the teeth of a similar wheel, so that one gear's turn-ing can cause the other to turn.

gear

gen·er·a·tion (jen′ ə rā′ shən) *n.* **1.** a group of persons born around the same time. **2.** one step in the line of descent of a family.

ger·bil (jėr′ bil) *n.* a small animal that lives in holes that it digs in the ground. Gerbils have a slender, tufted tail and a short, soft coat.

ges·ture (jes′ chər) *v.* **ges·tured, ges·tur·ing.** to make or use movements of

gerbil

the hands, head, or other parts of the body.

gin (jin) *n.* a machine for separating cotton from its seeds.—*v.* **ginned, gin·ning.** to separate cotton from its seeds with a cotton gin.

gleam (glēm) *v.* to shine or glow.

glimpse (glimps) *n.* a quick look; glance.

glis·ten (glis′ ən) *v.* to shine or sparkle with reflected light.

glis·ten·ing (glis′ ən ing) *adj.* shining or sparkling with reflected light.

glum·ly (glum′ lē) *adv.* in a gloomy, sad way.

gov·ern·ment (guv′ ərn mənt, guv′ ər mənt) *n.* the group of people in charge of ruling or managing a coun-try, state, city, or other place.

grain (grān) *n.* the lines and other markings that are found in wood and stone.

grasp (grasp) *v.* to take hold of firmly with the hand.

grate·ful (grāt′ fəl) *adj.* full of gratitude; thankful.

grate·ful·ly (grāt′ fəl lē) *adv.* in a grateful or thankful way.

grave (grāv) *adj.* threatening; serious.

graze (grāz) *v.* **grazed, graz·ing.** to feed on growing grass.

---

a bat, ā cake, ä father, är car, ãr dare; e hen, ē me, ėr term; i bib, ī kite, ir clear; o top, ō rope, ô saw, oi coin, ôr fork, ou out; u sun, u̇ book, ü moon, ū cute; ə about, taken

grind·stone
(grīnd′ stōn′) *n.*
a flat stone
wheel that can
be turned to
sharpen knives,
axes, and other
tools, or to
shape other
materials.

grindstone

grit (grit) *n.* bravery; courage.

grope (grōp) *v.* **groped, grop·ing.** to feel about with the hands, especially in the dark.

gump·tion (gump′ shən) *n.* determination; energy; drive; nerve.

gust (gust) *n.* a sudden strong rush of wind or air.

H

hab·it (hab′ it) *n.* **1.** a usual or customary way of acting. **2.** an action that is done so often that it becomes automatic.

halt (hôlt) *n.* a stop for a short time.

hal·ter (hôl′ tər) *n.* a rope or strap used for leading or tying an animal. A halter fits over the animal's nose and over or behind its ears.

halter

hard·ware (härd′ wãr′) *n.* metal articles, such as nails and tools, used for making or fixing things.

har·ness (här′ nis) *n.,* *pl.* **har·ness·es.** the straps, bands, and other fastenings used to attach a work animal to a cart, plow, or wagon.

harsh (härsh) *adj.* rough or unpleasant to the ear, eye, taste, or touch.

har·vest (här′ vist) *n.* **1.** the crop that is gathered. **2.** the time of year when ripened crops are gathered.—*v.* to gather in a crop when it is ripe.

hast·i·ly (hās′ ti lē) *adv.* in a quick or hurried way.

haul (hôl) *v.* **1.** to transport, as in a trunk or car. **2.** to pull or draw with force.

head·ing (hed′ ing) *n.* a title for a page or chapter.

hearth (härth) *n.* the floor of a fireplace.

herd (hėrd) *v.* to lead, drive, or group together in a herd.—*n.* a group of animals.

herd

herds·man (hėrdz′ mən) *n.,* *pl.* **herds·men.** a man who owns, takes care of, or drives a herd of animals.

her·on (hãr′ ən) *n.* any of various wading birds having a long slender neck, long pointed bill, and long thin legs.

hes·i·tate (hez′ ə tāt′) *v.* **hes·i·tat·ed, hes·i·tat·ing.** to wait or stop a moment.

hitch (hich) *v.* to attach, as with a rope; fasten; tie.

542

hob·ble (hob′ əl) *n.* **1.** a rope or strap used to hobble an animal. **2.** a limping walk —*v.* **hob·bled, hob·bling.** to tie the front legs or hind legs of a horse or other animal together to keep it from moving far.

hobble

hoist (hoist) *v.* to lift or pull up.

home·stead (hōm′ sted) *n.* a parcel of 160 acres of public land granted by the United States government to a settler for farming.

Home·stead Acts (hōm′ sted akts′) *n. pl.* a series of laws passed by the U.S. Congress to give public land for free to settlers who agreed to live there.

hon·or (on′ ər) *n.* a sense of what is right or honest. **in honor of.** as an expression of respect, esteem, or love for; in celebration of.

horned toad (hôrnd′ tōd′) *n.* an insect-eating lizard common to dry areas of the western United States, having spiny horns on its head and scales.

horned toad

huff·y (huf′ ē) *adj.* **1.** offended; sulking. **2.** easily offended; touchy.

hulk·ing (hul′ king) *adj.* very large and slow-moving or clumsy.

hu·mus (hū′ məs) *n.* a dark substance in the soil, made up of decayed plant and animal matter.

hunch (hunch) *n., pl.* **hunch·es.** a guess or feeling.

hur·tle (hėrt′ əl) *v.* **hur·tled, hur·tling.** to move fast, especially with much force or noise.

hus·ky (hus′ kē) *adj.* hoarse and deep in sound.

I

i·de·al (ī dē′ əl, ī dēl′) *adj.* being exactly what one would hope for; perfect.

i·den·ti·fy (ī den′ tə fī′) *v.* **i·den·ti·fied, i·den·ti·fy·ing.** to recognize; prove that someone or something is a particular person or thing.

i·dyl·lic (ī dil′ ik) *adj.* peaceful, simple, and charming.

ig·nore (ig nôr′) *v.* **ig·nored, ig·nor·ing.** to pay no attention to.

il·lus·tra·tion (il′ əs trā′ shən) *n.* **1.** a picture, diagram, or drawing used to explain or decorate something written. **2.** something used to make clear or explain, such as an example.

a bat, ā cake, ä father, är car, âr dare; e hen, ē me, ėr term; i bib, ī kite, ir clear; o top, ō rope, ô saw, oi coin, ôr fork, ou out; u sun, u̇ book, ü moon, ū cute; ə about, taken

im·age (im′ ij) *n.* **1.** a picture held in the mind of a thing or person that is not actually present. **2.** a picture, statue, or other likeness.

image

i·mag·i·nar·y (i maj′ ə när′ē) *adj.* existing only in the mind; unreal.

i·mag·i·na·tive (i maj′ ə nə tiv) *adj.* having a good imagination; showing creative ability.

i·mag·ine (i maj′ in) *v.* **i·mag·ined, i·mag·in·ing.** to picture someone or something in the mind.

im·mense (i mens′) *adj.* huge; of great size; very large.

im·pa·tient (im pā′ shənt) *adj.* not able to put up with delay or opposition calmly and without anger.

im·po·lite (im′ pə līt′) *adj.* not polite; not having or showing good manners; rude.

im·port (im pôrt′) *v.* to bring in goods from another country for sale or use.

im·pres·sive (im pres′ iv) *adj.* making a strong impression on the mind; exciting emotion or admiration.

in·cred·i·ble (in kred′ ə bəl) *adj.* hard or impossible to believe.

in·de·pend·ence (in′ di pen′ dəns) *n.* freedom from the control of another country.

in·de·pend·ent (in′ di pen′ dənt) *adj.* free from the control or rule of another or others; separate.

in·hale (in hāl′) *v.* **in·haled, in·hal·ing.** to breathe in; to take into the lungs.

in·sist (in sist′) *v.* to say something firmly and positively.

in·stall (in stôl′) *v.* to put in place for use or service.

in·struc·tions (in struk′ shənz) *n. pl.* directions, orders, or explanations.

in·tend (in tend′) *v.* to plan.

in·tent·ly (in tent′ lē) *adv.* with the mind firmly fixed or concentrated.

in·ter·rupt (in′ tə rupt′) *v.* to stop or break in on someone who is speaking or doing something.

in·ter·rup·tion (in′ tə rup′ shən) *n.* something that interrupts.

in·tru·der (in trüd′ ər) *n.* an unwanted visitor; someone or something that enters without being asked.

in·ven·tion (in ven′ chən) *n.* something that is invented, or made for the first time.

in·ves·ti·gate (in ves′ tə gāt′) *v.* **in·ves·ti·gate, in·ves·ti·gat·ing.** to look into carefully in order to find facts and get information.

irk·some (ėrk′ səm) *adj.* annoying; tiresome; bothersome.

is·sue (ish′ ü) *v.* **is·sued, is·su·ing.** to send or give out.

J

ja·cquette (zhä ket′) *French.* peel, as in apple peel.

jog (jog) *n.* **1.** *Informal.* a slight turn. **2.** a shake or push.

jour·ney (jėr′ nē) *v.* to make a trip; travel. —*n.* a long trip.

Ju·bas (jü′ bäz) *n.* a tribe in eastern Africa.

junc·tion (jungk′ shən) *n.* a place or station where railroad lines meet or cross.

June bug (jün′ bug′) *n.* any of several brown beetles that become adults in late spring, and can harm shrubs, trees, and crops.

June bug

jut (jut) *v.* **jut·ted, jut·ting.** to stick out; project.

K

kan·ga·roo rat (kang′ gə rü′ rat′) *n.* a small, burrowing animal that lives in the dry plains of western North America.

keen (kēn) *adj.* sharp or quick in seeing, hearing, or thinking.

Kla·wock (klä′ wäk) a town on an island in Alaska.

knick·ers (nik′ ərz) *n. pl.* loose-fitting pants ending just below the knee.

knickers

L

lack (lak) *n.* the state of being without or having too little.

lar·va (lär′ və) *n., pl.* **lar·vae.** an early stage in the life of an insect in which it looks like a worm and spends most of its time eating.

lease (lēs) *v.* **leased, leas·ing.** to allow someone to have or use something as a result of a lease or a written agreement.

leg·al·ly (lē′ gəl lē) *adv.* in a legal or lawful way.

leg·end (lej′ ənd) *n.* a story passed down through the years that many people have believed is true, but that is not entirely true.

leg·is·la·ture (lej′ is lā chər) *n.* a group of elected lawmakers.

lens (lenz) *n., pl.* **lens·es. 1.** a piece of glass or other clear material that is curved to make light rays move apart or come together. A lens can make an object look larger or closer. **2.** the part of the eye that focuses light rays onto the retina.

lens

life cy·cle (līf′ sī′ kəl) *n.* the series of changes through which a plant or animal passes. A life cycle includes birth, growth, and death.

ā bat, ā cake, ä father, är car, âr dare; e hen, ē me, ėr term; i bib, ī kite, ir clear; o top, ō rope, ô saw, oi coin, ôr fork, ou out; u sun, ů book, ü moon, ū cute; ə about, taken

limb (lim) *n.* a part of the body of an animal or person that is used in moving or grasping. Arms, legs, wings, and flippers are limbs.

limp (limp) *n.* a lame walk or movement. —*v.* to move or walk stiffly and with difficulty.

lit·er·al·ly (lit′ ər ə lē) *adv.* really; actually.

lit·ter (lit′ ər) *n.* young animals born at one time.

lone·ly (lōn′ lē) *adj.* **lone·li·er, lone·li·est.** unhappy from lack of friendship.

lum·ber (lum′ bər) *n.* wood cut as planks and boards.

lum·ber·jack (lum′ bər jak′) *n.* a person who cuts down trees and gets logs ready for transportation to the sawmill.

lu·mi·nous (lü′ mə nəs) *adj.* **1.** full of light; bright. **2.** sending out light of its own.

lux·u·ry (luk′ shər ē, lug′ zhər ē) *n., pl.* **lux·u·ries.** things that give much comfort and pleasure but are not really needed.

M

ma·chin·er·y (mə shē′ nər ē) *n., pl.* **ma·chin·er·ies. 1.** machines or machine parts. **2.** the working parts by which something is kept going, as in the machinery of government.

mag·nif·i·cent (mag nif′ ə sənt) *adj.* very beautiful and grand; splendid.

mag·ni·fy·ing glass (mag′ nə fī′ ing glas) *n., pl.* **glass·es.** a lens, or combination of lenses, that makes things look larger than they really are.

main·tain (mān tān′) *v.* to continue to have or to do; go on with; keep.

maize (māz) *n.* corn.

ma·jes·ti·cal·ly (mə jes′ tik lē) *adv.* in a majestic or grand way.

man·ners (man′ ərz) *n. pl.* polite ways of behaving or acting.

marsh (märsh) *n., pl.* **marsh·es.** an area of low, wet land covered with grasses or similar plants, such as reeds.

mar·vel (mär′ vəl) *v.* to feel wonder or astonishment.

marsh

mar·vel·ous (mär′ və ləs) *adj.* causing wonder or astonishment.

mas·ter·piece (mas′ tər pēs′) *n.* something that is done with great skill or craftsmanship.

me·an·der (mē an′ dər) *v.* to walk or wander without a fixed purpose or goal.

mere (mir) *adj.* nothing more than; only.

mes·sen·ger (mes′ ən jər) *n.* a person who delivers messages or runs errands.

meth·od (meth′ əd) *n.* a way of doing something.

mi·grate (mī′ grāt) *v.* **mi·grat·ed, mi·grat·ing.** to move from one place to another.

mill (mil) *n.* a building containing machinery to cut wood, weave cloth, make steel, or other goods.

min·now (min′ ō) *n.* any very small fish that lives in fresh water.

mi·rac·u·lous (mi rak′ yə ləs) *adj.* amazing; extraordinary.

mist (mist) *n.* a cloud of tiny droplets of water in the air.

moat (mōt) *n.* a deep, wide ditch, usually filled with water. In former times, a moat was dug around a castle or town for protection against an enemy.

mod·el (mod′ əl) *n.* a copy of something that is usually smaller than the thing it represents.

moist (moist) *adj.* slightly wet; damp.

mon·u·ment (mon′ yə mənt) *n.* an area of great natural beauty or historical importance set aside and preserved by the government.

mood·y (mü′ dē) *adj.* having changing moods, especially bad or gloomy moods.

moon·scape (mün′ skāp′) *n.* a picture or view of the moon's surface.

mot·to (mot′ ō) *n., pl.* **mot·toes.** a short sentence or phrase that says what someone believes or what something stands for.

moun·tain range (mount′ ən rānj′) *n.* a series of mountains forming a single group.

Muir, John (mūr) 1838–1914, American naturalist important in the establishment of the National Park System.

mul·ti·ple (mul′ tə pəl) *adj.* having more than one.

mu·ral (mūr′ əl) *n.* a large picture painted on a wall or ceiling.

mural

N

nar·ra·tor (nār′ āt ər) *n.* a person who narrates; one who reads or tells about something.

na·tion (nā′ shən) *n.* **1.** a tribe or group of tribes of North American Indians. **2.** a particular land where a group of people live under one government and share a common language.

na·tion·al (nash′ ən əl) *adj.* having to do with a nation.

na·tion·al mon·u·ment a monument of national importance under the care and control of the federal government.

Na·tion·al Park Ser·vice the federal office which preserves and protects the national parks.

---

a bat, ā cake, ä father, är car, âr dare; e hen, ē me, ėr term; i bib, ī kite, ir clear; o top, ō rope, ô saw, oi coin, ôr fork, ou out; u sun, u̇ book, ü moon, ū cute; ə about, taken

na·tive (nā′ tiv) *n.* one of the original people living in a region or country. —*adj.* belonging to a particular place or country.

nick·el·o·de·on (nik′ əl ō′ dē ən) *n.* in the past, a movie theater that charged five cents for admission.

nudge (nuj) *v.* **nudged, nudg·ing.** to push or touch gently.

nurs·er·y (nėr′ sər ē) *n., pl.* **nurs·er·ies. 1.** any place in which something is raised. **2.** a place where young children are taken care of.

nu·tri·ent (nü′ trē ənt, nū′ trē ənt) *n.* a substance that is needed by plants, people, and animals for life and growth.

O

ob·ject (əb jekt′) *v.* to be against; to make or raise an objection.

ob·serve (əb zėrv′) *v.* **ob·served, ob·serv·ing. 1.** to see or notice. **2.** to watch carefully.

ob·vi·ous (ob′ vē əs) *adj.* easily seen or understood.

of·fi·cial (ə fish′ əl) *adj.* approved by a proper authority.

o·kra (ō′ krə) *n.* a soft green pod of a plant that is used in soups and eaten as a vegetable.

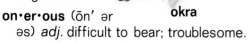

okra

on·er·ous (ōn′ ər əs) *adj.* difficult to bear; troublesome.

op·er·a·tion (op ə rā′ shən) *n.* the act or way of working or performing a task.

o·pin·ion (ə pin′ yən) *n.* a belief or conclusion that is based on what a person thinks rather than what is proved or known to be true.

or·chid (ôr′ kid) *n.* a plant with showy flowers that grow in different shapes and colors, but are usually white and bluish to reddish purple.

orchid

or·di·nar·y (ôr′ də nãr′ ē) *adj.* commonly used; regular; usual; not different in any way from others.

or·i·gin (ôr′ ə jin, or′ ə jin) *n.* the source from which something begins or comes.

o·rig·i·nal (ə rij′ ən əl) *adj.* **1.** fresh; new; unusual; creative. **2.** having to do with the origin or beginning of something.

o·rig·i·nal·ly (ə rij′ ən əl ē) *adv.* at or from the start; at first.

out·smart (out′ smärt′) *v.* to get the better of someone by cleverness.

P

pang (pang) *n.* a sudden, sharp pain or feeling.

Pap·a·go (päp′ ə gō′) *n.* a tribe of North American Indians who live in the desert areas of the United States and Mexico.

par·cel (pär′səl) *n.* **1.** something wrapped up; a bundle or package. **2.** a section or part, as of land.

par·ka (pär′ kə) *n.* a warm fur or cloth jacket with a hood.

par·lor (pär′ lər) *n.* a room in a house used for entertaining guests.

par·ty (pär′ tē) *n., pl.* **par·ties. 1.** a group of people who are doing something together. **2.** a gathering of people to have a good time.

Pas·cua Flor·i·da (päs′ kwä flō rē′ dä) the Spanish festival of flowers at Easter.

pas·sen·ger (pas′ ən jər) *n.* a person who travels in a car, train, plane, or other vehicle.

pas·tel (pas tel′) *n.* a chalklike crayon used in drawing.

pas·time (pas′ tīm′) *n.* something that makes time pass in a pleasant and happy way.

pa·tient (pā′ shənt) *adj.* being able to put up with hardship, pain, trouble, or delay without getting angry or upset.

pa·trol (pə trōl′) *v.* **pa·trolled, pa·trol·ling.** to go through or around an area to guard it or make sure that everything is all right.

ped·dler (ped′ lər) *n.* a person who travels from place to place selling goods.

peer (pir) *v.* to look hard or closely, as if trying to see something clearly.

per·i·scope (pãr′ ə skōp′) *n.* a tube in which mirrors are arranged so that objects not directly in front of the viewer can be seen. For example, a periscope allows people in a submarine to see things that are above the water.

periscope

per·mis·si·ble (pər mis′ ə bəl) *adj.* allowable; permitted.

per·suade (pər swād′) *v.* **per·suad·ed, per·suad·ing.** to cause someone to do or believe something by argument; convince.

pho·no·graph (fō′ nə graf′) *n.* an instrument that reproduces sound from records.

pho·to·es·say (fō′ tō es′ ā) *n.* a story or report that is told mainly through photographs.

pike (pīk) *n.* a large freshwater fish that has a slim body and a long duck-billed snout with many sharp teeth.

pin·a·fore (pin′ ə fôr′) *n.* an apron-like piece of clothing that is worn over, and covers, most of a dress.

pinafore

---

a bat, ā cake, ä father, är car, ãr dare; e hen, ē me, ėr term; i bib, ī kite, ir clear; o top, ō rope, ô saw, oi coin, ôr fork, ou out; u sun, ü book, ü moon, ū cute; ə about, taken

pi·o·neer (pi′ ə nir′) *n.* **1.** the first tree or trees to grow on a piece of land. **2.** a person who is the first to explore or settle a region.

pitch·fork (pich′ fôrk′) *n.* a long-handled tool with long, sharp prongs at the bottom, used especially for lifting and pitching hay.

plain (plān) *n.* a large area of flat or almost flat land.

plead (plēd) *v.* **plead·ed** or **pled, plead·ing.** to make a sincere request; beg.

plow·share (plou′ shãr′) *n.* the front edge or blade of a plow, which cuts the soil.

po·lite·ly (pə līt′ lē) *adv.* with good manners.

pol·i·tics (pol′ ə tiks) *n. pl.* the activities or affairs of government.

pol·lut·ed (pə lü′ tid) *adj.* made dirty or impure, as with garbage or other wastes.

pome·gran·ate (pom′ gran′ it, pom′ ə gran′ it) *n.* a round reddish-yellow fruit that has a tough skin, a juicy red pulp, and many seeds.

pomegranate

Ponce de Lé·on (pon′ sə dā lā′ ōn) 1460?–1521, the Spanish explorer who discovered Florida.

pon·der (pon′ dər) *v.* to consider or think over carefully.

pop·lar (pop′ lər) *n.* a tall, fast-growing tree.

pop·u·lar (pop′ yə lər) *adj.* well liked by many people.

port·fo·li·o (pôrt fō′ lē ō′) *n.* a case that can be used for carrying loose papers, drawings, and similar art materials.

por·trait (pôr′ trit, pôr′ trāt) *n.* a picture of a person, usually showing only the face and upper part of the body.

po·si·tion (pə zish′ ən) *n.* **1.** the way something is placed. **2.** the place where a person or thing is.

pos·ses·sion (pə zesh′ ən) *n.* something owned.

prai·rie (prãr′ ē) *n.* flat or rolling land covered with grass, having very few trees.

praise (prāz) *n.* an expression of high regard or approval.

prance (prans) *v.* **pranced, pranc·ing.** to move in a proud, happy way; strut.

prec·ious (presh′ əs) *adj.* **1.** having great value or worth; costly. **2.** beloved; dear.

preen (prēn) *v.* (of birds) to clean and smooth (feathers) with the beak.

pre·pare (pri pãr′) *v.* **pre·pared, pre·par·ing.** to make or get ready.

pres·ence (prez′ əns) *n.* the fact of being in a certain place at a given time.

pres·en·ta·tion (prez′ ən tā′ shən, prē′ zən tā′ shən) *n.* **1.** the act of presenting something. **2.** a showing or exhibition, as of a play.

pre·serve (pri zėrv′) *v.* **pre·served, pre· serv·ing.** to keep and protect.

prey (prā) *v.* to hunt or kill for food.

pro·ces·sion (prə sesh′ ən) *n.* a group of persons moving forward in a line or in order.

prog·ress (prog′ res) *n.* a forward movement.

proj·ect (proj′ ekt) *n.* a job or task that is to be done.

prompt·ly (prompt′ lē) *adv.* without delay.

prop (prop) *v.* **propped, prop·ping.** to support, hold up, or hold in place by placing something under or against.

prop·er (prop′ ər) *adj.* correct or suitable for a given purpose or occasion.

prop·er·ly (prop′ ər lē) *adv.* in a correct or suitable way.

proph·et (prof′ it) *n.* a person who tells what will happen in the future.

pro·por·tion (prə pôr′ shən) *n.* the relation of one thing to another with regard to size, number, or amount.

pro·test (prə test′) *v.* **1.** to make a point strongly. **2.** to object to; disagree strongly with.

prow (prou) *n.* the front part of a boat or ship; bow.

prow

pulse (puls) *n.* the regular in and out movement of the arteries caused by the beating of the heart.

pun·gent (pun′ jənt) *adj.* sharp and stinging to the smell or taste.

pur·chase (pėr′ chəs) *v.* **pur·chased, pur· chas·ing.** to get something by paying money; buy.

Q

quiv·er (kwiv′ ər) *v.* to shake slightly; tremble.

R

range (rānj) *v.* **ranged, rang·ing.** to move or wander over an area.

rap (rap) *v.* **rapped, rap·ping.** a quick, sharp, or light knock or tap.

re·al·ize (rē′ ə līz′) *v.* **re·al·ized, re·al·iz· ing.** to understand completely.

reap (rēp) *v.* to gather grain or a crop by cutting it down.

re·cite (ri sīt′) *v.* **re·cit·ed, re·cit·ing.** to repeat from memory.

reck·on (rek′ ən) *v.* **1.** to think or consider. **2.** to count or calculate.

rec·om·mend (rek′ ə mend′) *v.* to advise; suggest.

reed (rēd) *n.* a tall grass having long, narrow leaves and jointed stems that grows in marshes and other wet places.

---

a bat, ā cake, ä father, är car, ãr dare; e hen, ē me, ėr term; i bib, ī kite, ir clear; o top, ō rope, ô saw, oi coin, ôr fork, ou out; u sun, ů book, ü moon, ū cute; ə about, taken

re·fill (rē' fil') *n.* new material that replaces old material when it has been used up.

re·flect (ri flekt') *v.* to give back a picture of something; mirror.

re·flec·tion (ri flek' shən) *n.* an image given back by a reflecting surface; for example, the image of oneself as seen in a mirror.

re·gion (rē' jən) *n.* any large area of territory.

re·gret (ri gret') *v.* **re·gret·ted, re·gret·ting.** to feel sorry or upset about.

re·la·tion·ship (ri lā' shən ship') *n.* the connection between one person or thing and another; link.

re·lief (ri lēf') *n.* the freeing from or lessening of pain, worry, or other discomfort.

re·li·gious (ri lij' əs) *adj.* **1.** of or having to do with religion. **2.** showing devotion to religion.

re·main (ri mān') *v.* to stay behind or in the same place.

re·mark (ri märk') *v.* to say; mention.

rem·e·dy (rem' ə dē) *v.* **rem·e·died, rem·e·dy·ing. 1.** to correct, set, or make right. **2.** to heal, improve, or get rid of a bad or unwanted condition.

re·mote (ri mōt') *adj.* located in an out-of-the-way place; far away.

re·pre·sent (rep' ri zent') *v.* to stand for; symbolize.

rep·re·sent·a·tive (rep' ri zen' tə tiv) *n.* an elected member of a legislature or lawmaking body.

rep·tile (rep' təl, rep' tīl) *n.* a cold-blooded animal that has a backbone and dry, scaly skin.

reptile

re·pub·lic (ri pub' lik) *n.* a country where voting citizens control their government.

re·quire (ri kwīr') *v.* **re·quired, re·quir·ing.** to have need of.

re·ser·va·tion (rez' ər vā' shən) *n.* land set aside by the government for a special purpose.

res·pect (ri spekt') *v.* to have or show honor or consideration for.

re·spon·si·ble (ri spon' sə bəl) *adj.* **1.** being the main cause of something. **2.** having as a job or duty. **3.** able to be trusted; trustworthy.

re·store (ri stôr') *v.* **re·stored, re·stor·ing.** to bring back; establish again.

re·u·nite (rē' ū nīt') *v.* **re·u·nit·ed, re·u·nit·ing.** to bring back together again.

rim (rim) *v.* **rimmed, rim·ming.** to form a rim, or outer edge, around something.

rip·en (rī' pən) *v.* to become fully grown and ready to eat.

Roo·se·velt, The·o·dore (rō' zə velt) 1858–1919, the twenty-sixth president of the United States, from 1901 to 1909.

rot·ted (rot' id) *adj.* decayed.

rouse (rouz) *v.* **roused, rous·ing. 1.** to cause to awaken from sleep or rest. **2.** to stir up; excite.

rus·tle (rus′ əl) *v.* **rus·tled, rus·tling.** to make soft, fluttering sounds, as of leaves rubbing together in the wind.

S

sac·ri·fice (sak′ rə fīs′) *v.* **sac·ri·ficed, sac·ri·fic·ing. 1.** to offer something to a god as an act of worship. **2.** to give up something for the sake of something else.—*n.* something or someone that is so offered.

sal·a·man·der (sal′ ə man′ dər) *n.* an animal that looks like a small lizard. Salamanders live in or near fresh water and have smooth, moist skin.

sand·hill crane (sand′ hil krān) *n.* a large grey migratory bird with a notable red forehead.

sap·ling (sap′ ling) *n.* a young tree.

sat·is·fac·tion (sat′ is fak′ shən) *n.* the state of being satisfied or contented.

sat·is·fy (sat′ is fī′) *v.* **sat·is·fied, sat·is·fy·ing.** to make contented; meet the needs or desires of.

saun·ter (sôn′ tər) *v.* to walk in a slow, relaxed way.

scarce·ly (skãrs′ lē) *adj.* barely or hardly.

scene (sēn) *n.* **1.** view; sight. **2.** the place where something happens.

sched·ule (skej′ ül) *v.* **sched·uled, sched·ul·ing.** to plan or arrange for a specified time.

scorn·ful·ly (skôrn′ fəl ē) *adv.* with a feeling of scorn or hatred for someone thought to be low or bad.

scor·pi·on (skôr′ pē ən) *n.* any of a group of animals related to the spider, having a long tail with a poisonous stinger at the end.

scorpion

scowl (skoul) *v.* to frown angrily.

script (skript) *n.* the written text of a play, movie, or television or radio show.

scrun·gy (skrun′ jē) *adj. Informal.* dirty; unwashed.

sculpt (skulpt) *v.* to carve a figure or picture in wood or stone, model in clay, or cast in bronze or another metal.

scut·tle (skut′ əl) *v.* **scut·tled, scut·tling.** to move with short, rapid steps.

sec·tion (sek′ shən) *n.* a part of something separated from the rest.

seed·ling (sēd′ ling) *n.* a young tree less than three feet (about 1 meter) high.

seek (sēk) *v.* **sought, seek·ing.** to try to find; go in search of.

sel·dom (sel′ dəm) *adv.* not often; rarely.

---

a bat, ā cake, ä father, är car, ãr dare; e hen, ē me, ėr term; i bib, ī kite; ir clear; o top, ō rope, ô saw, oi coin, ôr fork, ou out; u sun, u̇ book, ü moon, ū cute; ə about, taken

se·lect (si lekt′) *v.* to choose or pick out.

se·lec·tion (si lek′ shən) *n.* something or someone selected or chosen; for example, a selected piece of writing.

sel·fish (sel′ fish) *adj.* thinking only of oneself; not thinking of others.

sen·si·ble (sen′ sə bəl) *adj.* having or showing good sense; reasonable.

se·quence (sē′ kwəns) *n.* the coming of one thing after another in fixed order.

Se·quo·yah (si kwoi′ ə) 1770?–1843, developed written form of Cherokee language.

se·ries (sir′ ēz) *n., pl.* **se·ries.** a number of similar things coming one after another.

set (set) *n.* the scenery and other objects used for a scene in a play or other show.

sha·man (shä′ mən, shā′ mən) *n.* a religious leader of a tribe who is thought to have magical powers.

shel·ter (shel′ tər) *n.* something that covers or protects.

shim·mer·ing (shim′ ər ing) *adj.* shining with a faint light.

shoot (shüt) *n.* a very young or new plant just after it has come out of the ground; sprout.

shoot

shrill (shril) *adj.* having a sharp, high sound. Shrill noises can hurt the ears.

sig·na·ture (sig′ nə chər) *n.* the name of a person written in his or her own handwriting.

sin·cere (sin sir′) *adj.* not false or pretended; honest and true.

sketch (skech) *v.* to make a rough, unfinished, or quick drawing.

skill (skil) *n.* power or ability.

slash (slash) *n., pl.* **slash·es. 1.** a sweeping stroke made with great force. **2.** a cut made by a forceful sweeping stroke.

slope (slōp) *n.* a stretch of ground that is not flat or level.

slump (slump) *n.* a sharp, sudden drop in performance.

smug·ly (smug′ lē) *adv.* in a smug or self-satisfied way.

snare (snãr) *n.* a trap for catching small animals.

snow·drop (snō′ drop′) *n.* a plant that blooms in the early spring and has a single white and green flower.

snuf·fle (snuf′ əl) *v.* **snuf·fled, snuf·fling.** to eat noisily while making loud snorts through the nose.

snug (snug) *adj.* comfortable and warm; cozy.

sod (sod) *n.* the top layer of soil that has grass growing on it. In the pioneer days, sod was often cut into squares to make "bricks."

sod

soot·y (sut′ ē, sü′ tē) *adj.* covered with soot, a black powdery substance that forms when wood, coal, or oil is burned.

sound (sound) *adj.* strong and healthy.

sound ef·fects (sound′ i fekts′) *n. pl.* sounds made to imitate other sounds.

source (sôrs) *n.* the place or thing from which something comes or begins.

sow (sō) *v.* **sowed, sown** or **sowed, sow·ing.** to spread or scatter seed over the ground; plant.

spe·cies (spē′ shēz, spē′ sēz) *n.* a descriptive grouping of plants or animals that have certain characteristics in common.

speck·le (spek′ əl) *v.* **speck·led, speck·ling.** to mark or cover with speckles, or small spots.

spell·bound (spel′ bound′) *adj.* held as if by a magical spell; entranced.

sprout (sprout) *v.* to begin to grow.

squat (skwot) *adj.* short and thick; low and broad.

stage man·ag·er (stāj′ man′ i jər) *n.* a person who manages the lighting, scenery, and props of a play.

stalk (stôk) *v.* to follow quietly and carefully in order to catch something.

stalk·ing (stô′ king) *adj.* hunting; tracking down.

star·tle (stär′ təl) *v.* **star·tled, star·tling.** to excite or arouse suddenly, as with surprise, fright, or astonishment.

stash (stash) *v. Informal.* to store or hide something for later use.

step·moth·er (step′ muth′ ər) *n.* the wife of one's father, after the death or divorce of one's mother.

step·sis·ter (step′ sis′ ter) *n.* a stepparent's daughter by a former marriage.

stern (stern) *adj.* strict; harsh.

still life (stil līf) *n.* a painting or photograph of objects that are not alive, such as bowls of fruit or flowers.

stoop (stüp) *n.* a small porch with stairs at the entrance to a house or other building.

stout (stout) *adj.* **1.** thick and heavy; fat. **2.** strong.

strain·ing (strā′ ning) *adj.* pushing beyond a normal or proper limit; overexerting.

stride (strīd) *n.* a long, sweeping step.

strug·gle (strug′ əl) *n.* a fight or battle.

stub (stub) *n.* a short part that is left after the rest has been torn, broken off, or used up.

stub·born·ly (stub′ ərn lē) *adv.* in a stubborn, willful, or headstrong way.

stur·dy (ster′ dē) *adj.* strong; hardy.

style (stīl) *n.* **1.** fashion, especially of dress. **2.** way of doing things.

sub·head·ing (sub′ hed′ ing) *n.* a heading below a main heading.

---

a bat, ā cake, ä father, är car, âr dare; e hen, ē me, ėr term; i bib, ī kite, ir clear; o top, ō rope, ô saw, oi coin, ôr fork, ou out; u sun, ů book, ü moon, ū cute; ə about, taken

sub·mer·gent (səb mėr′ jənt) *adj.* of or relating to plants that live entirely under water.

sub·way (sub′ wā′) *n.* a passenger railroad that runs mostly underground. Subways are usually found in big cities.

suc·ceed (sək sēd′) *v.* to turn out well; do well.

suc·ces·sion (sək sesh′ ən) *n.* the coming of one thing or person after another.

suc·ces·sor (sək ses′ ər) *n.* a person or thing that follows or takes the place of another.

sulk·y (sul′ kē) *adj.* in a bad mood; stubbornly silent or withdrawn.

sup·port (sə pôrt′) *v.* to show to be true; prove.

su·preme (sə prēm′) *adj.* greatest; highest.

sur·face (sėr′ fis) *n.* the upper or outer part or layer of a thing.

sur·rey (sėr′ ē) *n.* a light, four-wheeled carriage with two seats, usually covered with a top.

surrey

sur·round·ing (sə roun′ ding) *adj.* something that is on all sides of another thing.

sur·vive (sər vīv′) *v.* **sur·vived, sur·viv·ing.** to live through; outlast; endure.

sus·pi·cious (sə spish′ əs) *adj.* feeling or showing suspicion, or doubt and distrust.

sus·pi·cious·ly (sə spish′ əs lē) *adv.* with a feeling of suspicion or mistrust; questioningly.

swamp (swomp) *n.* an area of low-lying land flooded with water and usually covered with many plants including trees.

swarm (swôrm) *v.* to move in a large group.

sway (swā) *v.* to move back and forth or from side to side.

swine·herd (swīn′ hėrd′) *n.* a person who takes care of pigs or hogs.

swol·len (swō′ lən) *adj.* made larger by swelling.

syl·la·bar·y (sil′ ə bār′ ē) *n., pl.* **syl·la·bar·ies.** a set of symbols, each representing a syllable of a language.

syl·la·ble (sil′ ə bəl) *n.* a single spoken sound that forms a word or part of a word.

sym·bol (sim′ bəl) *n.* something that stands for, or represents something else.

T

tall tale (tôl tāl) *n.* a story that exaggerates or stretches the facts; for example, the story of Paul Bunyan, the giant lumberjack.

tamp (tamp) *v.* to pack down; force or pound down with light blows or taps.

tat·tered (tat′ ərd) *adj.* hanging or torn in shreds.

ten·der (ten′ dər) *adj.* not strong; delicate.

ten·der·ly (ten′ dər lē) *adv.* in a kind or loving way.

term (tèrm) *n.* a set period of time; length of time that a thing lasts.

ter·ri·to·ry (tãr′ ə tôr′ ē) *n., pl.* **ter·ri·to·ries. 1.** a large area of land; region. **2.** a particular area that an animal, or group of animals, lives in, used for nesting.

ter·ror (tãr′ ər) *n.* great fear.

thatch (thach) *v.* to cover with straw, reeds, or similar material.

thaw·ing (thô′ ing) *adj.* becoming free of frost or ice; melting.

ther·mo·stat (thèr′ mə stat′) *n.* a device that automatically controls temperature. Thermostats control the temperature in furnaces.

thermostat

threat (thret) *n.* a person or thing that could be the cause of danger or harm.

throb·bing (throb′ ing) *adj.* beating or pounding heavily and fast.

thrust (thrust) *v.* to push or shove suddenly or with force.

ti·dal (tī′ dəl) *adj.* relating to, or affected by the rising and falling of the ocean's tides.

time·ta·ble (tīm′ tā′ bəl) *n.* a list of times at which certain events are to happen, especially a schedule showing the arrival and departure times of trains.

ti·pi (tē′ pē′), *also* **te·pee, tee·pee.** *n.* a cone-shaped tent used by North American Indians, especially the Plains Indians.

tire·some (tīr′ səm) *adj.* boring; tiring.

Tlingit (kling′ ət) *n.* American

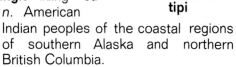

tipi

Indian peoples of the coastal regions of southern Alaska and northern British Columbia.

to·tem pole (tō′ təm pōl′) *n.* a pole carved and painted to represent animals or plants taken as family or clan emblems.

trad·ing post (trā′ ding pōst′) *n.* a store set up in an area where few people live.

totem pole

tram·road (tram′ rōd) *n.* a small railroad on which trams run. A tram is a small, four-wheeled wagon that is used to carry coal or lumber.

tread (tred) *v.* **trod, trod·den,** or **trod, tread·ing. 1.** to press with the feet; trample. **2.** to walk on.

---

a bat, ā cake, ä father, är car, ãr dare; e hen, ē me, ėr term; i bib, ī kite, ir clear; o top, ō rope, ô saw, oi coin, ôr fork, ou out; u sun, u̇ book, ü moon, ū cute; ə about, taken

tre·men·dous (tri men′ dəs) *adj.* very large or great; enormous.

trench (trench) *n.* a long, narrow ditch with the dug out earth piled up in front, used for the protection of soldiers in war.

tribe (trīb) *n.* a group of people joined together because they have the same ancestors, customs, language, and other characteristics.

tri·umph (trī′ umf) *n.* **1.** great joy caused by victory or success. **2.** a very great success, achievement, or victory.

tri·um·phant·ly (trī um′ fənt lē) *adv.* with a feeling of success or victory; in a triumphant way.

trol·ley (trol′ ē) *n.* an electric streetcar that runs on tracks and gets its power from an overhead wire.

trudge (truj) *n.* a slow, tiring walk.

twi·light (twī′ līt′) *n.* the time just after sunset or just before sunrise when there is a soft, hazy light reflected from the sun.

twirl (twėrl) *v.* to spin around quickly.

U

U.F.O. *n.* unidentified flying object; an object appearing in the sky that cannot be identified.

un·der·sto·ry (un′ dər stôr′ ē) *n.* a growth of different kinds of new trees underneath the branches of older, taller trees.

un·for·tu·nate·ly (un fôr′ chə nit lē) *adv.* in an unfortunate way; unluckily.

u·ni·corn (ū′ nə kôrn′) *n.* an imaginary animal that looks like a white horse with a long, pointed horn in the middle of its forehead.

unicorn

Un·ion (ūn′ yən) *n.* **1.** the states that remained loyal to the Federal government during the Civil War. **2.** the United States of America.

u·nite (ū nīt′) *v.* **u·nit·ed, u·nit·ing.** to bring, put, or join together.

ush·er (ush′ ər) *n.* a person who leads people to their seats in a church, theater, stadium, or other place.

V

vac·u·um cleaner (vak′ ū əm, vak′ ūm klē′ nər) *n.* a machine that is used for cleaning carpets, floors, and pieces of furniture. A vacuum cleaner works by suction.

val·ue (val′ ū) *n.* the worth, usefulness, or importance of something.

va·ri·e·ty (və rī′ ə tē) *n., pl.* **va·ri·e·ties. 1.** a number or collection of different things. **2.** lack of sameness; difference or change.

ve·ran·da (və ran′ də) *n.* an open porch, usually with a roof, that runs along one or more sides of a house.

veranda

ver·sion (vėr' zhən) *n.* a different or changed form of something.

Vic·tro·la (vik trō' lə) *n.* trademark name for a phonograph.

vi·sion (vizh' ən) *n.* **1.** something imagined. **2.** an image in the mind.

vol·un·teer (vol' ən tir') *n.* people who offer help or to do something without pay.

W

wad (wod) *n.* a small, tightly packed lump of soft material.—*v.* **wad·ded, wad·ding.** to roll, press, or pack into a wad.

wad·dle (wod' əl) *v.* **wad·dled, wad·dling.** to walk or move with short steps, swaying the body from side to side.

wag·er (wā' jər) *n.* an agreement to give or pay something to another if he is right and you are wrong; a bet.

war·ri·or (wôr' ē ər, wor' ē ər) *n.* a person who is experienced in fighting battles.

wa·ter spout (wo' tər spout') *n.* a pipe running from the roof down the side of a building that carries away rain water.

wear·y (wir' ē) *adj.* very tired.

well-stocked (wel' stokt') *adj.* having a large supply of many different goods or products.

wil·der·ness (wil' dər nis) *n., pl.* **wil·der·ness·es.** a place where no people live.

will (wil) *n.* **1.** a legal document that says what a person wants to have done with everything he owns when he dies. **2.** a strong desire; fixed purpose. **3.** the power of free choice.—*v.* to give away property by a will.

will·ful (wil' fəl) *adj.* determined to do as one pleases; stubborn.

wind·break (wind' brāk') *n.* a thing or group of things that is used to lessen the force of the wind. Fences and trees are often used as windbreaks.

wisp (wisp) *n.* a small bit or piece of something.

with·draw (with drô', with drô') *v.* **with·drew, with·drawn, with·draw·ing. 1.** to remove oneself. **2.** to take away.

with·stand (with stand', with stand') *v.* **with·stood** (with stüd', with stüd'), **with·stand·ing.** to be successful in resisting or holding out.

wit·ness (wit' nis) *n., pl.* **wit·ness·es.** a person who is present at a transaction, such as the signing of a contract or will.

won·der·ment (wun' dər mənt) *n.* the state or emotion of wonder; astonishment; amazement.

---

a **bat**, ā **cake**, ä **father**, är **car**, ãr **dare**; e **hen**, ē **me**, ėr **term**; i **bib**, ī **kite**, ir **clear**; o **top**, ō **rope**, ô **saw**, oi **coin**, ôr **fork**, ou **out**; u **sun**, ü **book**, ü **moon**, ū **cute**; ə **about, taken**

Y

yard goods (yärd′ gŭdz′) *n. pl.* fabric or cloth that is sold by the yard.

yarn (yärn) *n.* **1.** a long, exaggerated, or made-up story. **2.** thread used in knitting or weaving.

Yuc·ca (yuk′ ə) *n.* a desert plant found in dry areas of the United States and Central and South America.

Z

Za·ire (zä ir′) *n.* a country in central Africa, once known as the Congo.

Zam·bi·a (zam′ bē ə) *n.* a country in south-central Africa, once the British colony of Northern Rhodesia.

ze·nith (zē′ nith) *n.* the highest point.

zep·pe·lin (zep′ ə lin) *n.* a very large, cigar-shaped airship that is driven by motors and can be steered.

zig·gu·rat (zig′ ù rat′) *n.* an ancient temple built in the form of a pyramid with a series of large stages or terraces going up to the top. A ziggurat's sides appear zigzagged rather than straight.

Zim·ba·bwe (zim bäb′ wā) *n.* a country in south-central Africa, formerly Rhodesia.

zinc (zingk) *n.* a grayish-white metal. Zinc is used in batteries and in mixtures of metals, such as brass and bronze.

zin·ni·a (zin′ ē ə) *n.* a showy flower-bearing plant, growing in all colors except blue and green.

zinnia

zlo·ty (zlô′ tē) *n., pl.* **zlot·ys, zlo·ty.** a type of money used in Poland.

zuc·chi·ni (zü kē′ nē) *n., pl.* **zuc·chi·ni, zuc·chi·nis.** a green summer squash shaped like a cucumber, eaten as a vegetable.

---

a bat, ā cake, ä father, är car, âr dare; e hen, ē me, ėr term; i bib, ī kite, ir clear; o top, ō rope, ô saw, oi coin, ôr fork, ou out; u sun, ù book, ü moon, ū cute; ə about, taken